LISTENING TO
HARLEM

GENTRIFICATION, COMMUNITY, AND BUSINESS

DAVID J. MAURRASSE

Routledge
Taylor & Francis Group
New York   London

Published in 2006 by
Routledge
Taylor & Francis Group
270 Madison Avenue
New York, NY 10016

Published in Great Britain by
Routledge
Taylor & Francis Group
2 Park Square
Milton Park, Abingdon
Oxon OX14 4RN

Printed in the United States of America on acid-free paper
10 9 8 7 6 5 4 3 2 1

International Standard Book Number-10: 0-415-93305-6 (Hardcover) 0-415-93306-4 (Softcover)
International Standard Book Number-13: 978-0-415-93305-6 (Hardcover) 978-0-415-93306-3 (Softcover)
Library of Congress Card Number 2005026790

Library of Congress Cataloging-in-Publication Data

Maurasse, David, 1968-
    Listening to Harlem : gentrification, community, and business / David J. Maurasse.
      p. cm.
    ISBN-13: 978-0-415-93305-6 (hb : alk. paper)
    ISBN-13: 978-0-415-93306-3 (pb : alk. paper)
    1. Urban renewal--New York (State)--Harlem (New York) 2. Gentrification--New York (State)--Harlem (New York) 3. Harlem (New York, N.Y.)--Social conditions. 4. Harlem (New York, N.Y.)--Economic conditions. I. Title.

HT177.N5M38 2005
307.3'41609747--dc22   2005026790

Taylor & Francis Group
is the Academic Division of Informa plc.

Visit the Taylor & Francis Web site at
http://www.taylorandfrancis.com

and the Routledge Web site at
http://www.routledge-ny.com

DEDICATION

For my mother, Daphne Maurrasse, who is always there

CONTENTS

ACKNOWLEDGMENTS

As with past projects, I am ever so fortunate to benefit from many helpful and generous people who made this book a reality. I should first thank the Institute for Research in African American Studies at Columbia University for providing critical financial support. I want to especially thank Manning Marable, the Institute's director, and Kecia Hayes, his (now former) administrative assistant for feedback, advice, help in finding research assistants, and everything else.

I also want to give extra special thanks to Negin Farsad, my primary research assistant on the early stages of this project. Negin helped me put this project together in every possible way, from background research to arranging interviews, and even conducting some interviews herself. What a find! I also want to thank James Crowder, who provided research assistance in the early stages of the project. Karine Walther and Shanda Mays also assisted by transcribing interviews. Very special thanks should also go to Jackie Bliss, who provided monumental assistance in various stages of revision and in processing and analyzing survey data. Thanks to Cynthia Jones, who at the time was the Program Coordinator for the Center for Innovation in Social Responsibility for research assistance, especially transcribing—a most essential task for the qualitative researcher.

Both Jackie and Cynthia now work with me at my company, Marga Incorporated, which maximizes existing resources for societal gain through forging partnerships between major institutions and communities, and developing strategic plans. Others at Marga, such as Amaury Larancuent and Tara Wood helped in canvassing residents on the street about their perspectives on the changing landscape of their neighborhood. Through Marga, I—and the entire Marga crew—which also includes Rick Greenberg and Michael Price, have become closer to Harlem through our work. Since I began writing this book, Marga has worked closely with Harlem Congregations for Community Improvement (HCCI), and the Abyssinian Development Corporation (ADC), for which we facilitated the development of a strategic plan for the coming years. Lucille McEwan of HCCI and Sheena Wright of ADC both provided me with essential insight into the various dimensions of change in Harlem. Both of their organizations are significant players in the landscape of contemporary Harlem, each simultaneously engaging in residential and commercial (in ADC's case) development, yet attempting to maintain supportive environments for longtime residents. In many ways, their work characterizes the complexity and difficulty in seeking equitable solutions in an environment driven by demand and profit.

I have also gotten a bit closer to Harlem through the Alliance for Community Enhancement (ACE), which is actually both one of my classes, and a nonprofit organization for which I am the Board Chair. The class is running the organization. The organization seeks out partnerships with Harlem-based community organizations. Our first major partnership was with HCCI and our current one, a youth mentoring program, is with the Harlem Children's Zone. Everyone I have encountered through ACE, from the Board to the partners, and especially the many students who have passed through the class, has helped to shape the thinking in this book.

I am ever so grateful to all of those who agreed to be interviewed for this book. These issues are not without tension or controversy. In some cases, agreeing to be interviewed and tell it like it is was courageous in itself. Everyone was given the option of being anonymous, and very few interviewees chose to do so. This book seeks to improve the state of urban development, and all of the interviewees wanted to be a part of that. I can't thank them all enough. Also, finding interviewees leads to more interviewees, and thanks to all of those who opened up the network for me. The focus groups cited in the book, for example, emerged solely by the generosity of a couple of community based organizations— the Harlem Children's Zone's Community Pride initiative, at the time, headed by Lee Farrow, and the Valley, headed by John Bess.

Not everyone wanted to be interviewed around this delicate topic, and I just want to underscore that those who agreed to be interviewed made a monumental sacrifice for the sake of getting out the story and improving the situation. Overall, it is my impression, whether people agreed to be interviewed or not, that longtime residents in Harlem only want to make the situation better, and many of them have been tirelessly working to enhance their neighborhood for years. I can only hope that as Harlem's economic development unfolds, that same majority will be able to share in the resources being produced in the neighborhood's "new renaissance."

For continuous advice on the direction of this research, I should thank Jocelyn Sargent, Vicky Gholson, and Gail Aska. I also want to thank all of my students in my two Urban Planning classes, "Social Movements" and "Community Building and Urban Institutions." In both of these classes, students conducted research in Harlem as a part of their coursework. This research helped me think about the nature of economic development, access, and community building in contemporary Harlem. PolicyLink and the National Community Building Network also deserve acknowledgement, as both organizations, through their work on "equitable development," helped me shape my conceptualization of these issues. Indeed, the hope for development that prioritizes the needs of people in communities rests with organizations such as these.

At Columbia, other colleagues who have helped me get through this research include William Eimicke, Alan Yang, Lance Freeman, and Elliott Sclar. Thanks should always go to Aldon Morris of Northwestern University's Department of Sociology for continuous guidance. I will embark on no major research project without his input, and he is always willing to provide such.

Thanks to Community Voices Heard for building a system of checks and balances to ensure that low-income people have a voice, and that policy makers are accountable. Many of the members of this dynamic organization are from Harlem.

As always, thanks to Ilene Kalish, the original editor on this book, and the editor on two previous books of mine. She has now gone on to a different publisher. Nevertheless, I remain grateful for her insight and patience. Her disposition with me has brought joy to even the most arduous aspects of developing a book.

INTRODUCTION

From my thirteenth-floor office window at Columbia University, the highest peak of the Morningside Heights neighborhood, you can catch a panoramic glimpse of Harlem. I am always struck by the concentration of myriad towering red brick apartment buildings. Intermittent patches of greenery break the monotony. But, despite the overabundance of similar seemingly unimaginative mammoth structures, one cannot truly get a feel for Harlem from up so high. Nor can one actually see how much Harlem has changed; today's overhead view probably looks a lot like the one from a decade ago. After all, at its core, Harlem is and always has been a residential community.

To really feel Harlem's old grandeur and understand today's new developments, one must be on the ground, walking along the neighborhood's often teeming streets. On this one spectacular summer Sunday, the lights of the landmark Sylvia's Restaurant on Malcolm X Boulevard blink as if on the Las Vegas strip. One block up the Boulevard, a Black woman who appears to be homeless dons a straw hat, holding a denim piece of cloth in her hand, wearing jeans covered by an old skirt. Standing in front of a garbage can, she digs in her pockets. A few feet away, two middle-aged Black men sit next to each other. They appear to be marketing something to passersby. A White man in a beret passes, and crosses at 127th Street and the Boulevard. Further east, a number of

1

bow-tied, hat-wearing Black men, members of the Nation of Islam, congregate in front of a local Muslim mosque. Young men aggressively zip around on small-wheeled bicycles with long handlebars and high seats. On one corner, a man rides one of these bikes holding a baby in his arm. On 133rd Street, several African Americans of all ages sit on stoops, while a number of SUVs and vans are double-parked. At 136th Street, a car stops in the middle of the narrow block by the side of a pedestrian. The driver leans out of his window to talk to the man on the street, holding up traffic. On this warm summer's day, no one honks. It's not that people don't honk in Harlem as they do in Midtown. There is almost a "country" element to Harlem, likely influenced by the various cultures that converge on these streets, from the South to the Caribbean to Latin America to Africa. While this conversation continues, the feast for the ears is musical, blaring on each corner, spewing hip-hop in front of me, merengue behind me, and dance hall reggae on each side. The bounce of basketballs seems to move in rhythm with all of these beats, as every court in sight is in use. And those basketball games, whether pickup games or tournaments, are simply not complete without continuous howling and jabbering, rim ringing, and crowd cheering.

Whereas lower Manhattan streets are practically painted yellow with taxi cabs, Harlem's are filled with black or gray cars, usually old luxury sedans known as "livery" cabs. According to New York City policy, these independent taxi companies are not supposed to pick up passengers on the street. But they do so regularly, providing a service for Harlem residents that they would otherwise not receive. I flag down livery cabs myself when I am on Harlem streets. What else is one to do? The refusal of many yellow cab drivers to venture into Harlem and other New York City neighborhoods that are predominantly lower income and of color is well known.[1]

Turning to Harlem's legendary 125th Street, the typical bustle vibrates. But this present day scene can be distinguished from what one would have encountered ten years ago, when throngs of street vendors hocking their African wares and arts and crafts dotted most sidewalk spaces along the heart of this thoroughfare. In the commercial spaces, one would have found many smaller, independent, less-known establishments. The vibrancy of the street had a different character. It was unmistakable, uniquely Harlem, as crowds could only crawl along the sidewalks given the sheer volume of human bodies. Today's foot traffic is still significant but not quite as congested. The stores have changed vastly. Some street vendors dot these sidewalks, but many of them are new, as some of the seasoned ones were forced to move by Mayor Rudolph Giuliani during his administration. The Shabazz Market on 116th Street was to be the new haven for street vendors—a space designated by the city for these entrepreneurs. Business at this site has been spotty. On this glorious day, one would think this market would be flourishing. I counted twenty people shopping in this area on this day—a far cry from the foot traffic that these vendors would have encountered in a place where their consumer base would have been ready-made.

But the most noticeable change on 125th Street is the presence of chain retail stores. These stores could be anywhere in Manhattan or the rest of the country: HMV Records, Old Navy, Modell's, the Disney Store, H & M, and so on. To my eye, they almost appear out of place given Harlem's unique culture and history, but there they are. Change happens! One can also see commercial banking activity emerging on the street as well, such as Washington Mutual's new branch at the new Harlem Center, developed by the Abyssinian Development Corporation and Forrest City Ratner, one of the larger real estate developers in the New York City area. This space, at the corner of Malcolm X Boulevard and 125th Street, was once the open-air base for a number of African vendors. The Harlem Center is a small shopping mall including Marshall's and other retail establishments.

Although the sparkling new establishments leap out as you pass by, 125th Street's most well-known landmark, the Apollo Theatre, appears in need of renovation. Indeed, the scaffolding stretching across the front of the noted theatre suggests that repairs are underway. The sign for the old Blumstein's department store, having existed before the significant divestment of the '60s, '70s, and '80s, still stretches vertically above 125th Street. But a sign on the building now reads, "For Rent, 100,000 square feet, four floors, 25,000 square feet each." Mart 125, where independent vendors could sell their goods indoors on 125th Street, is completely closed down, and is now reduced to a two-story building with a glass storefront, surrounded by metal bars. This mart was a place where small entrepreneurs could sell any variety of goods from artwork to music to books and beyond. Not much has happened here for some time. Initially, these vendors received promises that they would be able to stay, but, in the end, Mart 125 became a real estate pricing casualty. Two massive American flags, flying in front of Old Navy, probably tell a story in itself. I can't recall ever having seen an

American flag of that size in Harlem, or any African American neighborhood, for that matter.

But one thing has not changed on 125th Street—the majority of the foot traffic is brown-skinned. A few White faces are dispersed among the African-descended masses, probably more than one would have seen ten years ago. The White population in the neighborhood has increased recently, but it doesn't appear that too many Whites partake in Harlem's vivacious pedestrian life.

Moving up Madison Avenue, the stretch of public housing from 132nd Street to 137th Street is unmistakable—the Riverton Houses, the Abraham Lincoln houses, public housing complexes. These rows of red brick buildings might be the hope for low-income residents to stay in the neighborhood. These are your quintessential public housing complexes. The Abraham Lincoln Houses, for example, contain fourteen buildings, six and fourteen stories tall, with 1,282 apartments and 3,117 residents[2]—a city unto itself. On 135th Street, the vast Harlem Hospital boasts a sign, "Harlem Hospital Physicians Acclaimed Among the Nation's Leading Black Doctors," and a sign at a nearby playground says, "Harlem Plays the Best Ball in the Country." Although many of the 125th Street businesses have been replaced by chain stores, the older African American–owned businesses there, such as funeral homes, barbershops, and beauty shops, remain.

Harlem is truly a neighborhood of neighborhoods. The housing stock reflects this internal diversity, as some areas contain concentrated housing, others public housing, and others tenements—those approximately five-story buildings lined in rows on many New York City streets, covered by their trademark fire escapes, and usually resting over small commercial businesses.

On this August Sunday afternoon, these are some of the sights in Harlem. Still predominantly populated by people of African descent, the neighborhood particularly comes to life in the summer. August, in fact, is known for its Harlem Week—once this was just a week long, now it lasts a whole month—when various local events bring out locals and visitors alike. For example, the plaza at the Adam Clayton Powell Jr. State Office Building on 125th Street is full on this day, as hundreds of people thunderously applaud a fashion show, which seems to have ended, as statuesque young women and men of multiple hues make a final sojourn down the stage.

As dusk approaches, the sun drapes itself like a yellow curtain over the neighborhood, from public housing to brownstones, and from parks to long stretches of concrete. The delicate transition from day to night that has always been my favorite time of day brings particular visibility to Harlem's many churches. They come in all shapes and sizes, and dot numerous Harlem corners and sometimes find themselves in the middle of blocks as well. I can see Metropolitan Baptist Church, a gigantic gray stone structure, favoring a castle, spreading its majesty, partly in light and partly in shade. Several other houses of worship join in observing the end of their holy day—some even in storefronts, sandwiched in between bodegas, right alongside the other more noticeable structures. Even on a residential street, like 136th, near Frederick Douglass Boulevard, one can find a church, Beulah Wesleyan Methodist, tucked into the middle of the block. It is hard to miss the significance of worship in this historic neighborhood. And as the wheels of economic development turn increasingly northward on the island of Manhattan, it would be hard to imagine the Harlem landscape without its many houses of worship.

Even though Harlem's economic development is well underway, at this stage, it is still spotty. The noted Striver's Row area of Harlem remains pristine, but is very close to poverty and blight. On one section of 137th Street, most of the brownstones lining the path are boarded up. The block has an almost ominous feel, as a man barbecues out of a barrel in the middle of the sidewalk, and a small group of folks have a picnic on a concrete slab. Going further west, toward Adam Clayton Powell Boulevard, 137th Street becomes tree-lined, renovated, and well kept. The trees on either side of the street literally form a tunnel as their branches meet overhead. There is no boarding on this block.

A few children play on this street, but the overall mood is far more sedate, almost suburban. At Frederick Douglass Boulevard, the housing stock changes again, but it is still decidedly developed and spotless, as a complex of three-story red brick townhouses represent a more modern incarnation of Striver's Row. But 136th Street changes again with far more varied architecture, and, like 137th, the eastern part of the street plays host to a number of boarded up buildings—"shells," in real estate parlance.

Making my way up St. Nicholas Avenue, a lovely park adorns the west side of the block, while five-story multicolored tenements line the other side. Emerging from the serenity is some kind of festive gathering on the concrete portions of the park. Hip-hop blares, and balloons are everywhere. What is most striking are the African Americans playing basketball in one section of the park, and the Latinos playing another sport in another section. It's hard to tell exactly what the Latinos are doing, but they play in a volleyball court with a soccer ball, bouncing it around, but not actually playing volleyball. I later came to find that foot volleyball is an actual sport! Indeed, this is volleyball where one can't use one's hands. One can use any part of one's body in this game that otherwise mirrors the rules of traditional volleyball.

Harlem has a few quite attractive enclaves. As one steers to the northern end of the vast neighborhood, this becomes even more evident, over the steeper hills and through the spaces of lush greenery. One truly picturesque spot rests at the northern end of St. Nicholas, at 151st Street, which plays host to a triangular small park in the middle of the street, surrounded by beautiful six-story residential buildings—simply regal.

Moving west over to Broadway, commercial activity overwhelms. Underneath seemingly endless rows of tenements, a diverse array of small retail shops contribute to a bustling aura. At Broadway and 139th Street, a Subway sandwich shop is next to a bodega, which is next to another bodega, which is next to the Santiago Deli, which is next to a pharmacy. It's all so crowded. More of a mix of Latinos and African Americans can be found walking about Broadway, but at this point, the pedestrians are primarily Latino. Even moving eastward on 135th Street, toward the top of the hill, Latinos of all ages sit at outdoor tables playing dominoes.

Going toward Central Harlem's southern tip, the neighborhood's proximity to the rest of Manhattan becomes very prominent, especially near the northern end of Central Park at 110th Street. At 114th Street and Adam Clayton Powell Boulevard, one can see spectacular prewar (built before World War II) residential buildings, almost resting in a bed of fertile greenery. Not surprisingly, in this area, a great deal of development is in process. Sandwiched between Morningside Park on the west and Park Avenue on the east, and bordered by 125th to the north and Central Park to the south, these Harlem flatlands could be emerging as an extension of Manhattan proper.

At 122nd Street, near Morningside Avenue, two White men peer into the window of a brownstone, maybe speculating about the unit's and the neighborhood's livability. Although some boarded-up buildings remain in this section, like one red brick structure on 122nd Street and St. Nicholas Avenue, one is far more likely to see various construction projects underway, ones that involve renovation of old homes or sites starting from scratch on empty lots. At 120th Street and Lenox Avenue, a new café/bakery called Settepani looks like something you'd find on 23rd Street. The storefront looks brand spanking new, the windows sparkling clean. The mostly White but still relatively multiracial crowd inside conjures up images of almost anywhere but what many would associate with Harlem. This is quite a nice café, by the way. And it is only one among a few others that have recently opened in the neighborhood.

A couple of blocks to the east, the various lamppost banners reading "Mount Morris Park Historic District" are hard to miss. This elegant square of classic residential architecture with a park in the middle offers the kind of living that most people dream about. Interestingly enough, Mount Morris Park was renamed Marcus Garvey Park in 1973, by a city councilperson, Charles L. Taylor. The mayor at the time, John Lindsay, signed it into law. Nevertheless, it does not appear that residents in the district have embraced the new moniker.

At Madison Avenue, the eastern end of this area, just south of this park, a sign reads, "Madison Court, your desire for affordable luxury is now addressed." All around this area are signs for the Fedders Development Corporation, a large developer that, like others, is creating new complexes. Simultaneously, local community development corporations are offering affordable housing and are helping to renovate existing residential properties.

Although the signs of development blossom at every turn, the metal gratings are pulled down over storefront windows; the graffitti scribbled across them can't be missed. Although commercial and economic development forges ahead, the public infrastructure of the area remains. For example, the Sojourner Truth School on 118th Street does not appear to be recently renovated. And at 5th Avenue and 115th Street and downward one can find a stretch of public housing, such as the King Jr. Towers and the Taft Houses, that does not appear any different than it was some years ago.

Visually, Harlem's overall landscape smacks of transition—a convergence of the neighborhood's past and future. I ended my long Sunday in Harlem gazing at a colorful sign on 119th Street. It depicts several flags—Jamaica's, the Dominican Republic's, Puerto Rico's and others—and reads, "Sharing Wisdom and the Dream of a Better Community."

Yes, Harlem is somewhat of a mosaic of different cultures, largely people of color. It represents the potential of these communities uniting around a collective idea of a better neighborhood. Yet, these cultures coexist in the face of a future that may or may not include them. The Harlem of tomorrow will likely be shaped by a peculiar amalgam of multiple racial and ethnic groups, community organizations, government, private funding sources, developers, churches, and corporations, sometimes operating with the same goal, and at other times moving with divergent views. Sometimes those views will, deliberately or accidentally, converge. Today's Harlem is already experiencing how varied interests and differing degrees of influence manifest in the effort to shape a suddenly desirable neighborhood. In this ever-so-unique area, the bandwagon has been built. The tickets to get on can be expensive, and some may get a free ride, but many are joining in the scramble to get the most out of this landmark, this goldmine called Harlem.

* * * *

Some understanding of the state of Harlem—why it's changing, and where it's headed—can be found through the voices of Harlem's long-time residents. They have lived through the area's decline and are now witnessing its apparent, yet debatable, resurgence. That significant economic development is occurring in Harlem is undeniable. However, the degree to which it leads to economic empowerment for longtime residents remains to be seen. The change in the neighborhood is well on its way—some of which brings clear benefit to longtime residents, and some of which exacerbates anxiety and shakes the security of, particularly, low-income residents.

John Bess, a Harlem native, reflected on the local changes he has witnessed over the last fifty years. I found Bess in his office at the back of the majestic Cathedral of St. John the Divine in Morningside Heights. The organization that he founded and still runs, The Valley, is located in this space. Tracking him down for an interview was no easy task as his organization, a nonprofit providing services to local African American and Latino youth, is comprehensive in scope and nationally renowned. Bess's busy schedule showed on his medium-brown face. A widely framed, fifty-ish African American man, Bess sat down across from me at a table in an open space of The Valley's office, and bestowed his experiential wisdom upon me.

The Harlem that I lived in was the Harlem where we as young people were revered and supported and nurtured. We could go into each other's houses at that time and doors were not locked … but someone dropped an atomic bomb on Harlem that traumatized us enormously. There was something called heroin. People who were upwardly mobile began to say, "I'm not living in this community." Then we had another neutron bomb called the crack addiction. No longer could you go in the people's houses, and no longer were people friendly, and no longer would people tell you what to do, because now people were behaving in a negative, violent, vicious, and malicious way.

In the decades of which Bess spoke, the 1960s to the 1980s, Harlem was rattled by drugs, crime, and the subsequent abandonment by those who had the option of moving. Boarded-up brownstone buildings lined various Harlem streets, some of which became havens for drug dealers and users. As Bess noted, the neighborhood became a place of fear. But Bess has recently been witnessing changes of an entirely different character. He said, "So now we are seeing a housing boom. Where there was once the stay away from, stay out of, there becomes an attractive community for people to live in. The transformation of Harlem is a radical change."[3]

Eighty-six-year-old Mary Baker has been living in the same building on 154th Street and Amsterdam Avenue for more than forty-two years. The long hallway of her first floor apartment is characteristic of pre–World War II architecture, before apartments were either cut into pieces or built as much smaller units in newer developments. She remembers all of the well-known African Americans who lived on her block and in her building—Coleman Hawkins, Joe Lewis, Billie Holiday, Ella Fitzgerald. Baker was born in Jacksonville, Florida, and, like many of her African American contemporaries, took the trek northward to the big city in the 1930s. "I wanted to get away from home, and I heard so much talk about New York," she told me in her slightly quivering yet decidedly strong voice.[4]

Her first apartment was on 119th Street, between Seventh and Lenox Avenues. She recalls how Seventh Avenue once played host to Mardi Gras, which ultimately became the West Indian Day Parade in Brooklyn—New York's most well-attended annual parade. In the 1930s, trolley cars moved about 125th Street and, although many residents were of African descent, few "coloreds" worked in any of the stores. The famous restaurant, "Charles," didn't even have a Black dishwasher, and only

Whites could eat there. Segregation in New York City was very much alive during this time, with only one difference from segregation in the South, according to Baker: "If you went anywhere, they wouldn't tell you; they wouldn't serve you. They'd pass by you, and just wouldn't pay you any attention. You didn't exist."[5] That segregation has been apparent throughout the history of New York City is well known, and I will discuss this later in this book. However, as Ms. Baker suggests, Black people have received inferior service and access absent of any explicit racial policy. This can be found in the school system, for example, to this day.

This can be found in other major aspects of the city's public and private infrastructure. In 1935, for example, a Black doctor at Harlem Hospital brought to light a de facto discrimination policy. Dr. Lucien Brown had resigned from his position at the hospital because of these practices. A *New York Times* article on his testimony at a hearing of the Mayor's Commission on Conditions in Harlem revealed "that although about 90 percent of the patients in the hospital are Negroes, only six internes [*sic*] out of twenty-seven on the junior staff are Negroes. The entire medical staff numbers 283, of whom 199 are white."[6]

In 1956, New York Senator Herbert H. Lehman called for "residential integration" in the city. In his eyes, it was segregation in housing, exacerbated by the presence of predominantly Black public housing complexes that made the segregation in all aspects of New York City life so palpable. He said, "Harlem is an area of poverty, congestion, substandard housing and sub-standard schools." He further noted, "Residential segregation is the other side of the coin of school segregation."[7]

According to Baker, it was Adam Clayton Powell, who could have passed for White, who broke segregation in Harlem. She can recall the first time she could enter the "five and ten" and sit down. "And we had a hot dog. I'll never forget it," she reminisced. She ultimately found work, cleaning up the hardwood floors in Jewish homes for fifty cents an hour. She "did everything" from cooking to washing to taking care of children in order to survive. But rent was much more affordable in those days. "You could get a nice kitchenette room for five dollars."[8]

Through her eyes, African Americans were gradually becoming more empowered in Harlem, as Black business ownership began to increase. "During the fifties and sixties, we had a lot of those Black shoeshine parlors, Black beauty parlors, and corner grocery stores, and fish and chip places," she remembered. She thought of "Mr. Sherman's," a barbeque restaurant at 151st Street. She said, "His barbeque stores were all over Harlem, and the thing that made him so unique is that not only did he own the store, he owned the whole building." In her view, this surge in Black ownership lasted "at least until the eighties."[9]

In their respective interviews, Bess focused on a rise in crime and Baker on a decline in Black ownership of homes and businesses. Both are aspects of Harlem's historical reality. Longtime residents of Harlem are not short on opinions, and they possess a strong sense of ownership over their neighborhood. Opinions can be as varied as the myriad types of personalities and backgrounds that one can find in the neighborhood. Harlem, throughout the twentieth century and to the present, has been a haven for people of African descent—the artists, the intellectuals, the workers, the poor, and beyond. With all of the richness inherent in Harlem's longtime residents, their perspectives are critical to shaping the future of the neighborhood. Seeing the neighborhood through their eyes can bring to light nuances that should not be overlooked as Harlem undergoes rapid changes.

My research assistants and I primarily interviewed longtime residents, nonprofit community organizations, and small business owners. Interviews were, at first, strictly qualitative, but eventually included a survey dimension, which allowed us to reach a broader cross section of people. This research assumes that through soliciting the opinions of those directly impacted by recent developments in the neighborhood, we can get a greater sense of the indicators of equitable and inequitable urban initiatives. We hoped that by conducting this research through this angle, we could develop a set of suggestions for more effective policies that will bring resources into urban neighborhoods without hurting longtime, especially low-income, residents.

However, this book is not simply about talking to people; it is ultimately an analysis of the paradox of urban development, where low-income neighborhoods are revitalized, but preexisting residents are not empowered in the long run. Harlem is in transition; but if the present day "renaissance" is to be truly groundbreaking, it will lead to improved economic opportunity for longtime residents, because it is the economic empowerment of individuals and families that has eluded communities of color, such as those residing in Harlem. A combination of jobs and business development coupled with improved training and education would be a good start.

Great learning can be found by listening to communities. Unfortunately, their perspectives have often fallen on deaf ears or their voices are simply ignored. In some instances, community voices are actually invited to the table, but often merely symbolically. Malcolm X said, "Sitting at the table does not make you a diner, unless you eat some of what's on that plate."[10]

In the presence of such dynamics, the process of this research intentionally focuses most of its energy on the perspectives of community residents and community-based organizations. Hopefully, the ideas emerging from these interviews can be beneficial to policy makers, scholars, community-based organizations, corporations, small businesses, and residents in similar urban communities.

Decisions always have consequences. The policies that determined Harlem's latest phase of development, whether public or private decisions, have had both positive and negative ripple effects on longtime, especially, low-income Harlem residents. What is the ratio of economic development projects to actual improvements in the economic livelihood of residents? Through working closely with and listening to community residents, it is easier to get an indication of how the damaging ripple effects of some tendencies in economic development can be turned even more in the residents' favor.

What are the ingredients of economic development strategies that advance opportunities for those who are less advantaged from the start? The impact of the ripple effects of development can best be understood through communication with the residents themselves. The residents can tell the story of how changes in the neighborhood directly affect their lives, and how alternate strategies can be more effective. Interviewees for this book were engaged in dialogue about the strengths, weaknesses, and future possibilities of Harlem's "new renaissance."

After decades of limited development initiatives, the concept of "impact" has come into vogue. It is in the slogan of the United Way, "community impact," and it is the lens through which many nonprofit, philanthropic, governmental, and community initiatives are critiqued and measured. The core question with which this view of urban economic development grapples is what kind of impact? We have reached a point where a higher standard can be placed on impact that enhances communities' capacity to exhibit greater control over their lives. Development does not necessarily lead to empowerment.

1

HARLEM THEN AND NOW

Throughout Harlem's rich history, the area has remained a compelling mosaic of all that is great and challenging about urban neighborhoods in America, and perhaps in the world. The majestic architecture, unique culture, commanding public figures, and overall vibrancy have coexisted with high crime, unemployment, struggling public schools, poverty, drugs, and potentially explosive racial and ethnic tensions. When Harlem is on an upswing, the media, real estate, speculators, politicians, and residents emphasize the neighborhood's many assets, but when it is down, all of the negatives can seem to eclipse what made Harlem the vibrant center of life and culture for the African diaspora.

The fact that Harlem is a part of New York City, where scale, energy, excesses, delights, and frights are all magnified, should come as no surprise. Harlem, in itself, is a vast area, taking up a solid chunk of Manhattan north of 110th street. The neighborhood spans three city districts—West Harlem, Central Harlem, and East Harlem, and boasts a population of nearly half-a-million people, essentially a city in itself.

HARLEM, HISTORY, AND ECONOMIC DEVELOPMENT

Before John Bess's time, Harlem was in its heyday—the Renaissance of the 1920s. But it was at the turn of the century when the Harlem that is associated with African American life and culture began to emerge.

We think of Harlem as an African American community, but that was not always the case. New York City's African Americans gradually moved up from the very southern tip of the Manhattan Island and eventually settled in Harlem. Much of this movement was facilitated by displacement from some Manhattan neighborhoods that few would imagine as Black communities today, such as the Wall Street area, the space currently occupied by Penn Station, and the area that is now Central Park. African Americans are the second oldest ethnic population in New York City, after the Dutch.[1] Of course, Native Americans predated both populations—the Algonquin Indians, in this case. Continually pushed northward by influxes of White immigrants and various commercial development projects, African Americans populated the Five Points district north of city hall, parts of Greenwich Village, and an area known as Little Africa, which is now Penn Station. Although Harlem's Black population remains significant, today's largest concentration of Black New Yorkers currently resides in Brooklyn. Nevertheless, Harlem's mystique persists, as it continues to dominate public consciousness with respect to the Black experience.[2]

It is important to note that, from the very beginning, the majority of New York City's Black population were of Caribbean origin. Of the enslaved and free Black residents of colonial New York, 80 percent could trace their African roots to the Caribbean.[3] In fact, it was a free African with roots in the Caribbean, Jan Rodriguez, who in 1613, helped to build a Dutch trading post in what we now know as Manhattan. The Dutch eventually named this area New Amsterdam in 1626, when New Netherland Director-General Peter Minuit purchased Manhattan island from the Algonquins for the equivalent of $24. One year before that, the Dutch brought in the first group of New York's enslaved Africans to be the city's labor force. These slaves built roads and homes, and cleared fields for farms, not only in Manhattan, but in the areas beyond New Amsterdam, which would become the Bronx, Brooklyn, Queens, and Staten Island.[4] As Africans gradually settled in New York, their status varied, from slave to free to half-free. Some of these Africans owned property and engaged in commerce, but in 1655, the Dutch turned all of

New Amsterdam into a slave trading post, leading to increased restrictions on the African population.[5]

The rights of Africans were even further diminished after the English wrested control of New Amsterdam from the Dutch and renamed it New York in 1664. Slave codes were developed to restrict enslaved Africans' behavior. The English also seized the property and rights of free and half-free Blacks.[6] Before English control, many Africans and Native Americans could aspire to be "cartmen," those who drove one-horse wagons to perform public works for the city—carrying commodities, maintaining roads, transporting rubbish, and other duties. They had actually formed a guild in 1667, enabling them to contract with the city. By 1691, however, the English-controlled legislature passed ordinances that made race a qualification for a carting license, prohibiting Blacks and Native Americans from these positions.[7] Carting and street vending were opportunities for people with almost no starting capital to make an income. These and other opportunities for Black economic empowerment were continually denied or severely limited. By 1712, Blacks, Native Americans, and "mulattoes" were officially prohibited from inheriting or transferring land to their heirs.

It was not until 1799 that the New York State Legislature passed an act that would lead to the gradual emancipation of African slaves (male slaves by the age of twenty-eight and females by the age of twenty-five).[8] An amendment of this act in 1817 called for the abolition of slavery on July 4, 1827. New York was an essential state in the cotton industry, which was buoyed by slavery.[9]

Seneca Village, near what is now Central Park West and 80th Street, was one of the African American neighborhoods that predated the Black migration to Harlem. Andrew Williams, a shoe shiner, bought three lots of land in this area for $125 in 1825.[10] The area ultimately became a haven for Black landowners and eligible voters. But, by 1858, the neighborhood was destroyed to make way for Central Park. The concentration of African Americans in Manhattan literally made a gradual shift northward. And it was often forces outside of Black peoples' control that led to the movement from one neighborhood to another. Between 1790 and the dawn of the Harlem migration in about 1910, Black communities in Manhattan were as follows: 1790–1840: Free African Community, near what is now City Hall; 1820–1863: Stagg Town, Mulberry and Baxter Streets, around what is now Little Italy; 1863–1890: Little Africa/Little Liberia: Thompson, Sullivan, Bleecker Streets, around

Greenwich Village; 1880–1910: The Tenderloin, 23rd Street to 42nd Street by 8th and 9th Avenues; and 1890–1910: San Juan Hill, 58th to 65th between 8th and 11th Avenues.[11]

New York's Black population gradually established their own institutions, churches, newspapers, and so on, with both success and failure. Economic power seemed to be the most elusive goal, but not for lack of trying. By 1851, a group of Black New Yorkers convened to discuss forming a Black bank from their own savings that totaled between $40,000 and $50,000 (the idea never came to fruition).[12] By 1853, Black economic power became more apparent, as investments in New York's business enterprises by African Americans totaled $839,100, and real estate holdings totaled $1,160,000.[13] As New York's population ballooned during the industrial revolution, the numbers of local African Americans grew as well. However, the extensive European migration to New York City shrunk the scope of jobs and other opportunities for income production for African Americans, particularly between 1870 and 1900.[14]

African Americans were well represented in the Tenderloin district in the western part of midtown, just before the migration to Harlem. The Black population grew even more rapidly as the turn of the 19th century approached; 1890's New York experienced an influx of about twenty-five thousand new Black residents, who tended to move to the Tenderloin, and another portion of Manhattan's western stretch of land, known as San Juan Hill, between 60th and 64th Streets and Tenth and Eleventh Avenues. Fifty-Third Street was the major thoroughfare in the Black community at the time, playing host to two Black-owned hotels, various small businesses, numerous churches, and a Black YMCA.[15] But on August 15, 1900, Blacks in the Tenderloin were attacked by a mob of several thousand Whites, who assaulted every Black person in their path between 27th and 42nd Streets around Eighth Avenue. The fatal stabbing of a White police officer by a Black man three days before the incident sparked the violence. During the funeral on August 15, Whites grew angry, and both civilians and police officers converged on the Tenderloin's Black community.

This brutal incident in many ways hastened the need for effective community organizing among Blacks that would lead them to strengthen their power as a collective and heighten their position and profile in New York, and around the world this thinking became the foundation of the Harlem Renaissance. New construction in the

Tenderloin early in the twentieth century also displaced many of the area's African Americans—another contributing factor in the last leg of African Americans' northern migration in Manhattan. In 1910, many of the Tenderloin's predominantly Black blocks were demolished, displacing thousands, to make way for the construction of Penn Station, Macy's, the U.S. Post Office, and the Hotel Pennsylvania.[16]

Overall, many of New York City's landmarks were once home to Black communities. Although gentrification is a relatively new term, the displacement of African Americans is not new. The history of African Americans in New York City is somewhat of a microcosm of the struggle of people of African descent in the United States and other parts of the world—even when advancing through their own collective endeavor, they are displaced, denied, prohibited, attacked, and even robbed by formal and informal policies through institutions that they have not controlled.

Harlem was established as a permanent Dutch settlement, a separate town, called New Harlem, in Manhattan in 1658. It is named for a town in Holland that fought tenaciously before falling to the Spanish in the sixteenth century.[17] The town was annexed by New York City in 1873. Even Harlem's landmark Abyssinian Baptist Church was located in the Tenderloin, on West 40th Street, before its own uptown exodus in the 1920s. Ethiopian merchants and Black members of the First Baptist Church who wished to escape segregated seating founded the church in 1808, on what is now Worth Street in lower Manhattan.[18]

Before the uptown movement of African Americans, Harlem was a primarily German and Irish neighborhood, which ultimately experienced an influx of Italian and Jewish immigrants. Before the arrival of the immigrants in the late 1800s, Harlem was home to the city's elite. One can still see remnants of the neighborhood's past wealth in various stunning works of architecture dispersed among dilapidated housing and more recent, less ornate, buildings. For all intents and purposes, Harlem was "New York's first suburb."[19] Living in Harlem was considered a symbol of high status in the 1800s—a destination for the wealthy.

In the early 1900s, African Americans from southern parts of Manhattan, then African Americans from the South, and ultimately immigrants from Africa and the Caribbean converged, making Harlem the capital of the African diaspora. In 1900, African Americans comprised less than 2 percent of New York City's population of 3.5 million.[20] Contributing to the growth of Harlem's burgeoning Black population, an additional infusion came from the South in search of a new, urban, northern life, and economic opportunity.

The proposal and eventual development of the subway—the Lenox Avenue IRT (Interborough Rapid Transit) to 145th Street (now going to the very edges of the Bronx) in 1910, created great anticipation among developers in the 1890s.[21] As a result, real estate developers built extensively and landlords rapidly bought property. The IRT was completed to 148th Street in October of 1904, carrying six hundred thousand passengers per day at forty miles per hour. Some of the greatest anticipation was in West Harlem, which was intended for wealthier people. Therefore, luxury housing, with elevators, maids' rooms, and butlers' pantries, was constructed. For example, William Waldorf Astor built an apartment house on Seventh Avenue, which cost $500,000—all part and parcel of what was to become "the loveliest Negro ghetto in the world."[22]

However, New York City as a whole was experiencing significant development at that time as well, and too many residential properties had been built in anticipation. These realities became apparent around 1904, as rents were cut, and a few months of free occupancy were offered. Some landlords and corporations succumbed to the pressure, and decided to rent to Blacks, whereas others relied on the threat of renting to Blacks in order to scare neighbors into buying them out at market rates. These were no simple economic transactions, as racism prevented many Whites from giving in to what was known as the "Negro invasion." As a reflection of their disdain, many White Harlem residents formed "protective associations," particularly on some of Harlem's more affluent streets (137th, 129th, 135th, as well as others). Signed agreements among residents, promising not to rent to Blacks for ten or fifteen years, and restrictive covenants that limited the number of Black janitors, servants, and other jobs, "White only" signs, and proposed evictions of existing Black Harlemites were all characteristic of the White resistance to the prospective African American uptown migration.[23]

But, ultimately, Harlem's Whites shared no uniform strategy or voice around real estate. Some were going to sell and could not be convinced otherwise. In their desperation to rent out vacant residential units, landlords began to relax their restrictions against African Americans, facilitating this uptown exodus. Between 1907 and 1914, many Whites entered a "panic selling" mode, sparking a staggering turnover in property; two-thirds of the homes near areas where African Americans were congregating were sold in this brief period.[24]

Of course, someone had to manage some of this activity. An ambitious African American named Philip A. Payton Jr. was one of the few African American landlords to benefit from this scenario. Through his Afro-American Realty Company, which he founded in 1904, he approached many of Harlem's existing landlords with the proposition of renting to select African Americans at above-market rates. Given their anxieties about finding paying tenants, landlords put some aspects of their prejudices aside in exchange for money. Payton embarked on a campaign, of sorts, to recruit Black residents to Harlem. He advertised on billboards and was one of the first to advertise in subway cars.[25]

Payton became the most successful real estate agent in the city and African Americans gained access to well-built homes; however, they were still paying more than Whites. Payton's clients paid at least $5 per month more than Whites for similar homes in Harlem.[26] Despite having been New Yorkers for centuries before many Whites, African American Harlem residents not only required landlords' desperation for tenants to gain access to decent housing but also had to pay more for it.

As has been the case in so many urban areas, significant increases in the population of African Americans influences "White flight." Therefore, Harlem rapidly shifted from a White majority to a Black one in a relatively short period of time, although the landlords were still mainly White. In Harlem, African Americans had managed to occupy some of the best real estate that any Black population has encountered en masse in the country at the time. As the people moved, the institutions followed: churches, branches of the Urban League and one of the founding chapters of the NAACP, the YMCA, YWCA, social service agencies, small businesses, and more, all made the northward trek.

In many ways, these institutions represented a form of self-government for African Americans. Given continued obstacles to empowerment in the country, the state, and the city, Harlem residents, through their own organizations, were able to maintain some semblance of self-determination. By 1921, Harlem boasted two newspapers, *The Amsterdam News* and the *New York Age*, sixty churches, and branches of the Elks, Pythians, and Masons.[27]

By the 1920s, Harlem was known worldwide as a Black Mecca of sorts, most notably through its arts and culture, made ubiquitous through the Harlem Renaissance. By 1930, Black Harlem had developed all the way down to the northern end of Central Park, with a population of two hundred thousand.[28] But even in the midst of the vitality that African Americans were infusing into this neighborhood, they continued to face discrimination and predatory economic practices. In a 1925 hearing of the Mayor's Committee on Rent Profiteering, a Judge of Harlem's Municipal Court, John Davies testified, "It is common for colored tenants in Harlem to pay twice as much as white tenants for the same apartments."[29] These continuous fiscal obstacles to the improvement of the livelihoods of African Americans weave together a theme throughout Harlem's history.

Black people moved to Harlem from the American South, and they also came up from the Caribbean. Different than the Caribbean population of colonial New York, this group of immigrants brought a strong sense of racial pride and a degree of political nationalism. The most notable Caribbean migrant of the time was Marcus Garvey, who moved to New York in 1916. His United Negro Improvement Association (UNIA), established in 1917, morphed into a global movement of people of African descent. To provide an indication of the UNIA's popularity, it filled Madison Square Garden with twenty-five thousand delegates during its first international convention in 1920.

The UNIA played a vital role in economic development for Black people in Harlem and elsewhere. A cruise ship, the Black Star Line, was probably Garvey's most well-known endeavor. However, lesser-known efforts, such as the Negro Factories Corporation, provided loans and technical assistance to Blacks wishing to create their own businesses. This separate business sold stock at $5 per share, which led to the development of a restaurant, a laundry, a chain of cooperative grocery stores, a publishing house, and other businesses.[30] Garvey stressed Black ownership of and control over enterprises, a radical notion for the time, as Harlem was still, largely, owned by outsiders, even though the population had shifted dramatically.

The UNIA's emphasis on Black pride and the idea of people of African descent forging a unified global agenda significantly influenced the Harlem Renaissance. It also should be noted that Garvey was not the only well-known Caribbean figure in Harlem during this period. One of his rivals, Richard B. Moore of Barbados, who was more of a pan-Caribbean militant activist,[31] and the Jamaican writer Claude McKay are other notables. Overall, various African American political artistic figures of the time also shaped the emergence of the Renaissance, such as W.E.B. DuBois, Langston Hughes, Georgia Douglas Johnson,

Countee Cullen, Nella Larsen, A. Philip Randolph, Gwendolyn Bennett, Charles Johnson, to name a few.

Although many of Harlem's residents were low income at this time, the neighborhood also was a bastion for the Black elite. Doctors, lawyers, famous artists, businesspeople, all actually owned some of the majestic homes recently vacated by Whites fleeing to the suburbs. Sugar Hill and Striver's Row, Harlem's wealthier enclaves, became synonymous with African American success. In many ways, the elite's opportunity to demonstrate talent and prove the vast capabilities of people of African descent was a major focal point of the Renaissance.

HARLEM RENAISSANCE

As is still the case today to a certain degree, the arts, in the 1920s, opened doors to African American expression and professional success. Along with the general enthusiasm around a predominantly Black neighborhood in New York City, north of Southern Jim Crow and lynchings, and central to the most vibrant part of America, came both a need to exhibit racial pride and assert the many talents pulsating throughout the African diaspora. The Harlem Renaissance filled this need, and Harlem was the ideal locale in which to launch an artistic and political movement. As a result, the neighborhood became a haven for artists. Writers, painters, poets, musicians, and artists of all variety came to Harlem from all over the world. The works of notables such as Langston Hughes, James Weldon Johnson, Zora Neale Hurston, Countee Cullen, W.E.B. DuBois, Jesse Fauset, Dorothy West, Nella Larsen, and countless others created and sustained this renaissance for which Harlem has become legendary. Although many of the most recognized names from this renaissance were in literature, it was also a golden age for Black music.

This renaissance[32] not only fostered a sense of pride among people of African descent, it also caught the attention of Whites. In New York, Whites began to consume African American literature, enhancing the celebrity of the cadre of brilliant renaissance artists. Harlem's jazz and dancing produced international stars such as Duke Ellington, and the myriad clubs and cabarets provided entertainment well into the night. The Savoy Ballroom, the Cotton Club, and Small's Paradise Club vibrated with Harlem's music. However, Blacks were often barred from entering these White-owned establishments. W. C. Handy, the composer known as the "father of the blues,"[33] after once having been denied entry into the Cotton Club, could hear his own music playing inside as he stood outside.[34] The Cotton Club, opened in 1924 at 644 Lenox Avenue at 142nd Street, explicitly excluded Blacks, despite the fact that most of the artists were African Americans. The club, owned by a White mobster, Owney Madden, sometimes admitted light-skinned Blacks.[35] Explicit exclusion was not the case at every club. For example, the Savoy, opened in 1926, was accessible to Blacks and Whites. However, in the grand scheme of things, admission was not the only issue. Much of the ownership of the Harlem institutions of the time rested in White hands outside of the neighborhood.

As Langston Hughes wrote of his early days in Harlem, "Downtown! I soon learned that it was seemingly impossible for black Harlem to live without white downtown." He continued, "The famous night clubs were owned by whites, as were the theatres. Almost all the stores were owned by whites, and many at that time did not even (in the very middle of Harlem) employ Negro clerks. The books of Harlem writers all had to be published downtown, if they were to be published at all. Downtown: *white*. Uptown: *black*. White downtown pulling all the strings in Harlem."[36] As the displacement of African Americans predated today's Harlem, so did limited Black ownership and job opportunities.

Whether or not Black people were truly in control of the renaissance, the period saw unprecedented opportunities for artists, helping to establish Harlem as a center of Black cultural expression. As a result, Harlem attracted Black artists from all corners. The neighborhood's appeal to African American artists has endured well beyond the renaissance. Harlem resident, Laconia Smedley, a musician, came to Harlem from Detroit, about forty years ago. Some of his friends, also artists, had moved to the neighborhood, and encouraged him to make the move. Smedley said, "… they called me, and they would say, 'You know you have to come here to New York; it's this big city. It's this that and the other.' So I did."[37] Although African Americans have been living in segregated conditions in large urban centers for many years, those who had moved to Harlem from cities such as Detroit, encountered an altogether different culture and environment.

Smedley continued, "The first thing that scared me was the taxi picking me up to take me up here. You know, I hailed a taxi. Zoom! And I jumped back…. 'Cause it's a totally different tempo…. a change of rhythm, 'cause when we were riding, coming up, at that time Fifth Avenue was two ways, and we were coming up Fifth Avenue, and this beautiful building and, of course, the park on the other side, and the rhythm was kind of like knocks, kind of stiff like that. Then when it turned to go to Seventh Avenue ... the rhythm changed. And that was the first time I recognized the difference in vibrations of people.... I picked it up right away, loose, just hanging loose kind of thing. I said, "Wow!" That was a shock. The other shock was when we did turn on Seventh Avenue, I saw all these people who, to me, I would consider downtrodden people, yet there was spirit there—loose and free, profane, colorful, angry, real ... and it was loud, you know, and very, very, like, to me, aggressive.... So it was a culture shock."[38]

For much of the twentieth century, despite the initial shock brought on by the personalities of the neighborhood and New York City, Harlem remained a draw for people of African descent of all occupations, levels in life, and cultures. The "Harlem Renaissance" was often referred to as the "Negro Renaissance," rendering Harlem and Negro synonymous. The symbolism of Harlem as a center for Black life and culture existed throughout the twentieth century. As Harlem native Vicky Gholson noted, "All of our leaders come through here. All of our young people that are aspiring—they want to get the flavor, get the feel—want to be able come up with the new cloth, the new cut, the new do, come through here. And it's something we publicize. It's something we do as a people because this is one of the important migration stops."[39]

Harlem has rekindled aspects of the allure of the renaissance recently, but the neighborhood has confronted drugs, crime, and abandonment from the Depression until the very recent past. After the 1960s, and into the following decades, Harlem lost one hundred thousand residents, many of whom fled to the suburbs. Landlords abandoned properties that were no longer profitable to keep, and New York City took over ownership of about 65 percent of Harlem's buildings.[40]

Today, Harlem has not completely changed, but is noticeably different than that of only ten years ago. But even before Harlem began to decline, life for residents was far from easy because of racism and socioeconomic inequality.

OBSTACLES TO GREATNESS

Although Harlem was generally accessible to African Americans, as noted, residents have often been charged above-market rental prices, resulting in limited home ownership. During the 1920s, Harlem's population of two hundred thousand resided in dense conditions. With the high cost of living, residents were often forced to double up. Although the renaissance brought great visibility for a few highly educated African Americans, most Harlem residents were employed as maids, cooks, and servants, usually in nonunion positions.[41]

Those who were actually employed were the lucky ones, as several Harlem retail establishments would not hire Black people. One department store, Koch's, closed in 1930 rather than hire a Black salesperson.[42] Despite these efforts to limit opportunities for Black Harlem residents, the spirit of pride and defiance encouraged by the renaissance either fanned the flames of protest or created the conditions for community-driven development efforts. The Young Negroes Cooperative League, for example, developed economic cooperatives in 1930. In the wake of the 1929 stock market crash, this effort, under the leadership of its founder George Schuyler and its first executive director, Ella Baker, uplifted the concept of communalism, that would enable the community to share in the profits of such endeavors as cooperative grocery stores, buying clubs, and food distribution networks.[43] And community protest forced Blumstein's, Harlem's largest department store, to hire Black elevator operators.

Despite the resistance and the community building, the Depression would bring even more challenging times to Harlem. By 1932, half of Harlem was on public assistance, the Harlem Hospital mortality rate was twice as high as Bellevue's (in Midtown), and the salaries of unskilled and semiskilled laborers had dropped by 43 percent.[44] By the next year, Adam Clayton Powell Jr. was becoming more politically active and visible, particularly through the "Jobs for Negroes" movement.

It was daunting for Black communities to address the full range of issues that affected their lives. If the issue of focus was employment, then just as much energy would be required for health. If not health, then housing, and so on. Rental units were the most accessible forms of housing for Harlem residents, but homeownership could have been in more people's sights without policies that either denied Black people mortgages or provided risky loans at exorbitant interest rates. The National Housing Act of 1934 ushered in the notorious color-coded maps to determine mortgage availability. Many predominantly Black communities were "redlined" in this system, explicitly discouraging housing investment in communities like Harlem. No one, regardless of color, wanted to put down unreasonably high downpayments or pay outrageously high rates. Low-income African Americans could not even hope to own homes, as they would not get mortgages in the first place. As of 1940, fewer than a thousand black New Yorkers owned their own house or apartment.[45]

The compounding pressure of the various forms of discrimination, and the lack of opportunity in so many areas, helped spawn the Harlem Race Riots of 1935. Actually, it was police brutality, or the rumor of such, in this case, that sparked the rebellion. The rumor that a Black high school student was beaten by the police led more than ten thousand Black people to protest on 125th Street. The windows of some of the White-owned businesses were broken. Ultimately, 200 stores were destroyed, 100 Blacks were arrested, 3 were killed, and 30 injured.[46] The incident led to a report, commissioned by Mayor LaGuardia, released one year later, which indicated that pervasive oppression caused the riot, and called for sweeping changes in employment, education, and police brutality. Federally funded low-income housing was one of the specific responses to the riot, as projects were built along the Harlem River Drive between 151st and 153rd Streets.

The onset of World War II created the need for various new jobs, opening up opportunities for African Americans in shipbuilding and other industrial trades. Conversely, the need for protest persisted also, as various forms of discrimination continued. In 1941, most notably, A. Philip Randolph along with twenty-two thousand other African Americans rallied at Madison Square Garden to demand an end to employment discrimination. Along with representatives of the NAACP and the Urban League, Randolph threatened to march on Washington if Roosevelt would not integrate the defense industry. This threat actually influenced President Roosevelt to issue an Executive Order to integrate the war industry and institute a Fair Employment Practices Committee.[47]

In the World War II era, some of the housing restrictions had been lessened, and the GI Bill enabled veterans opportunities to buy homes and pursue higher education. These opportunities helped to forge a Black middle class, which, in many cases, was less restricted, and sought to move out of neighborhoods such as Harlem. Nevertheless, protest still continued, as another riot, again in response to police brutality, erupted in 1943. On August 1, 1943, a woman interfered with the arrest of another woman. The son of the intervening woman, Robert Bandy, a soldier, got into an altercation with the police officer. He ultimately was shot by the officer. Although Bandy survived, the rumor that Bandy was killed spread, leading to crowds spilling onto the streets from 110th all the way to 145th Streets. When all was said and done, 1,469 stores were vandalized, 606 people were arrested, and 189 people were injured; 4 Black people were killed by the police and 2 by other Blacks.[48]

The overall economy began changing at this time, as factory jobs in the city began to decline after the war, and a service-based economy was beginning to emerge. The Federal Housing Act of 1954 instituted low interest loans for urban renewal and development, a part of what became known as "slum clearance." What was once a federal housing agenda became a local one with this act, placing the decision of spending on housing in the hands of businesses, developers, and local politicians.[49]

Between 1958 and 1964, the New York City metropolitan area lost eighty-seven thousand factory jobs.[50] Urban decline at this level spawned greater attention to the problems confronting the neighborhood. By this point, policy began to focus on youth, as the Harlem Neighborhood Association, founded in 1958, was funded by the President Johnson's Commission on Juvenile Delinquency in 1962 to implement Harlem Youth Opportunities Unlimited (HARYOU). HARYOU's "$100 million package of reforms are some drastic steps, such as a 'Reading Mobilization Year,' during which Harlem pupils would spend every classroom hour on reading." [51]

This program, widely perceived as unsuccessful, focused on the psychology of youth, "to discourage dependency through an increasing sense of pride, confidence, and initiative in the youth themselves."[52] Numerous such efforts to improve Harlem have been pursued over the years, often with limited success.

The depth of the challenge facing the quest to improve conditions for urban low-income African Americans, such as those residing in Harlem during the 1960s, becomes evident in various dimensions. In other words, the kind of economic and educational development required for noticeable, sweeping improvement would require change in numerous sectors. With respect to economics, the combination of overcharging by vendors and debt in the African American community creates a need to change both systemic economic practices and economic literacy among African Americans.

A businessman in the 1960s, Hope Stevens, said, "Harlem lives on credit—its future wages are to a great extent pledged for the consumer goods purchased to the present. African Americans are great shoppers."[53] Habits aside, African Americans historically have been overcharged for basic goods. Moreover, overcharging for housing extends from the moment Harlem was becoming a Black neighborhbood to the present. Black-owned small businesses also have been notably over-charged for rent. Additionally, small businesses have struggled to sur-vive in the face of incoming larger chain establishments. Stevens also noted, "The small shopkeeper is rapidly being eliminated by the com-petition of the chains."[54]

These circumstances have fueled racial tension in various aspects of business/consumer relations. This is not to suggest that all Black/non-Black consumer/merchant relations are contentious,[55] but in Har-lem, where new businesses forcing out older smaller ones (especially those owned by African Americans), contentiousness has become rela-tively common. Although some businesses still survive, the possibility of eviction caused by an inability to keep up with expenses or simple going out of business for similar reasons is becoming more of a real prospect for those small businesses that remain.

However economic activity unraveled in Harlem into the 1960s, one of the key reasons why Harlem further declined between the 1960s and 1980s was the gradually deepening concentration of poverty. Before the mid-1960s, Harlem already contained a significant concentration of poverty. However, it was more economically diverse than the era that immediately followed. Given the state of segregation, the Black middle class, working class, impoverished, and even the more well-to-do lived among each other in Harlem, as well as other urban neighborhoods. Although poverty was certainly widespread in Harlem, several profes-sionals and merchants resided alongside the less fortunate. However, during the Civil Rights era, the end of most legalized forms of segre-gation opened up opportunities for African Americans, ranging from access to education to expanded uses of facilities to greater freedom of movement, the latter meaning access to housing outside of major-ity Black neighborhoods such as Harlem. Before the Civil Rights era, Blacks in Harlem were "a class as well as a race,"[56] as they shared a com-monality of experience, and often found that their race was the deter-mining factor in the number and kind of opportunities they found. This is not to suggest that race is no longer significant or that pre–Civil Rights class differences did not exist, but it is to say that the Black com-munity is more economically diverse than ever before.

Many of the higher-income African Americans, who moved out of Harlem during the '60s, '70s, and '80s, took vital resources along with them. Harlem remained a predominantly African American neighborhood, and remained the capital of the African diaspora; however, its resources were diminished. Moreover, few of the remaining Harlem residents owned local businesses or real estate. As a result, residents, for the most part, were left with not only low incomes but also with little wealth.[57] In a free market economy, lack of ownership generally means lack of power and control.

Some of this sense of disempowerment translated itself into an increase in crime, including drug dealing and usage. The impact of drugs reached its most frightening stages during the crack epidemic of the 1980s and early 1990s, which turned abandoned buildings into crack houses and exacerbated an already prevalent local drug industry.

Although many Harlem residents were low income, they found ways to survive. Communities were kept afloat by their own economic systems. Ownership of property and businesses is one way to gauge a community's economic power. However, the African American community, and similar disadvantaged communities, developed alternative means of survival, which include forms of bartering or sharing. These exchanges, which did not involve cash, kept communities functioning in creative and independent ways.

Vicky Gholson, a communications specialist, Harlem native, and true aficionado of Harlem culture and history, recalled the development of these economic systems. She said, "We have community economics, which generate from how we live, depending on what we came from, and that's how we move the money around within our communities. A lot of people, a lot of times, talk too frequently about how we don't retain the money in our community, but if we didn't retain a certain amount of it, none of us would ... be here, so it's that woman who asks the senior to take care of her kids—that's an economic exchange—that is extra money for that woman to be able to do what she needs to do. That person may get somebody to clean her home, to tidy it up, and she pays that person a certain amount of money—who lives in the neighborhood."[58]

Survival and creativity are other key themes that capture the efforts of African Americans seeking economic stability in their lives. With barriers at every turn, many Harlemites found ways to survive and made this neighborhood a household word in many parts of the world.

Harlem is often in the news locally and beyond. As the neighborhood entered the 1990s, we began to see the clash of the high-crime, drug-dominated era transitioning into the era of commercial development and increased residential desirability. The continued White ownership in the area, alongside lower-income people of color who owned very little, played itself out in a heavily publicized incident on 125th Street.

A longtime Harlem small business, Record Shack, and Freddy's, a larger store next door, became embroiled in a storm of tension and ultimately violence. Freddy's, a clothing store owned by a White merchant, Fred Harari, sought to expand by ending the lease of its tenant, Record Shack, owned by Sikhulu Shange. The property was actually owned by a local church, to which Shange pled his case. However, neither the church nor Harari budged on their decision. Community residents organized a boycott in response to this occurrence—a protest that emerged into a more vigorous element of anger, by one person in particular. This man, Roland Smith, firebombed Freddy's with a gun and a can of paint thinner, killing himself and seven of the store's employees (all of whom were not Black).[59]

Shange continued to confront rising rents following this incident, an extreme example of the extent to which tensions can explode. However, it provides a sense of the complexity of a changing Harlem. With ownership comes power and control. In business, opportunity to raise prices to meet rising demand holds no natural social conscience. The Shanges of Harlem can protest, and the Roland Smiths of Harlem can take the most drastic measures, but the wheels of development in Harlem are, have been, and will continue to be rolling. The challenge for longtime residents and small business owners, particular those who do not own property, is to find ways to influence the direction of development, ensure that some aspects of change in the neighborhood meet their needs, and find mutually beneficial solutions that will help developers and businesses see where interests converge. Because the retail industry needs consumerism of Harlem's continuous foot traffic and developers need a climate characterized by a strong community spirit. One mighty task for contemporary Harlem will be bringing together key representatives to develop strategies that simultaneously address wide-ranging desires and interests in a relatively equitable fashion.

HARLEM NOW

As the twenty-first century has emerged, many will tell you that Harlem is on the rise again—experiencing a new "renaissance." Others will say that Harlem is on the rise but will also be quick to ask, at whose expense? The several new businesses dotting Harlem's main thoroughfare, 125th Street, and the omnipresent construction projects from block to block are indicators of a potential economic boom. Although real estate rates in the area have skyrocketed, and Harlem has become a more desirable destination for those who would have never imagined setting foot on the northern pavements of Manhattan, the neighborhood is still far from gentrified. A great deal of residential property remains public, abandoned buildings can still be found, and many residents still confront a litany of urban problems.

Although the neighborhood comprises three community districts (New York City districts 9, 10, and 11), Central Harlem (district 10) is the primary focus of this book. Central Harlem is an indelible part of African American history but also a haven for drugs and crime that have terrorized the mostly Black, low-income, and working-class population. Nevertheless, the residents have endured. But as Harlem returns to vogue, a glance at population changes in recent decades tells some of the story of Harlem's metamorphosis.

In 2000, the total population of Central Harlem was 107,109, a 7.6 percent increase from the 1990 population of 99,915. As has been stated, the drugs and crime of the '70s and '80s drove some residents out of the neighborhood. Subsequently, the 1990 population was a decline from the 105,642 in 1980. Therefore, the increase between 1990 and 2000 is striking. With so much abandonment, many properties were vacated, boarded up, and some were burned out or demolished. Harlem was dotted with vacant lots filled with garbage. Now that properties are being redeveloped, the neighborhood has received an influx of new residents.

Central Harlem remains predominantly African American—88.3 percent of the population over eighteen years of age is in the "Black/African American Non-Hispanic" category. Under the age of eighteen, African Americans make up 85.6 percent of the population. Hispanics account for 9.1 percent of those over eighteen and 13 percent of those under eighteen. Given that low-income people of color historically have been undercounted by the census, it is safe to say that Central Harlem is vastly of color. Whites are a very small minority. However, the White non-Hispanic population increased by 50.8 percent for those under eighteen and 44.1 percent for those over eighteen.[60] The African American population, despite the vast overall increase in Harlem's population, has decreased by .9 percent for those under eighteen, and by 6.5 percent for those over eighteen. The latter figure is eye-catching, as so many Harlem families have resided in the neighborhood for several decades. As seniors may be passing on or moving out, the vacant units may be filled by Whites.

In 1990, 48.9 percent of Central Harlem's population was on some form of public assistance—welfare, Social Security, or Medicaid. In 2000, the number was 34.3 percent, with the largest decrease of cases in welfare, down from 34,366 caseloads to 16,387.[61] One could deduce from all of this data that Harlem is on the path to some shifts in racial and economic demographics.

Also important to note in Harlem's latest phase of development is land use. Central Harlem is 899.1 acres, extending for 1.4 square miles. Of the 4,806 lots in this area, only 173 are commercial; 581 of the total are mixed residential and commercial, and 28 industrial. The largest category of lots in Central Harlem is designated for multifamily residents—2,721 lots.[62]

The cost of residential property is often the most controversial aspect of gentrifying neighborhoods. Although the quality of services and the upkeep of housing increase, rising housing costs have the potential to lead to displacement—pushing lower-income individuals and families out of the neighborhood. The rising cost of housing in Harlem certainly suggests that prices are moving out of reach. Increases in the average price of a residential home have been steady: $190,000 in 1995 to $224,000 in 1996 to $237,000 in 1997 to $296,000 in 1998 to $303,000 in 1999 to $391,000 in 2000 to $412,000 in 2001.[63] In a six-year span, housing costs more than doubled. Sales of these homes have been brisk. In 2000, 117 homes were sold, up from 67 in 1999. One home in 2001 sold for $995,000. Although the economy has turned downward and the horrific events of September 11, 2001, significantly affected New York City (and the world), housing costs continue to rise. Aided by historically low interest rates, the New York City housing market as a whole has remained desirable. And, in general, New York City's economy has rebounded quite resiliently to the present day.

A New Renaissance?

With gradually shifting demographics, new business development, and rising housing costs, some feel Harlem is entering a new renaissance. But it does not appear that this current concept of a renaissance resembles the very racially and culturally driven 1920's movement, the goal of which was to uplift people of African descent. Regardless of the containment of a vibrant African–descended life and culture in Harlem, the neighborhood does not exist in a vacuum. This renaissance is a function of national trends around the increased popularity of certain major cities and broader economic forces. Harlem's changes have been especially affected by downturns in the U.S. economy and the state of New York City as whole.

The late 1990s brought a convergence of an overall economic boom, and a particular shift in New York City. The city became more desirable than ever, with a flourishing financial industry, and apparently cleaner and safer New York. As real estate prices skyrocketed in downtown Manhattan, ripple effects spread to nearby neighborhoods, such as downtown Brooklyn, parts of Queens (especially those in close proximity to Manhattan), and Harlem. With greater disposable income, those who benefited from the economic expansion, especially in technology and finance, were willing to buy and rent at unprecedented high rates. This increased demand, coupled with a limited supply, sent vacancy rates tumbling and prices rising. In 1996, the vacancy rate in New York City as a whole was 4.01 percent and 3.4 percent in Manhattan. By 1999, the city's rate stood at 3.19 percent, and Manhattan at 2.4 percent. Between this same period, the number of rental units under $400 per month decreased by 6.5 percent, and the number of those costing over $1,750 per month rose by 34 percent.[64]

Higher-income African Americans and moderate-income Whites began moving into Harlem, as the first demographic shift in Harlem's burgeoning gentrification process. Many of these new residents purchased new properties and refurbished them. In 1995, 2.3 percent of all New York City mortgage loans for home improvement were in Harlem. By 1998, that figure stood at 15 percent.[65] The number of mortgage loans made in Harlem steadily increased between 1995 and 1998. The number of African Americans receiving mortgage loans jumped from 144 in 1995 to 348 in 1998. Even more striking is the number of Whites receiving mortgages for Harlem properties, which moved from 19 in 1995 to 107 in 1998[66]—a 563 percent increase.

It is also important to note Harlem's growth as a tourist destination. "Ground Zero," the former site of the World Trade Center, is currently the top tourist destination in New York City. But in the few years prior to September 11, 2001, Harlem was second to the Statue of Liberty among New York tourist destinations. "Upper Manhattan" receives 1.4 million visitors per year, who spend $25.7 million on food, admissions, and shopping during their trips. The overall economic impact of tourism in Upper Manhattan on New York City is over $154 million and over $4 million in tax revenue. Many of these visitors travel to New York City, and, when in town, head uptown. One in five visitors to Upper Manhattan primarily visit to see the local sights in the area. First-time visitors to Upper Manhattan primarily wish to visit the Abyssinian Baptist Church, Sylvia's restaurant, and the Apollo Theatre. Churches are an increasingly popular destination for tourists wishing to sit in on inspirational services. A bus tour, called Harlem Spirituals, focuses specifically on taking tourists to church services on Sundays. It is the music, gospel as well as jazz, which is the primary draw for tourists.

Despite Harlem's popularity among tourists, many of those visitors to New York City are not familiar with Upper Manhattan. Ironically fewer domestic than international travelers were even familiar with Harlem. The French, in fact, are the largest single group of visitors to the neighborhood. Japanese are also frequent visitors. Many of those who indicated that they were unfamiliar with Upper Manhattan, and not interested in visiting, listed concern about public safety as their primary reason for staying downtown.[67] Despite some remaining negative perceptions about Harlem and the rest of Upper Manhattan, the impact of tourism cannot be denied. If tourists can see Harlem's assets, others will follow.

Maybe Harlem's most newsworthy recent change was the controversial uptown migration of former President of the United States William Jefferson Clinton. In order to divert attention from his first office space choice, a lavish and expensive midtown suite, Clinton struck a deal that enabled him to do business out of 55 West 125th Street, right in the middle of the busiest section of Harlem. Some Harlem residents criticized this move, and, as will be discussed later, some residents do not think Clinton's presence improves the community. However, a late July 2001 ceremony at the plaza of the Adam Clayton Powell State Office Building (on 125th Street), brought out many well-wishers. A crowd of two thousand generally favored Clinton's presence, periodically chanting, "We love Bill."[68] Nevertheless, protestors chanting "slavemaster" made it clear that the range of responses to Clinton span the entire spectrum of possible opinions.

Clinton, himself, is aware of the potential perils of gentrification, and how his very decision to locate his office in Harlem could drive up prices. In a recent interview for the *New York Times*, Clinton said, "I want to make sure I'm a good neighbor in Harlem. I'm glad property values are going up, but I don't want small business people to be run out because I'm coming in."[69] This, of course, is easier said than done. As the noted journalist David Levering Lewis stated, "But even with the former president's good intentions, we would be a little naïve to think that large numbers of poor and working-poor families won't be displaced by increasing gentrification."[70] It is interesting that Clinton lauded the increase in Harlem's property values in this article. Often a sign of a strong economy, increased property values are usually treated positively, as if universally beneficial.

Under the Clinton administration in 1994, what is known as the Empowerment Zone became law—a ten-year designation accompanied by a $300 million grant to each cluster of neighborhoods in particular cities in need of economic development. In the Upper Manhattan Empowerment Zone (UMEZ) cluster, the goal has been to revitalize a vast area covering Central, East, and West Harlem, as well as Washington Heights, the neighborhood to the north of Harlem, and Inwood, which is at the northern tip of Manhattan.

Clinton particularly focused on small businesses in his remarks, and, indeed, this is an issue worthy of discussion in Harlem's recent changes. The business dimension of Harlem's economic shift is, in fact, one of the more visible indicators of a new day dawning. A central aspect of the Federal Empowerment Zone funding provided quite an additional infusion to Harlem's commercial development. This change is inextricable from the residential real estate prices and altered demographics. The Empowerment Zone legislation provided tax breaks and low interest loans to attract the Harlem USA shopping complex, Magic Johnson's movie theatre, a Starbucks, and several other retail establishments. Much of this development concentrated on 125th Street. More recently, it has begun to spread to other areas within the cluster.

Federal and state funding are only the beginning, as the Empowerment Zone is also designed to leverage private sector resources. As the former Upper Manhattan Empowerment Zone director Deborah Wright stated, "The idea is to take the Empowerment Zone funds and leverage them with private money. The private sector has a whole different set of criteria for investment than what's been used up here in the past. It's not about who owes whom or who's friends with whom. The numbers have to pencil out, and that, by itself, will fundamentally change Harlem."[71] The UMEZ certainly has leveraged dollars, according to their own data.

From its inception to 2002, for every Empowerment Zone dollar spent $5.20 was matched. The numbers are even more staggering for 2001 and 2002, where $7.87 was matched per Empowerment Zone dollar. To be more specific, the UMEZ invested $40,971,000 in this period, and leveraged $322,579,470.[72]

Wright's comments spoke not only of raw dollars but also of a mentality. She referred to the informal nature in which business historically had been conducted in Harlem, where most significant deals were brokered through relationships with notable local elites, such as Congressman Charles Rangel, former Mayor David Dinkins, or businessman Percy Sutton.

But it was those notable elites, particularly Charlie Rangel, who advocated for the Zone, not just for Harlem but also for distressed urban areas nationwide. I was fortunate enough to meet with former New York City Mayor David Dinkins, to discuss these issues. In his spacious office at Columbia University's International Affairs Building, one floor above my own, he squeezed in some moments within his hectic schedule. When we spoke, Dinkins said that Congressman Rangel was the key figure in bringing about the Empowerment Zone legislation. Rangel "recognized that there was really no federal plan for cities, and he went to the leadership in the Congress—in the House, and said that this was true and he wanted to revive the notion that Jack Kemp [former Congressman and Hud Director] and Bobby Garcia [former Congressman, who represented the Bronx from 1978—1990] had ... and he had a notion for what they called enterprise zones, as I recall."[73] Dinkins continued, "The leadership of the House told him [Rangel], 'Well, there's no more money, I mean if you want to spend money on any item, you have to get it.' And Charlie said, in effect, 'You get me the legislation, I'll get the money.' And he did; he got it out of the White House. It came technically from Health and Human Services, but it was administered by HUD, and there was a competition for them. They had a finite amount of money, and cities around the country competed.... And New York was a competitor for one of these Empowerment Zones. I was Mayor; we made an application. People here at Columbia [University] helped develop the application, and the area we chose included Congressman Rangel's district, for obvious reasons, and we won. And it called for three hundred million dollars over a ten-year period."[74] He uttered this figure as if it were merely symbolic—an important, but limited, amount.

The principle goals for the Zone include expanded economic opportunities, and improved overall quality of life. The program explicitly includes provisions to ensure that existing residents and community organizations benefit from improvements stimulated by the Zone.

Specifically, qualified employers in the Zone receive an annual tax credit of up to $3,000 for each local resident hired. Particular businesses in the Zone also can be eligible for tax-exempt bonds to finance renovations, expansions, and the purchase of new facilities. In order for a business venture to receive Zone support, it must demonstrate its ability to address the following stated "impact" criteria. The UMEZ Request for Proposal reads:

1. Does it expand economic activity by increasing jobs through the expansion and creation of businesses?
2. How will local residents, businesses and/or institutions benefit? For example, how does the initiative provide or protect essential support services necessary to facilitate residents' job readiness? Are local businesses or other institutions, including nonprofits a part of proposer's team in a way that empowers them to strengthen, expand or protect the scope of their activities?
3. Is the quality of life improved for residents, workers and/or visitors, e.g., is the physical environment of the EZ communities improved by blight removal or upgraded infrastructure (public safety, shopping environment, transportation, etc.)?

Evidently, pains were taken to ensure that the program would benefit local residents, organizations, and businesses. This language articulates a brand of development that, at least in words, leans toward economic empowerment. However, effective implementation of such goals may be more elusive than originally thought. Dinkins suggests that high expectations and misperceptions about the role and extent of the UMEZ were rampant. He said, "Now, to people in Harlem, Empowerment Zone, three hundred million dollars, sounded like there was this pile of money sitting over there—go get a handful! And, of course, it's not like that at all. Number one, three hundred million is over a ten-year period, and two, it wasn't money for grants."[75]

In order to address the multiple issues confronting an area of Harlem's size, greater investments are needed. As mentioned, additional funding was leveraged, but the question is, for what? From its inception in 1996 to 2002, UMEZ funds were concentrated in three areas:

business investment (58 percent of the funding), tourism and cultural industry development (27 percent), and workforce and human capital investment (15 percent). In 2001 and 2002, the figures shifted, with an increase in funding for business development (81 percent), a decrease in tourism (18 percent), and workforce development has been reduced to a tiny 1 percent.[76] Primary goals always surface in the implementation, and the increased investment not only suggests that the UMEZ is trying harder to attract businesses to the community but also the reality that Harlem is hot when it comes to new business. The arrival of new retail businesses in Harlem USA (including Old Navy, Magic Johnson's Theatre, and others), and in other spots on 125th Street is well documented. However, the UMEZ also has been supporting new small businesses and restaurants. Its "Restaurant Initiative" has funded new restaurants, such as Bayou, Moca Bar and Grill, Sugar Hill Bistro, Taste of Seafood, Amy Ruth's, Settepani Bakery, and Coogan's. Small businesses, such as the Hue-Man Bookstore and MIKSU Cosmetics, also have received funding.[77]

Larger projects include Gotham Plaza and the Gateway—office buildings, three stories each, totaling forty-five thousand square feet, and the Langston Hotel, a three-thousand-square-foot boutique hotel. Other new businesses have arrived, including Jennifer Convertibles furniture store and AT&T Wireless. The presence of banks is also of note, as quite a number of new financial institutions have either already opened or will soon open, such as JPMorgan Chase, Fleet, Washington Mutual, Amalgamated, and HSBC.[78]

It should be noted that when discussing the investments in Upper Manhattan through the Empowerment Zone, the target area expands well beyond Harlem's boundaries, reaching further uptown into Washington Heights and parts of Inwood (the northernmost neighborhood in Manhattan). Because this book focuses essentially on Central Harlem, much of the discussion focuses within these boundaries. However, the boundaries are not so rigid, and some of the recent investments are so large that they affect the entire area. For example, one of the largest developments underway is in East Harlem, the East River Plaza, which will become a 500,000-square-foot, four-story retail development, stretching from 116th Street to 119th. Tenants already signed on include Home Depot, another Gap, another Old Navy, Staples, Costco, Best Buy, and Marshalls; $15,000,000 of Empowerment Zone funds are being contributed to make this effort a reality.[79]

Although small businesses are included in the UMEZ approach, the funding to small businesses in 2001 and 2002 was a mere fraction of the funds going to larger business projects. Total funds to small business development stands at $2,813,500,[80] whereas those funds under the category of "business investment" stand at $28,725,000.[81] It appears that the flow of dollars has leaned toward larger commercial businesses. From the outset, UMEZ prioritized creating jobs and leveraging funds, certainly their approach is working in this sense. But what are the ripple effects of these decisions, as they relate to longtime, especially low-income, Harlem residents? What is the impact of these efforts on the everyday lives of preexisting Harlem residents?

Although the presence of federal policy to develop inner-city areas is essential, the kind of comprehensive approach necessary is far more costly. The level of change required to improve the circumstances of the low-income residents, in particular, will take commitment from government, business, nonprofits, and community residents. On the surface, UMEZ might declare success given its stated goals.

The business development taking place in Harlem capitalizes on the great potential for retail stores to thrive in a heavily populated, pedestrian-oriented, conveniently located area. In some ways this is consistent with business development before Harlem's less desirable periods in the '70s and '80s. The primary thrust of this period of development has not focused on "buying Black" and other similar ideas that had flourished in the neighborhood throughout its history. As Harlem was becoming predominantly African American, Black-owned local business emerged as an extension of Harlem's culture. Residents were able to create small businesses, such as funeral homes, law firms, medical practices, barbershops, and beauty shops. Among the more successful businesses were Carver Savings and Loan and United Mutual Life Insurance Company. These businesses were Black-owned and served a local, Black clientele; dollars circulated within the community. Although small business was not the economic panacea for Harlem and its residents, entrepreneurs could aspire to create local businesses given the opportunities, residents could patronize establishments that catered directly to their needs, and the Black-owned small businesses were part and parcel of the unique culture and life of Harlem.

The current business development in Harlem has focused largely on attracting national chain retail corporations, which do not target specific audiences, and are not locally owned or controlled or uniquely reflective of any particular culture. Ironically, what made Harlem so attractive during the original renaissance were the unique elements cultivated by Harlem's African American population. What could be found in Harlem could not be found anywhere. A Gap, an HMV, a Starbucks, an Old Navy, and other similar chains can be found in just about any American city or suburban strip.

On the whole, it does not appear that the primary emphasis in business development, through the UMEZ, in the neighborhood is focused on turning the ownership trend toward local residents. Although businesses new to the area provide certain conveniences for residents, it does appear that Harlem's current renaissance targets a population yet to arrive as much if not more than the population that has been present. The original renaissance promoted the unique contributions of a new African American population poised to assert its significance. This is not to suggest that Black businesses are completely ignored. Some small Black-owned businesses are receiving subsidies and technical assistance, as I will discuss in the next chapter. This is only to say that the primary focus has been on large retail chains.

Looking forward, the myriad commercial and residential projects slated for development in Harlem could blur your vision. In addition to what was already indicated, the planned arrival of Edison Schools, Inc., a corporation that operates private schools, might be the first national corporation to headquarter in Harlem. A new Museum for African Art is in the works, a gourmet food store with locations in some of the ritzier parts of Manhattan, Citarella, should open on 125th Street in the near future. In addition, Citarella will move its food preparation center to a former Taystee Cake Bakery on 126th Street. Additionally, a 220,000-square-foot complex at Duke Ellington Circle, overlooking Central Park, at the southern end of Harlem is under construction. I could go on, for example, mentioning the various condominium buildings and redeveloped residential units underway.[82]

Harlem is beginning to look more like the rest of Manhattan. But as Harvard fellow John Jackson notes in his book, *Harlem World*, Harlem is not Manhattan.[83] Harlem's significance as a center of African American life and culture may very well be in jeopardy in the long run. But as these resources enter the neighborhood, the challenge of ensuring that longtime residents benefit rather than lose is of utmost concern. It could be that the residents are expected to sink or swim in an increasingly competitive environment. If development is going to result in widespread empowerment, residents, community organizations, corporations, government, and real estate developers all must take some action, beyond market forces, to ensure some degree of balance in Harlem's current and future economic development.

2

HARLEM RISING

Harlem residents and community organizations have been traditionally active in the pursuit of some sense of justice in the neighborhood.
Throughout the twentieth century, Harlem residents and community
organizations have been addressing a number of injustices from higher
prices and lower service to redlining, the process by which banks deny
lending within specific geographic boundaries. The engine behind
African American pride and socioeconomic advancement in Harlem
has rested in community-based institutions. From churches to small
businesses to activist organizations to block associations and beyond,
Harlem residents have stressed organization as a means to improved
social change.

It should never be said that Harlem's development is only taking
place at the top. Much of the change that has occurred has been facilitated by grassroots efforts to clean up blocks and engage residents in
improving their overall surroundings. However, the development from
above—at the level of large developers and corporations—creates significant ripple effects in the lives of longtime low-income and working

class Harlem residents. Many see the impact of local development as diluting rather than strengthening resident empowerment. This reality has encouraged some to increase their community building efforts and raise their voices.

With rising prices, organizations such as the Harlem Tenants' Council have stepped up their efforts to organize residents and protest the nature of change in the neighborhood, whereas community building agencies such as the Harlem Children's Zone have secured additional funding to provide multiple services to the existing Harlem population. Both of these organizations share the goal of enabling residents to stay in their homes and take advantage of a safer, cleaner, better-serviced neighborhood. Both attention to social services and community organizing are required in order to stave off the potentially damaging ripple effects of urban development.

The Harlem Tenants' Council, headed by Nellie Bailey, has held town hall meetings on the neighborhood's rising prices and has organized various protests as well. The Council tells a story that gets lost in the myriad articles and discussions about Harlem's renewal. A Council-sponsored survey of Harlem residents revealed that 70 percent of minority households in the community earn less than $15,000 per year.[1] Given that the definition of "affordable housing" in New York City includes homes priced between $300,000 and $600,000, it is little wonder why some residents are outraged.[2] An October 2000 "Citywide Anti-Gentrification March and Rally" sponsored by the Citywide Tenants' Coalition—a broad coalition of community based organizations moved across 125th Street, starting at Old Navy at Harlem USA, amidst chants of "Harlem for the needy, not for the greedy!" and "Harlem is not for sale! This is our home!"[3] The March ultimately ended in Morningside Park (the West Side of Harlem, just below 125th Street), where a rally ensued, with other chants, such as "No housing! No peace!" and "No lease! No peace!"[4]

Protesters coexist with those who would prefer to cooperate with the changes taking place. The Mount Morris Park Community Improvement Association, for example, has emphasized the upkeep of its immediate neighborhood. Not far from the center of 125th Street, residents of this part of Harlem have welcomed some of the changes. The head of the Association, Valerie Jo Bradley, has said, "There is a real need to bring in the supermarkets, bookstores, boutiques, restaurants, dry cleaners, shoe repair shops—anything you can get in any other neighborhood."

Despite this cooperative spirit, even those residents who would like to see change worry about damaging ripple effects. Bradley also said, "But I also think there's a real willingness by ordinary people to keep Harlem on the scale that it is, and not a great desire to see this place get yupped up or see an overabundance of franchises and big corporate stores running out a lot of the small businesses. There has to be a delicate balance."[5]

As I will discuss later, many Harlem residents feel insecure over the recent economic changes in the neighborhood. Many fear displacement as a result of rising real estate rates. With all of Harlem's recent popularity, it is the longtime residents who made Harlem what it is today. Although the neighborhood faced numerous social and economic trials and tribulations in recent years, residents stuck it out. Community organizing on blocks and in buildings enhanced a sense of community but also cleaned up blocks, built community gardens, fought crime, and held landlords accountable to meeting tenant needs. Many of those new to Harlem don't always realize how much the way had been paved for those coming in. Harlem resident Cynthia Simmons said, with respect to new residents entering the community, "... there is a tremendous conflict between the new buyers and the old ones, you know, they call them "low-income tenants"—not understanding that if they had not taken charge of those buildings, that there would be nothing there for them to rent. Or, I mean none of those people would have lived in those buildings when there was no heat or no hot water for stretches of weeks."[6]

Laconia Smedley's block association, on 121st Street, has spent a great deal of time addressing crime and drug concerns. They began their crusade to clean up the area in 1983, and it did not start "clearing up" until 1999. Smedley laments that new residents coming into the neighborhood "have no idea what it was like." When asked where he thought the block would be without their efforts, he said, "At best, it would be—it would hold at the same level it was. And I feel with the kind of intellect these people [drug dealers] have, of takeover, it would be worse, because they will take the place over if you let them. They put fear in people...."[7] According to Smedley, the drug activity that brought Harlem to its knees was not accidental. He said, "... people will put drugs in a neighborhood where people are depressed, and you know, they'll take over the drug because that's their savior; you know that will make them feel better."[8]

Drug dealers were able to take over entire buildings and blocks throughout Harlem because some residents were susceptible to addiction. However, many of those residents who stayed in Harlem did fight to clean up the neighborhood, assisting mightily in Harlem's redevelopment. Therefore, the changing Harlem is not merely a top-down effort; residents played a crucial role in positioning Harlem for change. The question that remains is whether or not the residents will benefit or be shortchanged in the long run.

GENTRIFICATION AND THE URBAN FUTURE

During the '70s and '80s, American urban areas faced significant capital flight. Although this trend has not ceased in all or even most cities around the country, we have seen a more recent movement of capital to the central city in places such as New York, San Francisco, Chicago, and some places outside of the United States as well, such as London, which has led to increased real estate rates as well as displacement particularly of low-income residents who rent. As a result, inner-city residents, often with little economic means, are forced to leave neighborhoods they have called home for—in some cases—generations. This makes way for a wealthier population, a sort of modern "gentry," to move in. This new population desires increased services and new establishments to suit its tastes. The old population becomes priced out of the area and has little hope of returning. This process, known as "gentrification," is becoming increasingly apparent in the United States from Boston to Chicago to Atlanta to San Francisco. The term came into vogue in Britain in response to the redevelopment of London neighborhoods and the subsequent entry of middle-class residents.

One of the more apparent aspects of gentrification is the close proximity of low-income and wealthier populations during the process of change. Whereas low-income people traditionally have had their circumstances exacerbated by distance from those who are more economically stable, the kind of urban development facing Harlem actually fosters mixed economic communities. However, what has been lacking in other neighborhoods undergoing gentrification has been mixed *opportunities*. On another side of New York City, in the Park Slope section of Brooklyn, for example, the population has shifted drastically from a more diverse, less well-to-do population to one that is far Whiter, and wielding significantly greater means. Even though the neighborhood may become cleaner, safer, and more convenient, unless specific opportunities to improve the lives of low-income people are instituted, mixed economic communities will remain temporary phases in neighborhood transition, from affordable to exclusive.

In other words, the main issue at stake in urban development is in the realm of access and opportunity rather than merely cleaning things up and increasing property values. The lack of opportunity for low-income people is apparent in the persistently vast and continually increasing worldwide and America-wide gap in income and wealth. This gap has, in fact, become an increasing barrier to low-income and low-wealth communities. The capital that vacated urban areas in the '70s, '80s, and '90s carried with it stable manufacturing unionized jobs either to the outskirts of urban areas or to other countries. The majority of jobs available to lower-skilled labor and those with less formal education are in the service industry, and for less income and stability and fewer benefits. Gentrification is a daunting threat to many urban communities because of sheer mathematics.

MANAGING RIPPLE EFFECTS

Neighborhood change is inevitable. Urban development, often designed to improve the quality of low-income neighborhoods, while improving some services, and enhancing some opportunities, also can spawn ripple effects that exacerbate or create economic, social, political, and cultural challenges for those of limited means. Urban development that can positively impact a critical mass of longtime low-income residents requires attention to several factors—an anticipation of the potentially damaging consequences of decisions, and a commitment to achieving a common good.

In some ways, Harlem's recent economic changes have benefited longtime residents, but not enough mechanisms are in place to avoid or limit negative consequences for low-income residents in particular. One of the key reasons that low-income communities suffer is the lack of connection to opportunity. Harlem's focus on bringing new businesses to the neighborhood is one way in which residents can gain access to jobs, but even this strategy, in the absence of a full complement of other interrelated efforts, has significant limitations.

Over the last few decades, an entire field has emerged, focusing on comprehensive community development designed to improve inner-city conditions by addressing multiple issues simultaneously, while leveraging a complement of existing resources through collaboration.

As a result of this growing movement, the Aspen Institute, a nonprofit think tank, convened a "roundtable" of people who have been engaged in this kind of work to reflect on the strengths and weaknesses of such efforts, and help the field think about how to most effectively revitalize urban communities. Aspen, as a result of numerous conversations with its roundtable, emphasizes two key principles for urban development: "comprehensiveness," simultaneously addressing social, economic, and physical conditions; and "community building," promoting widespread participation in forging development efforts.

Standing alone, any strategy that tries to address everything at once and include everyone probably sounds a bit too utopian to support. However, in practice, these principles have merit, and can be applied to productive efforts. Development efforts can focus on "strategic drivers," or particular social issues, such as employment, housing, and so on, in which the focus may be on one issue but the analysis remains broad. This enables those participating in development initiatives to hone in on particular short-term goals, while keeping the bigger picture in mind.[9]

In many ways, community building is a means of creating new vehicles through which residents can impact policy. Too often, the perspectives of those impacted by policy are not addressed when decisions are made. The philosophy behind this thinking has logic—if the recipients of policy do not have a say, they will not own the results. The philosophy behind comprehensive approaches also makes sense in that the issues confronting communities are deeply intertwined, to the point where it is difficult to separate one's ability to access a job from the state of schooling from the relative affordability of housing. Although, with limited resources, it is practical to focus on one issue, the broader context must be kept in mind at all times.

While keeping the big picture in constant view, it is easier to anticipate the ripple effects of particular development decisions. For example, if an employment development strategy is pursued, how does it impact small businesses, real estate, the environment, and other issues? Ripple effects occur with any decision, but how can potentially negative ripple effects be transformed to create positive ones? How can development lead to widespread empowerment? In thinking about development, I recommend what I call *ripple effects management*. What I mean by this is a development strategy that is thoughtful enough on the front end to anticipate how particular decisions can affect other areas, especially concerning low-income communities, and increase the chances of this development yielding positive ripple effects. The intent is to turn potentially negative consequences for low-income communities into positive ones. A *ripple effects management* strategy cannot be successfully conducted without including the participation of those who will be affected.

No matter how many ideas around comprehensive development might be developed, policy makers, corporations, and developers may not have the best interest of communities, particularly low-income ones, automatically in mind. However, if those residents are involved, it is more likely that various influential figures and institutions will have a greater understanding of their point of view, and become better positioned to collaboratively craft mutually beneficial strategies. The other continuous challenge to the pursuit of such broad, contextual development approaches is decision making. Involving community residents is not new, but opening up genuine avenues to shared governance between communities, institutions, and government is a more elusive proposition.

THE SIGNIFICANCE OF URBAN COMMUNITIES

Urban areas are not just residences for lower-income communities. Most cities are designed with extensive public services to meet the needs of their citizens. From public schooling to public hospitals to public housing, cities remain destinations for those at every economic level. But although cities contain extensive public services, the distribution of these services has been a topic of constant debate among residents, public officials, academics, and others. Low-income urban neighborhoods often have faced slower responses to emergencies, sporadic garbage collection, crumbling public schools, and dangerous, neglected public housing complexes. When neighborhoods are gentrified, some of these issues are addressed. More specifically, the issues that directly affect the more affluent new residents, such as garbage collection might receive sufficient attention. However, other issues, like the conditions of public schools, might not be, as new residents very well may send their children to private schools or not have children at all.

Ironically, in many gentrified or gentrifying neighborhoods, older residents organized around and demanded greater resources from the public and private sectors, such as cleaner streets, fresh produce, convenient stores, and so many basic services. This has been occurring in Harlem, and a variety of New York City neighborhoods, especially in

Brooklyn. These residents paved the way for greater investment, responsiveness, and accountability from businesses, real estate developers, and local government. For a neighborhood such as Harlem, in the (albeit early) process of gentrifying, longtime lower-income residents face the challenge of gaining access to new resources in the neighborhood they made desirable.

Gentrification often has been addressed largely in the context of housing and the relative access to affordable residential units. However, gentrification has many interrelated dimensions and affects neighborhoods at a variety of levels. In addition to real estate, commercial development and interpersonal relations should be addressed as well in painting a broader picture of dynamics in gentrification. A *residential real estate* dimension is obvious, as housing ultimately becomes a central obstacle for low-income communities once gentrification is underway. *Commercial development* is another key dimension, as new businesses enter changing communities, and real estate developers become increasingly interested in properties and land use. Finally, an *interpersonal* dimension is also critical as neighborhoods undergo demographic shifts during gentrification, and tensions arise between old and new populations. Many other issues also come into play; however, in the study of gentrification, residential real estate and interpersonal relations are often key focal points.[10] Another key variant is culture, as the nature and character of communities change.[11]

A fully gentrified area no longer caters to the previous population economically, socially, culturally, or politically. Because of the extent of corporate subsidies to attract retail chains, commercial development is particularly significant in the case of Harlem. Community Development Corporations in the neighborhood, the Empowerment Zone, and others made a conscious effort to attract businesses to the neighborhood in order to connect residents to jobs and improve consumer services. Although some residents have been employed as a result of this effort, and new services have entered the area, the presence of many of the new businesses alters aspects of Harlem's culture that have made the neighborhood unique and compelling. A comprehensive view of the various dimensions at work in neighborhood change is essential in shaping how we craft solutions to the negative consequences that can occur as a result of urban development. It is, in fact, heavy attention to one aspect of development, while overlooking other key aspects that fosters unbalanced approaches that benefit only those with resources. Extant literature on gentrification and related issues has begun to address the strengths and limitations of urban development, and resident efforts to leverage accessible directions. However, research has only begun to address a more holistic, solution-based approach that could lead to greater equity in urban communities undergoing development.

In *Resisting Gentrification and Displacement,* the sociologist Vicky Muniz analyzes the community organizing of Puerto Rican women in the Brooklyn neighborhood of Sunset Park. She rightfully maintains that gentrification is often met with community resistance. Gentrification, according to Muniz, is a struggle. Not only must several external institutions and individuals organize to comprehensively restructure neighborhoods but also existing residents must organize on behalf of their interests as well. Muniz discusses the overall awareness of Puerto Ricans of the history of displacement of their community throughout New York City. This awareness, which she notes is across class, further facilitates the organized resistance of Puerto Rican residents. According to Muniz, much of the literature on gentrification portrays the "gentrifiable working class as passive and conformist."[12]

Muniz largely focuses on how communities address the housing dimension of gentrification, but her work is critical because it addresses the issues through the perspectives of residents—longtime residents, who stood everything to gain from opposing processes that would result in displacement from their neighborhood. Even in the absence of formal avenues to shape the direction of urban development initiatives to their advantage, residents create spaces through which their voices are heard. The focus of this book is not on resistance to urban development in Harlem; however, any attempt to understand the relative success of urban development initiatives includes residents' interactions with the social, economic, and political dimensions affecting their lives. Additionally, resident perspectives provide deeper insights, shedding light on the true complexities at work in neighborhood change scenarios, helping to crystallize the potential ripple effects of various decisions. They are usually less interested in glossing over the hard issues, and often interested in finding realistic ways to improve their neighborhoods.

Because gentrification is a relatively new concept, rooted in a very particular history of urban decline, followed by a return to vogue for certain inner city areas, we have only begun to understand this concept. Today's reality is that urban development takes place in stages. Therefore, we now have enough examples to think about the phases of neighborhood change that could result in gentrification. Taking a stab at this, and the phases are probably many, a crude way to look at this might be the following:

- *Stage 1:* Grassroots-level organizing—cleaning up streets, holding public officials accountable to the community, and so on.
- *Stage 2:* Planning—policy makers become involved in actively developing strategies, working with CDCs and business—explicit solicitations to a more affluent potential residents.
- *Stage 3:* Pioneer—new residents begin to move in, a few new shops appear appealing to that population; real estate prices begin to rise.
- *Stage 4:* Intensive investment—policy makers, businesses, new residents, developers intensify their investment.
- *Stage 5:* Population shift—demographics and businesses are noticeably different, and the previous culture appears out of date.
- *Stage 6:* Displacement—fewer and fewer low-income residents can hold onto their rent-stabilized apartments or longtime residents have sold their properties.
- *Stage 7:* Full transformation—the old neighborhood is largely unrecognizable, and most residents are of the newer population, their culture dominates, and most businesses cater to them.

Quite a number of factors shape these stages, such as the size of the neighborhood, the availability of affordable housing, the strength of the pre-existing community, and certainly the level of resources and determination among those wishing to see substantial change. The neighborhood known as Park Slope in Brooklyn is probably somewhere between Stages 6 and 7. Certain parts of San Francisco are indeed at Stage 7. The Upper West Side of Manhattan, below 96th Street, is pretty much at Stage 7. Harlem is probably somewhere between Stages 4 and 5. The fact that data has not pointed to significant displacement in Harlem has received significant press. But this does not mean that Harlem's changes will not evolve to later phases in gentrifying. Quite a bit of Harlem's housing stock had been abandoned, and the neighborhood contains extensive public housing. Furthermore, rent stabilization keeps many people in their apartments. They don't want to move; they can't afford to move. But they rely on the continuance of housing policies such as rent stabilization to allow them to stay. Without it, they would have to move. Therefore, gentrification can be a slow process depending on land use policy, housing policy, and availability.

Although Harlem is by no means fully "gentrified," it is experiencing redevelopment. We can already see some Harlem residents losing out as a result of increased prices. Many could argue that these are simple market forces at work. One could say that Manhattan is the engine behind the nation's economy, increasing its desirability for residents and visitors. With this increase in demand for space and services catering to the elite, Harlem is ripe for transformation. Given its close proximity to Midtown Manhattan, Harlem is potentially valuable to a host of parties who previously overlooked or even dismissed the area's potential. Now, wealthier individual house or apartment hunters of all races, retail businesses, restaurateurs, and real estate developers are all taking note of the emergence of a new era in Harlem.

Harvard Business School professor Michael Porter's landmark *Harvard Business Review* article published in 1995, "The Competitive Advantage of the Inner City," argued that inner-city communities must create wealth, and do so by capitalizing on "strategic location, local market demand, integration with regional clusters, and human resources." In order to do this, according to Porter, communities must abandon antibusiness sentiments, and accept a "new model." As previously noted, the attraction of new businesses to Harlem has the potential to leverage new resources for existing residents.

Porter is right in that communities like Harlem could benefit from new local businesses and wealth-creation strategies. However, context is essential; business-focused strategies absent of safe guards for the community, accountability for newer companies, business opportunities for residents themselves, avenues for training and advancement in new jobs for residents, and multiple other factors, merely replicate existing inequalities. Being a predominantly African American neighborhood, and knowing what the sociologists Melvin Oliver and Harvey Shapiro,[13] in their landmark book *Black Wealth/White Wealth,* have highlighted regarding the racial gap in wealth, local business, and economic development strategies are essential.

Healthy partnerships with external businesses and the regional economy are also critical, as region is another key contextual factor to include in conceptualizing and implementing urban development efforts. Given the wealth in outer ring suburbs and in some downtown areas, communities like Harlem require pathways to those areas. Few inner-city communities possess such a strategic location as Harlem, which is effectively New York's gateway to the rest of the world—minutes from LaGuardia Airport, the George Washington Bridge, and Westchester County. But the question remains: If Harlem successfully leverages its competitive advantage, to what degree do those resources reach low-income, longtime residents?

When the panoply of social contextual factors does not receive sufficient consideration in urban development strategies, market forces are left to their own devices. This is not to suggest that every single real estate developer or corporation is inherently greedy or only self-interested. In fact, the significance of personal will cannot be ignored in this respect. However, the lack of measures to ensure benefits to low-income residents worsens security in already unstable life situations. Does the market have any responsibility to disadvantaged communities? Is there any way in which a disadvantaged neighborhood can experience significant economic development without displacing residents or increasing pressure on their lives? It does not appear that policy makers have figured out how to foster successful economic development that benefits and does not displace existing low-income populations. Maybe the suggestions of residents and community organizations might help policy makers, businesses, and developers arrive at solutions that produce widespread benefits that don't totally derail their efforts, and simultaneously improve the lives of greater numbers.

The limited formal avenues through which inner-city residents and community organizations can influence those who ultimately make the decisions decreases the likelihood that urban development will take a holistic direction, because the resident voices and experiences recognize, understand, and reflect the need for comprehensive approaches. Anyone would be hard-pressed to find a completely unified community voice. In most communities, some own homes while others rent, for example. Self-interest and experience foster differing opinions. And in some cases, people simply don't agree. However, in general, the voices of disadvantaged communities often do not become incorporated into high-level discussions about the market impacts on poor neighborhoods. This missing piece is part of the reason why urban development initiatives have not succeeded in substantially improving the lives of low-income communities.

Organizations such as the National Community Building Network, a national membership organization that brokers information and connections among community builders, and PolicyLink, which seeks to advance new policies that emphasize equity based on the experiences and ideas of local communities, have been, through research and dialogue, developing various concepts and strategies for "equitable development." In fact, PolicyLink's website lists examples of ways in which low-income communities have been able to leverage resources to their advantage, and stave off displacement or other potential negative consequences associated with gentrification. These examples help advance society's understanding of the significance of resident leadership and involvement in ensuring that multiple avenues have been addressed in the process of development. They also add innovation to the limited scope of merely attracting new businesses and building and refurbishing housing. Some of these examples, further discussed in Chapter 6, don't dismiss the need for business development, but they prioritize the needs of low-income residents.

Urban development does not automatically foster inequality. Economic improvements in poor urban neighborhoods can stimulate opportunities. Low-income residents could benefit from linkages to the resources housed in major institutions and industries. On the one hand, market forces left to their own devices can be highly detrimental to low-income people. But, on the other, low-income people do not always have the access, skill, or knowledge to take advantage of market forces. Both dynamics are at work in Harlem. The residential housing market, for example, has exceeded the reach of many residents and some simply do not have the knowledge to make the housing market work to their advantage. Key barriers to mortgages, for example, have remained, but government regulations against redlining have enhanced access to mortgages to varying degrees. But even with increased access, some residents require education in terms of investigating the housing market, approaching banks, brokers, and so on. In other words, approaches seeking equitable development require both new strategies to increase access as well as efforts to educate and enable low-income people to take advantage of preexisting opportunities. If new jobs are created, residents should be able to access those positions *and* receive the training and supportive services needed for them to succeed in those jobs.

Harlem is vast, heavily populated, world-renowned, and part of the even more renowned New York City. It boasts incredible access to public transportation, bridges, and highways, and is in close proximity to some of the most abundant resources in the world. Nevertheless, the issues of gentrification appear to be the same in many other vastly different cities.[14] The opinions of Harlem residents certainly do not determine the feelings of every other community, nor do they apply in every neighborhood.

Today, a central part of Harlem's economic development is being fueled by a federal initiative that includes other cities around the country—the Empowerment Zone Initiative. Moreover, Harlem has historically been a test site for various other urban development initiatives throughout the twentieth century. Harlem native Vicky Gholson, an independent communications consultant, maintained, "When they want to try something, they just try it out in Harlem. When they want to test something, just like they'll test an ATM in Yellow Springs, Ohio, the next place they are testing it is someplace like Harlem. If it works here, then it is going to be exported to the various Harlems around the world. That happens with health programs—IUD—when the IUDs were done, they came out in Europe; it was tested in Harlem. Platform shoes, jheri curls, they were tested in Harlem."[15]

When I spoke with these longtime residents of fifteen or more years in the neighborhood, employees of various local nonprofit organizations, and small business owners, I started to develop a picture of some of the ingredients that would be necessary for urban development that does more good than harm, and increases opportunities for low-income residents. Those with whom I spoke are from all walks of life and experience the current changes in the neighborhood differently. They don't agree on everything, yet common themes became apparent from interview to interview.

Overall, comprehensiveness is essential; approaches taking account of numerous interrelated issues and potential consequences enhance the chances of widespread benefit. The availability of *avenues for resident ownership* arose as a core theme from the interviews—a critical factor in determining who can benefit from continuous and rapid economic development. Ownership is not the panacea for everything, but those positioned to own fair better than those who are not in urban development. Creative efforts to own property and businesses that benefit the entire community, instead of a smaller cluster of individuals, can be pursued. Collective ownership of land, economic activity, or other areas, enhance the decisionmaking capacity of residents—the ability to decide for themselves how they wish to relate to their neighborhoods.

While the presence of larger businesses can increase local jobs, *attention to small business needs* can provide additional options. Technical assistance and skill development is a prerequisite for effective business management, and many of Harlem's small businesses have received such. It is also important that resident-owned and -run businesses have some priority in terms of access to capital. An equitable approach would strengthen small businesses as well as attract large corporations.

Given the significance of displacement in many urban development initiatives, the availability of *affordable housing* is crucial. Set asides in buildings and affordable developments can mean the difference between staying and going. Rent control policies are also important but still not guarantees when residents don't own. Again, ownership potential is the best possible scenario. And it is difficult to imagine realistic ownership opportunities without access to *employment with advancement and training opportunities.* New businesses may bring jobs, but if residents only have access to lower-rung positions, absent advancement or training opportunities, then the community is not much more empowered than it was before those new resources arrived. Indeed, jobs in themselves are important, as unemployment is a persistent challenge, but jobs accompanied by training and advancement opportunities create more effective paths to economic empowerment.

Resident concerns are more likely to be understood and heeded when *effective partnerships* between community residents and various major institutions, such as corporations, universities, banks, and others are in place. Government/community partnerships can lead to *logical and useful planning and design.* Zoning and land use issues are essential in that the types and locations of commercial and residential property should correlate with resident interests. For example, too many of one type of business might concentrate in a particular area, whereas another type of business is sorely needed but altogether nonexistent in the neighborhood.

Similarly, resident *involvement in actually setting policy* can place community interests and government decisions in greater accord. Resident advisory committees have become relatively commonplace. Although it is important to solicit resident opinions beforehand, this input goes only so far, and can be easily ignored once policy is actually set. Not only should residents be extensively involved in advising; they also should have some role in making the actual decisions that affect their neighborhood. For example, residents could be able to veto certain development projects before they occur, beyond community boards (which do not always reflect the interests of the majority).

As new residents and businesses enter an area, ethnic and racial demographics change. In a neighborhood such as Harlem, preserving culture takes significance far beyond New York City. It is important that those new to the area *appreciate the existing local culture*. For example, if the new establishments in a changing neighborhood cater more to the new population than the old, the signal becomes clear—that old residents are unwanted. If businesses want to do well in new areas such as Harlem, it is important to recognize that the old residents still keep them in business, making attention to existing residents' needs in their best interest.

Although the creation of formal avenues to resident participation in policy making can enhance the likelihood that development will lead to empowerment, no democratic structure will work without *informed, involved, and organized residents*. In fact, it is probably not likely that any of the aforementioned ingredients for effective equitable development will come to fruition without resident involvement. On the one hand, policy makers, businesses, developers, and others should consult residents; on the other, residents should actively seek out information, and take advantage of opportunities that will enable them to benefit from their neighborhood's assets. An organized community is better positioned to advocate on its own behalf. *Strong community-based organizations* are central to continuous effective community participation, and very well can be the portal through which resident concerns can be voiced and acted on. But, in terms of information, there is a lot that residents already know; it is important to build on this collective wisdom in community and economic development. Conversely, given that residents don't know everything, it is important that communities have access to technical knowledge, meetings, resources in educational institutions, and more to increase their chances of not only developing ideas, but acting on them.

How we perceive the world and our individual roles within it will continue to drive everything from our personal every day decisions to sweeping national policy. It may seem this goes without saying, but *a spirit of common good* could probably go a long way toward equitable development. If everyone focuses on only their gain, ignoring the interdependency between renters, homeowners, developers, banks, corporations, new residents, small businesses, street vendors, community-based organizations, and others, development will likely foster inequality. Too many decisions have been made at the expense of, particularly, low-income people.

Other factors could most likely be added to this list. The nuances from the interviews bare this out in these pages. One word is worth mentioning—interdependency. One of the reasons why comprehensive approaches make the most sense is that all of these issues are naturally related. *Attention to residents' social concerns,* for example, is another essential factor. The state of residents' health, for instance, influences their ability to be engaged in their community. If health needs are not addressed, then everything else is impacted.

It is important that the drive toward economic development does not eclipse the importance of tending to a range of other needs. Because of the multiple dimensions at work in making communities whole, urban development is highly complex and often unlikely to please all constituents. But great potential lies in the effort to transcend the errors of the past.

3

EQUITABLE URBAN DEVELOPMENT

In 2003, the number of poor Americans rose by 1.3 million, resulting in a total of 35.9 million Americans living in poverty.[1] For a family of four, the poverty rate is an income of $18,810, a family of three, $14,680, a couple, $12,015, and an individual, $9,393. For African Americans, the poverty rate remained essentially the same, at a rate of 24.4 percent, and Hispanics at 22.5 percent. Between 2002 and 2003, the median household income for the Black community saw little change at approximately $30,000.

The income for the top 5 percent of households, even in the face of a floundering economy, still rose by $1,000 to an average of $260,464. Half of all household income is in the hands of the most affluent fifth of the American population. This number stood at 45 percent in 1985. This can be contrasted with the poorest fifth, which controls 3.4 percent of all household income, which happens to be lower than 1985 figures, where this population controlled 4 percent of income. The number of severely poor, those possessing less than half of the official poverty level rose as well: up to 15.3 million from 12.6 million in 2000. The ranks of the poor continue to swell, even in the wealthiest country in the world. These figures do not engender any sense of promise for the future stability of low-income people or of the Black community in particular. Evidently, new strategies are required in order to turn this tide.

One of the more interesting census statistics happens to be the increase in poverty in the suburbs. In 2002, the number of poor people in the suburbs stood at 13.3 million—up 16 percent since 2000.[2] This figure has a direct relationship with the dynamics of urban and regional development. As many cities began to sprawl[3] away from the urban core, inner-city areas became further isolated[4] and dilapidated, whereas certain suburban areas grew. Low-income people began to move to suburban areas, especially those on the "inner ring" or those closer to city boundaries—in the New York Metropolitan Area, Hempstead, Yonkers, Mount Vernon would be some examples—to be closer to jobs and better-funded school systems. As a result of this wave of suburban migration, higher-income communities moved to go to outer-ring suburbs, further away from the city, even bulldozing rural areas in the process. These dynamics are particularly striking in more recently developed metropolitan areas, often in "Sunbelt" states, where population growth is highest.

As some of the more affluent communities settled in the outer ring, some residents grew annoyed by long commutes into the city for work and play. Simultaneously, efforts to revitalize once-abandoned urban areas were emerging and expanding. On the one hand, this development was welcoming for the lower-income communities that had been left behind. On the other, it made cities increasingly attractive to higher-income people from outside of the city. Those who once thought the city was too dangerous were changing their minds as they witnessed cleaner, safer streets in many urban areas. As they began to move back, they raised the stakes for everyone, as they were willing to bid up residential real estate, and encourage city governments and industry to tailor policy and commerce to their needs.

I began this research when we were still pointing to the wondrous "economic expansion," partly fueled by unprecedented technological advances that changed the speed and scope of everything we do. This economic boom appeared to present great promise. Could we leverage abundant resources and information on behalf of low-income and disenfranchised communities? The census figures give us a picture of poverty and wealth in the face of a recession. Statistics prior to the aforementioned census data show that, long before the recession, the income and wealth gap was continuing to grow.

Most Americans lost wealth between 1983 and 1998. The top 1 percent of households possess 40 percent of the wealth (wealth statistics, as many have noted, provide an even truer picture of inequality than those focusing solely on income).[5] That same top 1 percent doubled its share of national wealth from the 1970s to the late 1990s.[6] Toward the end of the last decade, the height of the economic boom, almost 90 percent of the value of all stocks and mutual funds were in the hands of the richest 10 percent of households; debt, as a percentage of income, rose from 58 percent in 1973 to 85 percent in 1997; the bottom 40 percent of households lost 80 percent of their net worth.[7] The gap is both economic and racial. For example, African Americans' net worth decreased by 17 percent between 1994 and 1999 to $7,000. The median U.S. household net worth rose 9 percent, during that same period, to $59,500. For White households, median net worth, at this time, stood at $84,400.[8]

Technology, with the ability to become somewhat of an equalizer, has not advanced low-income communities either. This "digital divide" has likely hindered the chances of less privileged communities catching up. Gaps in technology are staggering in any number of categories, from access to the Internet and e-mail to ownership rates of computers. For those with incomes over $75,000, significant percentages have computers at home, as well as access to e-mail and the Internet at home and at work. The gap becomes most apparent at around $25,000 annual income. Those below that mark tend to have far less access.[9] This data also highlights particular divisions along racial lines.

It is also essential to analyze the state of wealth, poverty, and access in the United States in the context of the wider world. Although the United States is the richest nation in the world, it also is a nation with a substantial, recognizable gap between its rich and poor. One-third of people in the world live in "abject poverty." Over the past fifty years, even the global gap between rich and poor has become wider. Although money is not everything, access to wealth—and, increasingly, access to information as well—impacts myriad social issues from health to housing to education to the environment. When addressing the state of the economy, we paint a picture of the state of communities. Low-income people often grapple with poor education, health, and other social concerns.

In the poorest countries, for example, we will find the greatest hunger and health crises. Approximately 790 million people in the developing world are chronically undernourished.[10] These worldwide gaps in wealth have not subsided in our now declining economy; they have simply left those at the bottom more vulnerable to downturns. The elimination of jobs often hits the lowest rung workers hardest. In New York City, the loss of one hundred thousand jobs since September 11, 2001, greatly affected some professionals, but low-income people remain the biggest losers, as the aforementioned statistics demonstrate. Vast increases in the number of homeless bear this out.

THE URBAN DIMENSION AND GENTRIFICATION

Even in historically agrarian economies, urban areas have become havens for low-income people seeking opportunity and access to the array of services that cities provide. Gaps in wealth can be most stark in metropolitan regions (cities and suburbs). Post–World War II urban policy stimulated the development of the suburbs, which sparked a flight of, largely, White professionals outside of urban areas.[11] Many refer to this as "White flight." The corporations and the jobs often went along with these demographic shifts. The growth of the suburbs created urban sprawl but simultaneously fostered the decline of the urban core, where most low-income residents remained.

Various initiatives, some engineered by residents and some by policy, attempted to improve conditions in these inner-city areas. Ultimately, many of these approaches turned toward economic development. Addressing the economic dimensions of the state of the inner city made sense. Even as the Civil Rights movement made some strides concerning race and policy, economic inequality remained largely intact. African Americans, for example, were *de jure* free from certain forms of discrimination but, in many cases, still living in impoverished urban conditions that were low in services and high in crime. Only by changing those conditions could one truly begin to see some enhancement in life opportunities for African American residents in these areas.

The urban economic development approach, from the late 1960s to the present has often sought to bring back those professionals and businesses to the inner city in order to stave off urban decline and revitalize city life. In some cities, this has worked better than in others. However, in many of those areas in which it has worked, the life circumstances of low-income, inner-city residents have not significantly improved. In fact, the results of some of these initiatives has sometimes directly hurt low-income residents. In the more extreme cases, longtime residents have been forced to move out of the neighborhoods that they called home, as a result of increased prices.

As previously stated, gentrification has often been analyzed primarily with respect to housing, without taking account of many other important factors. The housing issue, however, is no small factor in itself. Home ownership can often be the springboard to stability. Those who own homes in areas experiencing significant economic development can reap enormous benefits as their property values soar. However, when we address low-income communities in particular, housing is often a question of rent. Home ownership in the United States is on the rise. Homeowners receive significant tax benefits, and public policy has generally supported homeownership over renting dating back to the Sixteenth Amendment, instituted in 1913, which established the federal income tax and continued support for federally backed mortgages.[12] Despite intermittent attempts to support rental housing through policy, such as rent subsidies through the New Deal, homeownership has received preferential treatment at the expense of renting, and ultimately low-income communities. This is a painful reality caused by diminishing access to affordable rental housing.

One-third of households in the United States are renting—nearly 36 million. Thirty-five percent of these households are in urban metropolitan areas, but 24 percent are in rural areas.[13] The figures on housing accessibility capture the significance of inequities when income is brought into the equation. In the calculation of Fair Market Rent, housing affordability is based on the fact that no more than 30 percent of a household's income should be devoted to housing costs. Taking this into account, along with the cost of rent, the median hourly income required to afford a two-bedroom rental home is $14.66.[14] Multiplying that hourly figure by forty hours, and multiplying that total by fifty-two (weeks in a year), this means an annual income of over $30,000, well over the poverty rate, and also over the average household income in Harlem, which is $26,000. Knowing that the cost of living is far higher than the median in New York City, the reality is even more grim for low-income people there. In New York State, the hourly housing wage is $18.24, the fifth highest in the country, behind Massachusetts, California, the District of Columbia, and New Jersey, respectively.[15] Given that these are statewide figures, they also do not capture the full reality in New York City, which has far higher rental costs than most of the state.

This essentially means that economic development strategies should be producing jobs paying a few times the $5.15 federal minimum wage (which has not changed since 1997). With most job opportunities for low- and semiskilled people resting in the service sector, we are witnessing a swelling in the ranks of the "working poor," who "are perpetually at risk for becoming the poor of the other kind: they are one paycheck away from getting fired, one missed rent payment short of eviction."[16] Certainly, several people make far less money than $18 an hour, and they may live in smaller rental units, and double and triple up with other families and individuals. This is the state of survival in urban America. However, it is hard to fathom that over 90 percent of the renter households in the nation have a housing wage that is between three and four times the minimum wage.[17]

Given these realities, one would imagine that mobility among long-time residents in gentrifying areas would be rather high, as they would be displaced, and ultimately forced out as a result of high costs. However, circumstances are not that straightforward. The presence of public housing or rent control, or the aforementioned tendency to double and triple up, are factors that enable low-income people to stay in some instances. Undoubtedly, residents are displaced by evictions, changes in the land use of properties, and by landlord decisions about the future of their properties. Developers can buy out landlords, and individual multiunit homeowners can decide to sell, leaving renters at the mercy of new owners. So many scenarios can lead to displacement. And all of the above situations have occurred in Harlem.

Recently, Columbia University professor Lance Freeman and Frank Braconi, executive director for the Citizens Housing and Planning Council, analyzed New York City Housing and Vacancy Survey (NYCHVS) data to determine the mobility of residents in gentrifying areas.[18] They found that, contrary to previous assumptions, lower rates of mobility have been found among low-income residents in gentrifying neighborhoods. Does this mean that gentrification actually helps low-income communities?

If I were a low-income person, and my neighborhood gradually began to receive more services and resources, I would try to figure out a way to stay. But do low-income people truly have such options? The community development field has repeatedly lauded the potential merits of mixed economic communities. Yet, when affluent households reside alongside low-income households, many such neighborhoods end up closer to monolithic. In other words, if the low-income people stick around, the more affluent ones want to leave or move the low-income people out. Or, if the low-income people enter a neighborhood, higher-income people leave. Low-income people are often faced with limited options; and even if a neighborhood has become better-serviced, cleaner, and safer, low-income people, renters in particular, possess fewer choices. They are, in effect, hanging on. Factors such as public housing that may allow residents to stay, are by no means guaranteed.

A recent report defined gentrification as "the process by which higher-income households displace lower-income residents of a neighborhood, changing the essential character and flavor of that neighborhood."[19] It is hard to disagree with such a definition when thinking about neighborhoods that have been fully transformed, such as New York City's Chelsea or the Upper West Side. However, this is where phases of neighborhood change are important to acknowledge. Harlem remains a few stages away from full-scale gentrification. It could take many years, or it could turn in another direction. On the Upper West Side, for example, the gentrification process accelerated in the late 1960s with the construction of the Lincoln Center. Although the entire face of the neighborhood has changed, one can still find longtime Latino residents who have held on to apartments for decades. This is the case with some of the less-affluent Whites, who lived in the neighborhood pre–Lincoln Center as well.

With all of the significance of residential housing shifts in urban development, it is essential to take account of changes in commerce in order to understand gentrification. This dimension of urban change and development is often understudied in the literature and discourse around gentrification. In Harlem, recent commercial development has been hard to ignore as a major driving force toward changing the demographics of the neighborhood's population. A key aspect of the gentrification process is the conscious effort of businesses to cater to a more affluent clientele. Although some longtime residents might be able to remain in their altered neighborhoods, are they the desired market? Do they experience greater harassment? Do they feel insecure? These are some of the nuances that broaden the consequences associated with urban development. When observing quality of life, those able to stay in gentrified areas probably experience conveniences that they may have never enjoyed, but have their public schools gotten better? Has their income increased? Low-income people have not been getting any richer, and it is not uncommon to find troubled public high schools in very gentrified areas. The new residents change what is tailored to them, not things such as public schools that they may choose not to use—the same schools to which low-income residents must send their children, because they still lack options.

THE BUSINESS PERSPECTIVE

Businesses in communities such as Harlem could play a critical role in enhancing not only the economic but also social infrastructure. Because the availability of jobs and resources is critical to the livelihoods of communities, the corporations that house them have the potential to provide direct opportunities to residents. Government can go only so far in spurring greater opportunity and access for communities, given devolution, leaner bureaucracies, and outsourcing. Many government responsibilities have been shifted to for-profit or nonprofit institutions.

Over the last three decades, corporate social responsibility, as a movement, has gradually gained steam, to the point at which businesses now seek recognition for their social programs and philanthropic initiatives. Some businesses have even crafted a brand that is closely aligned with their social endeavors, such as Ben & Jerry's, the Body Shop, Newman's Own, and others. Even IBM, a true megacorporation, is a perennial presence at or near the top of *Business Ethics* magazine's socially responsible corporations list. But given global poverty, and the increasing gap in access to resources and information, it does not appear that development of a corporate social responsibility industry has made a significant dent in our most pressing social problems.

Corporate social responsibility takes multiple forms. From corporate giving to socially responsible investing[20] to community partnerships[21] to ethics in labor and the environment to compliance with legal regulations to pricing to diversity to cause-related marketing to corporate/nonprofit partnerships,[22] and more. This almost endless list provides a moral compass for corporate behavior, but it does not necessarily guarantee significant impacts on societal inequality. Moreover, it still appears that the corporate sector requires external prodding despite growing evidence of the benefits (to corporations) of socially responsible practices.[23] With Enron, WorldCom, and the slew of other corporations in the spotlight for corporate irresponsibility, public faith that the corporate sector actually will effectively take on social causes has declined.

Ironically, the exposure of negative corporate behavior surfaced in the wake of September 11, 2001, a time at which we might have expected an increase in social responsibility. The fact of the matter is that corporations did not recently become irresponsible; they were recently caught. Because corporations are generally first concerned with the profit bottom line (many suggest social responsibility to the public constitutes a second bottom line), corporate social responsibility and giving programs are often vulnerable in the overall context of priority allocations. Jericho Communications recently surveyed CEOs of 264 Fortune 1,000 corporations regarding social responsibility in the wake of September 11. Thirty-six percent of those CEOs indicated that they were more conscious of corporate social responsibility since September 11. However, only 1 percent indicated that they are allocating more money for socially responsible practices.[24]

Despite the limited evidence for hope, I would hate to imagine the state of responsible corporate citizenship without the lengthy history that produced today's movement to foster a more caring, careful, and conscious corporate global society. Given the aforementioned preeminence of corporate power worldwide, even with recent declines, the need for corporations to step up and increase their responsiveness to public needs is more crucial than ever.

As previously mentioned, the void left by the departure of corporations from cities led to the loss of jobs, which impacted overall local economies, which influenced flight (many corporations moved to the suburbs, and the people followed), which created despair among remaining residents, which influenced crime. This is not to say that all of the problems of inner cities, and many rural towns as well, are a result of the lack of loyalty of some corporations. In fact, government policy opened up avenues for corporate movement, to seek out cheaper land and labor. Withered global boundaries have exacerbated some of these circumstances.

But, even in terms of policy, corporations continue to wield incessant influence over public officials due to their vast resources. Those local and federal policy makers who developed the Empowerment Zone legislation underscored their recognition of the significance of corporations to urban development by providing subsidies to encourage retail corporations to locate in inner city areas and provide jobs to local residents. In the case of Harlem, new businesses, not all based in the neighborhood because of the Empowerment Zone, are bringing jobs, resources, and services. In many ways, this approach is new to Harlem in that it has been and remains a predominantly residential neighborhood.

Nevertheless, as the residents have indicated, additional factors must be addressed in order to make the presence of these various new establishments more beneficial to the neighborhood. But it is important to note that, whereas corporations doing business in inner-city environments is one of the latest manifestations of corporate social responsibility, this should not be perceived as a mere act of benevolence. Indeed, they are doing business and capitalizing on Porter's "competitive advantage."[25] The longer term question is: How far can corporate social responsibility be extended to foster and maintain equitable development and enhance opportunities for low-income people?

SMALL BUSINESSES AND THEIR FUTURES

Although corporations had left many inner-city areas (and this still happens), small businesses sought to fill the void. They provided goods and services tailored to the needs of the local population. Oftentimes, these services have been inferior and offered at unreasonably high prices. In historically African American neighborhoods, significant racial tensions surround inner-city small businesses.[26] The merchant class has often been composed of immigrants who do not resemble the majority of the residents and sometimes faced difficulty grappling with the local culture.

Historical redlining by banks, refusing business loans to Black residents, only made business ownership more elusive for African Americans. It was often through the informal economy that many local residents survived in inner-city areas, including both legal and illegal activities. In Harlem, as will be discussed further, the "numbers" gambling racket was underground, but extensive and sophisticated. The drug trade was also a persistent and imposing force in the neighborhood, but it was, and still is, some people's livelihood. Street vending, home-based businesses, bartering, and other systems are some of the various ways that residents have created economic systems of survival. Lacking opportunities, residents created their own.

Despite the barriers to creating formally registered businesses, the number of Black-owned businesses in the United States has increased. The number of Black-owned businesses in 1997 was up over 25 percent from the number of such businesses in 1992. The increase in the same period for all U.S. firms was 6.8 percent.[27] In no way, however, does this suggest that African American businesses are outpacing other firms in revenue. Despite owning 4 percent of all U.S. businesses, African Americans account for only .4 percent in receipts and .7 percent in the number of employees.[28] A key factor in this picture is the preponderance of individual proprietorships in these statistics, as somewhere around 90 percent of Black-owned businesses are in this category.[29] It should be noted that these figures are not totally out of step with the broader population, as nearly three-quarters of all U.S. businesses have no payroll. These "nonemployers" account for only 3 percent of receipts among all businesses.[30] Therefore, the question is not simply to own or not to own, but to succeed or not to succeed. Starting a business is not difficult, particularly a sole proprietorship, but it is far more grappling to maintain a living through self-employment.

The fact of the matter is that Black American business, like the African American community, and America as a whole, is intensely stratified. Of the 823,499 Black-owned businesses, 8,682 (or 1.1 percent) of them have receipts of $1 million or more. These businesses account for 56.4 percent of all of the receipts of the entire sum total of Black businesses. Only 11.3 percent of all Black-owned businesses have employees, and these firms account for almost 80 percent of the receipts among all African American businesses.[31]

Interestingly enough, more Black businesses are located in New York (86,469) than any other state, and more of such enterprises are concentrated in New York City (63,327) than in any other U.S. city. The New York Metropolitan Area also leads in the number of Black-owned businesses.[32] Within New York City, the county with the most businesses is Queens; New York County (which includes Harlem) is second. Although Black businesses tend to specialize in services and retail, such firms do not come near all U.S. firms in receipts in any single category.[33]

Between the 1960s and 1980s, large corporations were not paying significant attention to inner city areas. The challenge to urban policy makers was to find ways to attract larger corporations to neighborhoods that they had been neglecting for years. Not every neighborhood resembles Harlem in this respect. With its Manhattan location and extensive transportation, Harlem brings more to the table than many other inner city areas in the United States. It is, therefore, not surprising that, with the effort and additional incentives, the Empowerment Zone has been able to convince large corporations to set up shop in Harlem.

These entities can provide quality services and jobs, on the one hand, but, on the other, the presence of large corporations in inner-city areas brings a level of competition that forces most residents to be employees rather than owners. Therefore, small businesses, and those in the informal economy, such as street vendors are left vulnerable to increased real estate values, significant competition, and raised expectations around quality, service, and management. Although outsiders have often owned many Harlem small businesses, some of those owned by longtime African American residents have not had the easiest time. Some are closing or are in danger of doing so. This will be discussed in further detail through the experiences of current small business owners in Harlem.

Comprehensive approaches to equitable urban development are important because attention to one area has consequences for another. Unless those consequences are anticipated up front, ripple effects can cause damage. Attention to those potential consequences can help move development toward empowerment. In the case of business development, the intent to bring in large retail corporations may bring jobs and services, but a number of additional questions must be posed in order to maximize community benefit. What is the nature of the jobs? What will the corporate presence do to small business opportunity? How might the corporations impact housing prices? What role should corporations be required to play in community development? In other words, policy decisions should be accompanied by contingency plans.

THE QUEST FOR EQUITABLE DEVELOPMENT

As previously discussed, African Americans, throughout the history of New York City, have not enjoyed security and have often been cheated. According to the journalist Mamadou Chinyelu, Harlem is akin to a Third World country, where resources are taken out at the expense of an indigenous population. Chinyelu explicitly suggests a rather disingenuous intent among Harlem's power elite, as they cooperate with business to take the neighborhood away from the masses of African Americans. Harlem, according to Chinyelu, has been a "crown jewel" that fell out of the hands of the affluent and powerful, and this is the time when they wish to retake the neighborhood.[34]

The approach of the UMEZ, according to Chinyelu, is consistent with the exploitation of the Third World, where outsiders decide the terms, and focus on making the indigenous population consumers rather than owners. Low-income people, he argues, are being "ethnically cleansed" from the neighborhood because their earnings "are not substantial enough to support the retail and entertainment establishments that are currently being developed in Harlem." He continues, "And if your income is not high enough to support the business establishments of the masters of capitalism, then you must be removed to make room for moderate-, middle-, and upper-income households that can afford to support those businesses."[35]

Here, Chinyelu not so subtly implies cooperation among corporations, UMEZ, Rangel, and others in shafting low-income Harlem residents to benefit big business and wealthier populations. Comparisons between the circumstances of African Americans and Third World countries are not new.[36] Nor are discussions of the circumstances of African Americans as a byproduct of capitalism.[37] The idea of a middle or "buffer" class that cooperates with powerful and influential people and institutions to oppress the less advantaged sectors of its own community has been widely discussed and debated.[38]

Urban development in present-day Harlem is more than an issue of Black and White, as it is fraught with socioeconomic class dynamics. Many of those moving into Harlem are of African descent, despite the gradual increase in the White population, and although small business opportunities have diminished for some Black people, they have not entirely dissipated. The UMEZ has been funding the development of a noticeable number of small African American–owned businesses.

As a result of an extension in the federal program, the deadline for spending down funds from the Empowerment Zone is December 31, 2009, giving the UMEZ a fifteen-year period in which to spend the money. According to Ken Knuckles, the current director of the UMEZ, alternative funding sources are being investigated to supplement the funding. Knuckles speculates about the degree to which their effort can develop an "agenda for the poor." Not long after he accepted this position, Ken Knuckles, a former administrator at Columbia University, and I sat down at Columbia's Faculty House, to discuss his vision for the UMEZ.

Knuckles wishes to see enhanced workforce development tied to the jobs that have been stimulated by the UMEZ. Knuckles said,

"Workforce development is necessary because many people in Upper Manhattan are undereducated and underskilled." Training that "lends itself to long term employment," according to Knuckles would be a sensible approach for the UMEZ to take at this juncture. With respect to his desire to bring a hotel to 125th Street and Park Avenue, Knuckles indicated, "If I bring a hotel, I want to be able to go to trained workers."

Another important direction that Knuckles has been envisioning is an emphasis on culture and tourism. "Culture," said Knuckles, "is everything—business, politics, religion …" He wants to see greater support for Harlem's cultural institutions, large and small. At this point, the UMEZ had already spent $4 million on the restoration of churches. He wants to see the tourists visiting Harlem's churches and other cultural institutions to spend money in the community.

Knuckles will also be working to develop other corridors in the neighborhood, such as 145th Street, 116th Street, and 135th Street. Much of the initial thrust of the UMEZ had focused on the commercial development of Harlem's major thoroughfare, 125th Street. Knuckles sees so much more potential in the neighborhood's other major arteries. He also senses opportunities with the expansion of Columbia University into a part of West Harlem, called Manhattanville. He wonders about the kind of industrial corridors that can be created in close proximity to Columbia, as well as the City University of New York, which is also located in the West Harlem.

One division of the UMEZ is the Business Resource and Investment Service Center (BRISC), which serves as a "One Stop Capital Shop" that helps small businesses "obtain capital, pro-bono professional support, and technical assistance."[39] Some examples of small business owners recently supported by the UMEZ include Leon Ellis, owner of two restaurants, Emily's and Harlem Underground, and soon-to-be-owner of Moca Bar and Grill, and Teresa Kay-Aba Kennedy, CEO of Youforia, a burgeoning yoga center that proposes to create thirty-two jobs.[40] Both of these examples either are or are aspiring to be among the tiniest percentage of Black-owned businesses—employers and higher-revenue earners. Numerous other businesses owned by people of African descent and other persons of color are receiving support from UMEZ and are creating jobs. But the characteristics of those with access to business opportunity is limited, and the target consumers of many new businesses are not low-income people.

The UMEZ approach is undoubtedly filling a void in terms of business opportunities for African Americans, and these firms are receiving support. Services from BRISC include:

- loans from $50,000 to $250,000, and assistance in securing funding from other institutions
- technical assistance
- needs assessment and planning assistance
- business plan development
- counseling in financial management and marketing
- loan packaging
- credit counseling
- referral assistance (to lending programs)
- small business seminars
- community outreach[41]

Evidently, some thought has been put into small business development. This approach does not necessarily lead to widespread empowerment, because business opportunities are limited. One must demonstrate resources from the start in order to secure resources from elsewhere. The rules are not so different in the nonprofit sector, in which the organizations that can demonstrate greater levels of management capacity and resources up front have a better opportunity to obtain funding from foundations and other grant-making sources for the future.

The closing of Mart 125 is one example of how small business people with fewer resources have lost rather than gained opportunity. Opened in 1986, Mart 125 was intended to house about fifty small merchants, marketing a variety of products. With so many vendors on the sidewalks of 125th Street at this time, the mart was an opportunity for small-scale vendors to operate in an enclosed environment. It was developed by the now-defunct state agency, the Harlem Urban Development Corporation, which signed the agreement to develop the Mart in 1979. In 1995, New York State Governor George Pataki shut down the Corporation, and New York City took control of the mart. But, in the midst of the Empowerment Zone, and the wave of new investment, this mart with its prime location in the midst of the 125th Street shopping district appeared unprofitable in comparison with what could be achieved with another tenant. As a result, the city evicted the tenants in 2001. Angry evicted vendors were dismayed by the lack of protection they received from the UMEZ.[42]

Harlem, a neighborhood that endured decades of divestment, is experiencing such an influx of investment that the new opportunities are working against some longtime residents and small business owners. Although Harlem is on a larger scale than the vast majority of neighborhoods, the principle of pushing out old residents and businesses is a common occurrence in the process of gentrification. Other urban areas, such as Camden, New Jersey, or East St. Louis, Illinois, might hope to have the kind of investment that is taking place in Harlem, as they continue to be plagued by effects of decades of disinvestments. Indeed, these are cities that remain poor and are not experiencing a potential for gentrification. Quite simply, many of the traditional approaches to urban policy have not benefited low-income people. When policy stimulates urban disinvestment, low-income people are left behind, and when it stimulates inner-city investment, low-income people are hanging on to stick around.

As a result of the damage that gentrification or disinvestments in the inner city can cause, many in the urban community development field have been seeking equitable development strategies. Such efforts seek to economically develop inner-city areas, but with the explicit goal of benefiting longtime, especially low-income, residents. By elevating and promoting equity before all else, these organizations and individuals are exploring strategies to maximize economic opportunity for as broad a cross section of residents as possible.

One community development effort that brought such strategies into light was the Dudley Street Neighborhood Initiative[43] in Boston. This diverse coalition of residents in a gentrifying area was able to secure eminent domain status, during the late 1980s, as a nonprofit organization. Eminent domain has historically been reserved for the government to control land use decisions within its boundaries. As a community-based nonprofit organization, the Dudley Street Neighborhood Initiative was able to control the various real estate projects slated for the area, leading to the development of affordable housing, which would have otherwise been overlooked. This enabled residents to remain in their neighborhood. The Dudley Street Neighborhood Initiative continues to operate today.

As I will later indicate, the Harlem Children's Zone's Community Pride initiative enabled low-income Harlem residents to take ownership of public rental buildings at staggeringly low prices. Other examples of equitable development strategies have been employed worldwide. PolicyLink and the National Community Building Network are two national community building organizations that take inventory of various equitable development strategies in order to guide communities on how to ensure that residents benefit from the resources in their neighborhoods and regions. PolicyLink has gone as far as creating a "toolkit," containing a variety of "resident ownership mechanisms."

Although equitable development strategies might bring some sense of hope, the larger landscape underscores the magnitude of work that must be done. The state of the economy and of low-income people in particular, the dynamics of the housing market and limited affordability, the nature of urban policy, and the priorities and decisions of corporations are some of the larger forces that shape urban development. In addition to the efforts of low-income people, other residents, and community-based organizations, some effort on the part of government, real estate developers, and other corporations and influential institutions would be required in order to foster development that works in the interest of the least advantaged.

The interrelationship of these broader social forces as well as the interconnected web of social issues make problem solving in today's society painfully complex. Without recognizing the broader context up front, and emphasizing the interests of low-income people, policies will not remedy the harmful ripple effects of urban development. In focusing on a neighborhood such as Harlem, it is important to draw on this bigger picture, going beyond a limited approach to urban development. Policy in neighborhoods such as Harlem should be place-based as well as (simultaneously) people-based, focusing on the well-being of existing residents along with the state of the geographical area. The reality of the lives of those residents rests within a wider context. Given that the economic boom led to an increased gap in wealth; given that urban policy has historically worked against low-income people; given that housing is less affordable; given that corporations are not allocating enough resources to social responsibility; there is little reason to believe that the kind of urban development occurring in Harlem will naturally improve the life circumstances of low-income people. Innovative strategies must explicitly benefit longtime residents, in Harlem and in other gentrifying neighborhoods, to ensure that the least advantaged are not the biggest losers in urban development.

4

RESIDENT PERSPECTIVES

Although the prospects for the future for low-income people in neighborhoods could prove insecure, given the broader socioeconomic dynamics of our times, none of the skepticism around gentrification should suggest that Harlem is not deserving of redevelopment. Nor is it to suggest Harlem is undeserving of cleanliness, safety, new jobs, or anything of the sort. The issue of urban development brings with it a constant dilemma—the quest to improve conditions in communities, yet certain improvements can bring dire consequences for some residents. To say "what's good for Harlem is good for its residents" does not quite tell the whole story. Harlem, as a place, was once a wealthier neighborhood, which became accessible. It deteriorated, but now it is undergoing significant revitalization.

Having seen Harlem's many faces over the course of their lives, longtime residents have formulated a variety of perspectives on the direction of their neighborhood's development, and its consequences for themselves and their neighbors. In-depth interviews with longtime Harlem residents formed the core of research for this book. This qualitative approach was designed to capture the nuances of how residents are experiencing the new and improved version of their neighborhood. A different group of residents filled out a survey to provide a "quick and dirty" statistical view of the opinions of a random and varied sample of Harlemites.

With the assistance of numerous research assistants from Columbia University and my company, Marga Incorporated, along with select Harlem community-based organizations, a random survey of Harlem residents was conducted to complement the qualitative interviews of residents and community-based organizations.

Survey participants reflected various walks of life, and, not surprisingly, a wide variety of perspectives about recent economic and real estate changes in Harlem. The survey included ninety-one respondents, who were approached through numerous methods, including street canvassing, community board meetings, church services, and neighborhood/block meetings. As a result of the varied approach, the survey reached the hands of a fairly diverse demographic in terms of age (see Appendix, Figure A) and years of residence in the neighborhood (see Appendix, Figure B). Given the desire to reach longtime residents, over 28 percent of survey participants exceed the age of fifty-five, whereas just under 8 percent were under eighteen. The largest concentration of respondents was between the ages of twenty-six and fifty-five.

With respect to the number of years in the neighborhood, over 23 percent were relatively new to the neighborhood (between one and five years). Just about 10 percent have resided in Harlem between six and ten years, 8.8 percent between eleven and fifteen years. The remainder of respondents exceeded fifteen years of residence in Harlem—the primary target population for this research. This remaining 67 percent, included some elders who have lived their entire lives in the neighborhood. Five and one half percent of respondents have resided in Harlem for over fifty-one years; the same percentage has been in the area between forty-six and fifty years.

The income level of respondents reflected its own diversity, as indicated in Figure 1. The number of participants with an income of $30,000 per year or under approached 40 percent. Over 15 percent of respondents did not indicate an income. The unemployment status data (see Appendix, Figure C) helps illuminate the presence of unemployed persons in the findings. Over 34 percent of participants indicated their unemployment status—a figure that one might imagine would approach

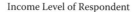

Income Level of Respondent

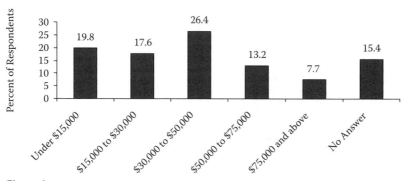

Figure 1

the lower side given that some would not wish to indicate that they are not employed.

The degree of property ownership among respondents provides another compelling picture, as almost three quarters of survey participants were home renters instead of owners (see Appendix, Figure D). As will be discussed later, limited ownership inhibits residents' ability to take advantage of new economic opportunities and build assets rather than face vulnerable circumstances and potentially succumb to displacement.

In terms of race, ethnicity, and gender, the chosen approaches to finding survey participants yielded a heavily "Black" response. As indicated clearly in the historical demographics of the neighborhood, those calling themselves "Black" varied from African American to Caribbean to African to Latino (see Appendix, Figure E). The majority of respondents categorized themselves as "African American." Very few who categorized themselves as "White" responded to the survey. Despite a demographic increase of Whites in the neighborhood, one generally sees a far greater concentration of people of African descent on the streets, in churches, and in neighborhood meetings.

Respondents were also predominantly female (see Appendix, Figure F)—another demographic likely affected by our methodological choices, especially in the case of churches.

This collection of survey respondents provided us a variety of perspectives on the status and future of recent changes in Harlem. Their collective perspectives demonstrate the complexities of approaches to urban economic development. When asked what they liked most of about recent changes in the neighborhood, responses varied

What do you like most about changes in Harlem?

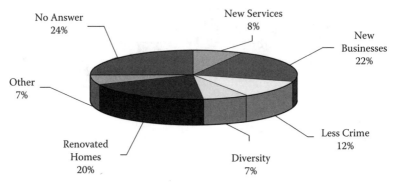

Figure 2

significantly, as indicated in Figure 2. Twenty-four percent did not even answer the question, but 22 percent indicated the new businesses, 20 percent pointed to renovated homes, 12 percent noted crime reductions, and 8 percent indicated new services. New services and new businesses likely overlap in some viewpoints. Some preference for new businesses and services is consistent with results from qualitative interviews.

When asked about what they like the least about changes in the neighborhood, responses were less varied, as indicated in Figure 3. Overwhelmingly, cost of living was the response to this question.

What do you like least about changes in Harlem?

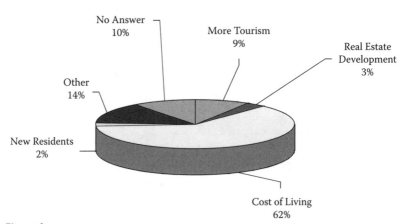

Figure 3

Sixty-two percent of respondents indicated the rising cost of living as their least favorite aspect of recent changes, with very little competition, as 14 percent suggested something other than any of the choices, and 10 percent did not answer at all. This is also consistent, as discussed later in this book, with the more detailed commentary from those who were interviewed in depth.

One of the more challenging aspects of any research project on urban development and change is providing evidence of displacement. Some instances, that is, a multifamily unit converting to a single family unit as a result of the preference of a new owner, suggest displacement against one's will but not necessarily economically. Other instances, when residents relocate, could be influenced by a variety of factors. Instances in which developers secure new zoning regulations that influence relocation also could suggest some form of displacement against one's will. The manifestations of what drives any individual or family to move are numerous. As a result, it is awfully difficult to accurately or scientifically identify that the process of gentrification is primarily a function of forced relocation.

However, as previously noted, the stages of a gentrifying neighborhood are periodically driven by economic and political choices that prioritize some shift in a population, from one that is lower in income to one that wields greater resources and influence. As a result of the complicated dynamics associated with gentrification and displacement, we decided to ask a very straightforward question of survey participants: Do you know anyone forced to move because rent became too high? We were specific in terms of being "forced" to move and in terms of economic drivers. Over 58 percent of the respondents answered that they

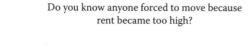

Do you know anyone forced to move because
rent became too high?

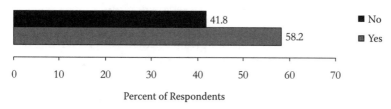

Figure 4

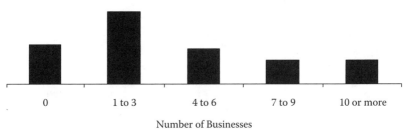

How many Black-owned businesses do you know of that have closed
in the last five years?

Number of Businesses

Figure 5

know of someone who was forced to move as a result of rising rents, as
indicated in Figure 4.

In conversations with residents, another lively aspect of the displacement factor is the challenge facing longtime small businesses,
particularly those owned by persons of African descent (see Figure 5).
Approximately 36 percent of respondents indicated knowledge of one
to three Black-owned businesses that have closed in the last five years.
Only about 20 percent did not know of any. Roughly 42 percent indicated that they know of over four Black-owned business closings in the
last five years. Slightly over 1 percent of total respondents could identify
over ten recent Black-owned business closings.

Not surprisingly, the forecast of this mix of survey respondents for
the future of Harlem brought some varied responses. However, quite a
significant number, 63 percent, see a positive change in the quality of
life in the neighborhood on the horizon. When specifying the future
for longtime residents, the responses were closer to a split, with just
about 40 percent suggesting recent changes would prove harmful to
Harlem residents, and a little over 36 percent imagining positive effects
for longtime residents (see Figures 6 and 7).

As will be discussed in the rest of this chapter, participants in qualitative interviews distinguished between owners and renters and lower-
income and middle-class longtime residents. They generally pointed to
the distinctions in how those longtime residents of greater means can
far more easily benefit from changes than those who are lower income
and not property owners.

The final critical factor emerging from the survey focuses on local
participation and decision making. And it is in this area, that the
most overwhelming responses emerged. A whopping 92 percent of

Overall, the recent changes in Harlem are:

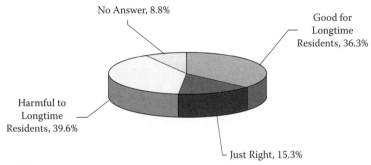

Figure 6

As you look to the future of Harlem, do you think your quality of life will:

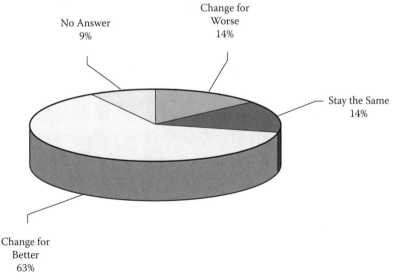

Figure 7

respondents desired more input into major decisions made about the future of Harlem. Only 25 percent of participants feel they have any say in the major decisions affecting the neighborhood (see Figures 8 and 9).

This finding captures the spirit that led to the research for this book, soliciting the perspectives that may not have been incorporated into

When major decisions are made about the future of Harlem,
would you personally like to have:

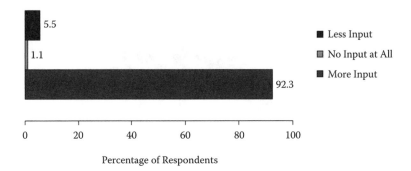

Figure 8

Do you personally feel like you have any say in the major decisions
affecting Harlem?

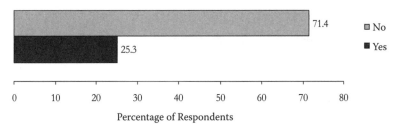

Figure 9

the path of economic development in Harlem. These survey findings
should make more sense complemented by the elaborations of the residents who graciously agreed to be interviewed for this study.

In-depth interviews did not provide a radical departure from the
survey results. Their principle value was in identifying the dynamics of
the changes occurring from resident points of view—in demonstrating
how social, economic, housing, cultural, and other changes are experi-
entially manifesting. These qualitative interviews also, better than any
survey ever could, capture the emotions, pride, passion, and spirit ema-
nating from these residents' attachment to their home. Indeed, what

also comes through in these interviews is that Harlem is more than a neighborhood or home for these residents. It carries a level of identification and meaning unparalleled in many settings.

With respect to the ever controversial displacement concern, the vast majority of residents who were interviewed in depth, like their surveyed counterparts, knew of other residents who have been displaced from the neighborhood as a result of an increased cost of living. As previously noted, rents have always been high, particularly higher for African Americans, in Harlem. However, current rents are simply outpacing what residents can afford. In recent decades, New York City's rent control laws preserved dwellings for residents. Those laws are gradually shifting, enabling higher annual rent increases. Moreover, landlords sensing opportunities have been creatively finding ways to evict longtime tenants in order to bring in new ones at market rates. Many longtime renters are effectively stuck in their current apartments because they cannot afford to move in the neighborhood (or anywhere nearby), and they are vulnerable to the decisions of their landlords, who may sell or even evict.

Owning and renting residents experience the new renaissance differently. While renters confront insecurities, owners can think about opportunities. As real estate rates plummeted in Harlem, working class residents could actually afford some of the majestic old properties originally designed for the elite. Many of these residents may have newfound retirement capital, as their property values likely exceed what they had ever anticipated.

Small businesses have experienced some difficulties as well, as they have been forced to compete with larger, established, well-resourced retail corporations, many of which received financial incentives from the Upper Manhattan Empowerment Zone (UMEZ). Some small businesses have subsequently been forced to close.

With all of these changes, is Harlem as we know it coming to an end? David Dinkins said, "Harlem is sort of coming alive to a degree. People are coming back in. As a matter of fact, some people are concerned that some of the folks coming back in didn't live there before, or are white, or whatever. Needless to say, they have as much a right as anybody else to live in Harlem, 'cause we say Harlem is a state of mind anyway."[1] However, one might address this from another angle, in which Harlem represents a geographical homeland of sorts for people of African descent—a place where people of African descent can go, live among each other, share in each other's culture, and collectively forge a social, political, and economic agenda. If this historical significance is not one of the many factors sufficiently addressed in Harlem's development, then it is no surprise that residents are upset about recent changes. One can find tensions of this sort in any neighborhood undergoing change, but these feelings become magnified in Harlem because of its importance to, not only Harlem residents, but also to many other people of African descent and others who have been touched by the neighborhood's unique qualities.

Lorraine Gilbert, a Harlem-based real estate broker for twenty years, sees Harlem's changes in the context of development in several other neighborhoods. By no means are these changes unique to Harlem, Gilbert maintains. She said, "The same change that took place over on the Upper West Side, near Columbus Avenue, fifteen years ago, is starting to happen now. I mean, all over America, money grew. If you're not financially prepared to do what you need to do, you can't always blame somebody else who comes in and has the money, and can outbid you."[2] Gilbert speaks to the hard realities of urban development, which often spawns gentrification. Change is difficult for anyone, and change is often necessary, but is the current road to a revitalized Harlem the most appropriate path, particularly for longtime low-income and working-class residents?

The residents themselves are more directly affected than anyone by all that has transpired in Harlem in the last decade. Some of the recent changes were made with existing residents in mind, and have improved services and some other aspects of the neighborhood. Interviewed residents generally provided a balanced assessment of the state of affairs. Their opinions touched multiple topics from business to real estate to demographics to culture. These interviewees shed light on some of the opinions one can find on the stoops, in the living rooms, in the churches, on the sidewalks, in the barber shops and beauty salons, and in the coffee shops of Harlem.

These interviews were not gripe sessions for disappointed residents; they were asked to consider both the strengths and weaknesses of recent changes. Some residents are upset, and it appears they have legitimate concerns given that they have put so much into the neighborhood over the years. Many residents feel insecure; they are concerned that the new renaissance is not for them, but is in fact against them.

ADVANTAGES

Overview

Overall, interviewees were candid about their feelings. Because they were longtime residents, which I defined as having lived fifteen or more years in the neighborhood, they understood the issues in historical context. Some feel they are benefiting far more than others, largely based on one's socioeconomic position—those who own homes, for example, feel they benefit more than those who do not. Owning a home in Harlem does not make one wealthy. Real estate rates had hit pretty close to rock bottom in the '70s and '80s. Well-built homes with character, attractive to anyone's eyes, were being sold for a few thousand dollars. This enabled some working-class people to purchase property. Now that real estate rates have risen so much (brownstones now selling in the $1 million range), some of these homeowners have opportunities of which they may never have dreamed. It is also important to note, as John Jackson (2001) maintains, that Harlem residents have a great deal of interclass communication, largely because of race. Therefore, it is not surprising that some socioeconomically privileged Harlem residents might share opinions with low-income residents. In fact, despite some variety in opinions, a general amount of agreement has emerged concerning the strengths and weaknesses of this new renaissance.

Because of the aforementioned popular reticence to even set foot in Harlem, for many years, local residents received limited access to a number of the basic services found in many other neighborhoods. Access to fresh produce, taxis, bank machines, restaurants that deliver, and many other goods and services thought to be commonplace in traditionally higher-income neighborhoods had been limited. Harlem residents tended to count on a trip downtown for access to a decent grocery store.

Interviewees generally agreed that they benefited from goods and services that have become recently available in the neighborhood as a result of the Empowerment Zone, as well as other economic changes. Residents lamented the days when they would have to gather as much as they could downtown before heading home. Now many more residents can actually walk from their doorsteps to grocery stores and other services.

Minnette Colemen, a Harlem resident for about eighteen years, lives in a brownstone with her husband, Robert Roach, and their two children. In January of 1985, they moved from Upper Marlboro Maryland.

Minnette works for the New World Foundation, and Robert for IBM. This middle-aged African American couple has witnessed significant change in their neighborhood. Although many of the interviewed residents had been in Harlem much longer, this family represents the first wave of newer pioneers to the neighborhood. They essentially moved to their West Harlem home a few years before the area became fashionable; although the plans for extensive development were underway, the 1980s was considered one of Harlem's more troubling decades.

Coleman welcomes the addition of services brought on by recent development. She described the course of change, "When we first moved here, there were two or three very shoddy grocery stores in the neighborhood. There were bodega-type drug stores, and where we live now, there are major drugstores—I'm talking about walking distance, major drugstores." She continued, "They'll do Chinese food delivery where they wouldn't do it before. Cab service is a little easier to get, and there are more restaurants and there are more specialty food shops." She also welcomes the presence of banks, particularly Chase (JP Morgan Chase), which agreed to waive ATM fees in Harlem.[3] The improvement in bank services, according to Roach, is a result of the community's changing economic base. With a higher overall income among residents, banks have a larger pool of potential new customers. Therefore, the presence of a more recent higher-income population can improve services for the entire neighborhood. According to Roach, this applies to all types of business. He said, "People look at the bottom line. And if you have a certain clientele in the neighborhood, the stores are going to try to cater to that clientele, so they can move the goods."[4]

Overall, Roach is relatively pleased with recent changes. He further described some of the conditions during their earlier days in the neighborhood. He said, "When we first moved here, there was like a homicide near Amsterdam or around the corner every four months, and it was basically dealing with drugs. And there were apartments in city-managed buildings that they were selling crack out of; you could see the lines around the corner."[5] On seeing and experiencing the array of local problems, Roach joined the local block association and began working with local government. Residents having lived through some of Harlem's harder periods, through this sort of community participation made valuable contributions to the neighborhood's revival. The developers, politicians, and corporations have the power to craft and implement decisions, but the residents made Harlem's improvement possible. The involvement of Roach and other interviewees is a testament to the potential of community building at the most local of levels to make neighborhoods safer, cleaner, and more convenient.

However, Roach maintains that it took a while for a greater sense of civic participation to set in. He said, "One of the things that surprised us when we moved here to New York was the lackadaisical attitude of people in the neighborhood. In other words, I would challenge people in a city-managed building to own their building, manage their building, because they could buy their apartments for like two hundred and fifty dollars per room, and to my astonishment and amazement, nobody wanted the responsibility."[6]

Coleman wishes that more residents would take advantage of the presence of new resources. She said, "We have a tendency to say that these changes came because white folks were moving into Harlem, and that's how many people feel. And those of us who are smart, take advantage of the changes and of the situations."[7] Many residents lack the information and the skills to take advantage; this is why education is an essential factor that should be incorporated into understanding how to make urban development work for most people. However, Coleman is also speaking to a certain lack of will or desire among residents to at least try to take advantage. She said of her own personal resolve in relation to new businesses and residents, "I am not going to let them take over where I am and what I am doing, but if they can benefit or if they can bring something good to the neighborhood, then that works for me." She does think that racism has played a major role in determining how services enter the neighborhood. She said, "These changes happen not because more affluent Black people live here. I have friends who bought their houses thirty years ago—three million dollars worth of property in Harlem. And, so these were well off people. They still didn't get good services. These services started changing the more you got White people, but you can say also Asians; Asians came in by the busloads and bought property."[8] In the end, the services have and are continuing to come to Harlem, and Coleman feels she is just going to take advantage of them, and she wants to encourage other African American residents in particular to do the same.

Harlem native John Bess also welcomes some of the neighborhood's improvements. He said, "… you have variety—you have diversity; you do not have to go downtown to see the movies. You can go to Magic Johnson's theater and go see movies. If you're thinking about a restaurant, you can go to Londell's, Emily's, Sylvia's, 145th Street Bistro (Sugar Hill Bistro), you can go to a whole other host of restaurants that didn't exist. Harlem didn't have a supermarket; now you have a supermarket that's booming. The Pathmark had no idea ... that it would be one of its hot-selling Pathmarks. A community that was losing supermarkets—now having supermarkets begging to come in...."[9]

Supermarkets

As Michael Porter's research has demonstrated, and has been known in urban communities for many years, neighborhoods like Harlem are ideal for the retail industry. Given the sheer size of the population, and its pedestrian nature, the Harlem community takes advantage of services such as supermarkets en masse.

The Pathmark near the East and Central Harlem border on 125th Street did not emerge without controversy. When the proposal to build a fifty-three-thousand-square-foot Pathmark became known to the public in 1995, two hundred local merchants and over five thousand community residents signed a petition demanding a smaller store,[10] suggesting this behemoth structure would wipe out local small businesses. The fact that East Harlem is predominantly Hispanic and the Charlie Rangel–backed, Central Harlem–based UMEZ sponsored the project added another dimension to the debate. The Empowerment Zone provided $1 million in grants for the project. Actually, the Abyssinian Development Corporation and Pathmark had been in discussion about this effort before the existence of the UMEZ. On top of UMEZ money, a city loan and tax abatement package kicked in another $6.2 million. Seen as "corporate welfare"[11] by some, the project still managed to come to fruition, despite a 1994 Human Resources Administration study that found Pathmark to have the highest prices among local supermarkets.[12]

Proponents of the $12 million project maintained that the Pathmark would offer reasonable prices and high quality, in addition to three hundred jobs and two hundred construction jobs. At the time, the project was the largest development endeavor in East Harlem in twenty years.[13] The tension was resolved when New York Mayor Rudolph Giuliani intervened, allowing the Harlem-based nonprofit overseeing the development of the project, the Abyssinian Development Corporation to control only 51 percent of the interest in the project because it is a Central Harlem–based African American organization. Because East Harlem is predominantly Latino, the City's Economic Development

Corporation held the other 49 percent of interest on reserve for a to-be-announced Latino nonprofit organization.[14]

The Latino community's opposition to the project stemmed not only from the fact that the supermarket was to be located in East Harlem. Their perspectives also were influenced by the ubiquitous small bodegas (corner delis), some owned by Latinos. These small businesspeople, they feared, would be put out of business by unbeatable competition, and opportunities for small business in general would be diminished.

Ironically, some similar issues emerged around another Pathmark. Indeed, some have argued that Harlem's development is far too concentrated on and around 125th Street. As the street has seen its share of new commercial projects over the last few years, discussions about other parts of Harlem are well underway. Another major thoroughfare, 145th Street has not received much new commercial attention. That is changing quickly, and one 1999 proposal involved bringing a Pathmark to 145th Street and Bradhurst Avenue. This address is actually in Central Harlem, making this project the first for a major supermarket in Central Harlem. Before coming to fruition, the project encountered numerous hurdles. It was opposed by the Community Board for Central Harlem's District 10, which believed too much traffic would ensue, changing the character of this residential neighborhood. Proponents suggested it would spur other developments along the street. In fact, a developer proposed to build a ten-screen movie theatre on the block. The project also faced competition from a couple of young Latino entrepreneurs, who owned a few local smaller grocery stores. The Fernandez brothers, however, "could not match what Pathmark offers,"[15] thus the City's Department of Housing Preservation and Development chose Pathmark's bid over those of the young locals.

In December 2001, Pathmark signed a lease to build on forty-five-thousand square feet at the 145th Street location. A $52 million project, financed by $6.4 million in grants and low-interest loans from the city also will include 126 "middle-income" cooperative apartments and six thousand square feet for other retail space, along with underground parking for 118 cars. This project actually never received UMEZ funding, as a group of Latino politicians and Giuliani's Deputy Mayor, Rudy Washington blocked its funding in support of the Fernandez brother's appeal. Slated for a 2004 completion date, the Pathmark should create two hundred jobs, three quarters of which must be from the local community.[16]

The supermarket issue is paramount in many urban areas, as stale produce and various inferior products in small local groceries give residents little choice, as nicer supermarkets tend to be located in higher-income areas. Harlem native and community activist Gail Aska said, "I think that the residents have suffered in quality. We haven't had it in terms of food." She noted how the Pathmark supermarket made her feel as if she were "in a different town or state because we didn't have a quality type market we could go to and get fresh vegetables—vegetables that you could tell what they were. And the color—the green vegetable was not green, it was grey; it had spots on it, and yet the prices were astronomical, and you'd stand there and say, 'you've got to be kidding!'" The presence of the Pathmark has given residents a choice in this matter. She said of the Pathmark, "It's helped that because the quality of the produce alone is much better than most of the markets if not all of them. They also, because it's such a big market, they sell bulk things, where a person with a limited budget can go and stock up and get the most out of their money in terms of people who are on welfare and get the most of their food stamps."[17]

Robert Roach is also happy that his choices of produce and other food products have improved dramatically. He said, "You don't see rotten meat anymore, or vegetables that are rotten, and they were trying to sell it." As will be discussed further, the threat posed to small businesses by the advent of large retail corporations stirs emotions in the neighborhood. The question of the quality of service for residents versus ownership opportunities for small entrepreneurs will likely remain a lasting debate in Harlem. For Roach, quality is the priority regardless of the demographics of business owners. He said, "Businesses were small and the prices they charged were exorbitant. Buy Black? There's no problem with that, but you got to offer me what I want. I'll buy Black, but I'll buy any color, as long as you are offering a product that I want. Why should I buy a product from you just because of your color when I don't want it? Don't work that way! Not that way in the business community, and now what you have is going back to the bottom line."[18]

According to Lorraine Gilbert, Harlem residents were persistently treated rudely in local stores; this recent commercial competition has altered various merchants' behavior. She said, "There was a time when we weren't treated with respect when we patronized a business, and a lot of times, we've had to patronize because we had no other choice; there were no other competitors."[19] Increased access to services is one identifiable advantage for Harlem residents, but it extends to treatment and behavior. How people are treated is the kind of factor that might be overlooked when assessing quality of life in a neighborhood. Although it is a byproduct of larger political and economic decisions, sometimes quality of life can boil down to something as basic as being treated with dignity and respect.

Jobs

As previously mentioned, a key initial goal of the Empowerment Zone was to stimulate jobs for local residents. For example, the 125th Street Pathmark employs about three hundred people, 78 percent of whom live locally.[20] According to UMEZ, Harlem USA, with Old Navy, HMV, and others, created five hundred permanent jobs. Businesses attracted to Harlem as a result of incentives incorporated into this federal legislation have been required to hire locally. Despite this reality, residents have mixed opinions regarding the extent and/or impact of these jobs.

Laconia Smedley thinks the new jobs are generally positive, "… I mean they may not be getting big sums of money, but at least it's more than what they had. Some of them didn't even have jobs; they can (now) walk to the job. So I think in a way, the stores that opened up on 125th Street are a good thing for that, because these people are making some money. And if a person can get a job making some money, that makes them feel good—some sense of pride within themselves, and that gives them self esteem."[21]

Gail Aska also put a positive spin on the new jobs, although she was a bit skeptical. She said, "I guess time will tell whether they've maintained it—whether people are getting jobs there and being given decent wages and all of that. But the beginnings seem to be with the consideration of the residents of Harlem being given priority to hire them as opposed to other people. So that's an example of something that came in and we tend to benefit…."[22]

Vicky Gholson was less enthusiastic about the jobs coming into the neighborhoods. From her experience and conversations with residents in the neighborhood, the jobs are not quite as plentiful. She said, "People have said to me as we walk across 125th Street—friends of mine who work in the movies—you know, there are plenty of jobs. I say, there are no jobs. We walk across 125th Street, and I say, do you see any for hire signs in the windows? There are no jobs here. I say that's a misnomer."[23]

In addition to jobs provided through Empowerment Zone incentives, the tourist industry provides employment as well. About 723 full time jobs with an annual salary of a little over $27,000 per year are directly associated with Harlem's landmarks, cultural institutions, tours, and other aspects of the tourist industry. However, only 32 percent of those jobs are held by residents of Upper Manhattan. When professional positions are isolated among the 723 jobs, the number of jobs held by locals reduces to 14 percent.[24] For many of its investments, the UMEZ lists the projected amount of jobs that will be created by the initiative. The massive East River Plaza, for example, is projected to bring in twenty-two hundred jobs. The Gotham Plaza, 586, the Langston Hotel, 112.[25] Therefore, although jobs may be located in the neighborhood, quite a number of them, and especially the higher-paying and more stable positions, go to outsiders.

As previously noted, the Harlem community's income is not particularly high. Moreover, while it is difficult to attain actual 2002 through 2004 unemployment data in the neighborhood, the state of the economy suggests that fewer jobs are available. We do know that New York City, post–September 11, lost quite a number of jobs. It is interesting that the promotional materials of the UMEZ focus on the projects underway, money distributed, and funding leveraged, but not on the state of unemployment, income, and other social characteristics.

Mixed Economy

In previous decades, the flight of capital from Harlem meant concentrated poverty. The lack of a mixed economic community contributed to the lack of services, the lack of jobs, and the lack of opportunity for local residents. Several scholars have found that concentrated poverty creates a vicious cycle, limiting opportunities for generations of residents.[26] Recent changes in Harlem have attracted middle-class employed new residents, many of whom are African American. On various blocks in Harlem, one can now find a broad mix of economic classes—the kind unseen for decades. This mix exposes low-income residents to people with education and access. But the hard reality is that the presence of middle-class professionals, and the prospect of their arrival, attracts resources and services that would generally elude low-income people had they been living only among others in the same socioeconomic class.

John Bess said of the demographic shift, "People who are now professionals once fled. This upper working class never thought about living in Harlem ... a community of low income, no income, poverty devastates the community."[27] On the surface, it would appear that mixed economic communities are the solution to concentrated poverty. However, creating mixed economic communities that work has been a persistent challenge. The movement of low-income people into more affluent areas has tended to stimulate an exodus of existing residents, often known as "White flight." In the reverse situation, known as gentrification, in which more affluent people move into low-income neighborhoods, low-income residents become priced out, which is the fear concerning Harlem's future.

Although it is difficult to tell if Harlem will become far too inaccessible for less advantaged populations, in the present, some residents feel, the increased existence of professionals in the neighborhood is helpful to low-income people. According to Roach, "I think with the neighborhood being diversified the way it is now, what I mean by diversified, I'm talking about the professionals, regardless of color, professionals because it gives the kids an opportunity to see a different side of life."[28]

Although he is not a new resident, former President Bill Clinton has brought increased attention to Harlem. His moving into an office on 125th Street does indeed provide local residents a glance at another style of life. The reviews as to the significance of Bill Clinton's Harlem office location are mixed, as previously noted, but his presence certainly brought attention to Harlem. For some, this might say, "If Harlem is good enough for Clinton, it should be good enough for anyone." When asked if Clinton's presence will improve the community, Smedley answered, "Bill Clinton had nothing to do with the changes happening in Harlem. The plans were already on the board—long time ago. People planned twenty, thirty and forty years ahead."[29]

Safety

Crime was also one of the key roadblocks to Harlem's advancement throughout the '70s and '80s. Although policing practices have been credited for crime rate reductions in New York City during the 1990s, many have argued that crime reduction has been a national trend as a result of other factors, such as the decline in the prevalence of crack-cocaine. Others would maintain that increased incarceration rates and incidents of police brutality were sorry trade-offs in exchange for crime reduction. Some would suggest that innovative community policing strategies reduced crime. Overall, the issue is controversial, but reduced crime has facilitated some aspects of urban community development.

Although it may be difficult to determine the source of crime reduction, given national trends in crime reduction throughout the '90's, less prevalent crime in Harlem has contributed to the neighborhood's recent heightened profile: "… you do feel safer when there are more lights, when there are people who you know are working, people who are purchasing homes, and if you have three buildings … on this block, which were vacant at one time. People were running in and out of it, they're in a vacant building, by the way, to do their drug business. That (new home owners) eliminates that definitely."[30]

Whatever one's opinions about how crime data is gathered, the reduction in crime rates in Harlem and Northern Manhattan as a whole are quite noticeable. The reasons why are debatable. But when people say that New York feels safer, that Harlem feels safer, evidently, the reasons are grounded in data. In New York City as a whole, crime is down, having steadily dropped since 1997—240,008 crimes in 1997, and 161,977 in 2001. Robberies, assaults, and burglaries appear to have the biggest dips. Overall crimes dropped 12.02 percent between 2000 and 2001. In all of Northern Manhattan, however, the figures are far more significant, especially taking a nine-year view; between 1993 and 2001, crime dropped 65.18 percent. Central Harlem shares three police precincts, numbers 28 at 2271—89 8th Avenue, 30 at 451 West 151st Street, and 32 at 250 West 135th Street. The 28th Precinct witnessed a 69.99 percent drop between 1993 and 2001. The 30th saw a 59.11 percent dip in the same period, and the 32nd Precinct saw a 58.15 percent decrease. Large reductions occurred in murders and burglaries, both of which were often associated with the drug trade.[31]

Tourism

One of the ways in which developing countries have generated resources has been through tourism. As an economic development tool, this concept can be applied to low-income communities, especially if they have something to offer tourists. Given Harlem's rich history, and myriad legendary sites from the Apollo Theater to the Abyssinian Baptist Church, the neighborhood has become a chosen tourist destination in New York City. Although most residents and community organizations have not found ways to directly benefit from tourism, the presence of tourists from around the world brings additional services and attention from local government. As previously noted, Harlem's tourism is a significant economic generator for the neighborhood and New York City as a whole.

UMEZ has been putting resources into tourism. In their eyes, the ripple effects would be jobs as well as resources from outsiders. Tourism is an often-tried strategy, but not one that has always benefited low-income people. Nevertheless, UMEZ has made investments in the Harlem Strategic Cultural Collaborative, including some of Harlem's most well known cultural and tourist attractions. These include the Apollo Theatre, the Boys' Choir of Harlem, the Dance Theatre of Harlem, the Schomburg Center for Research in Black Culture, the Studio Museum in Harlem, and others. This $25 million Cultural Investment Fund is likely to strengthen the neighborhood's local attractions. Since the renaissance of the 1920s, Harlem's art and performance has been a global attraction. Additionally, investments in this area can serve to preserve some of the cultural traditions for which Harlem has been known and respected. Another large investment of note in UMEZ's repertoire of support to arts institutions is the $2.5 million allocated to the Museum for African Art, which will top off the Manhattan's Museum Mile on Fifth Avenue. The new museum, to be located at the northeastern edge of Central Park, will be a state-of-the-art facility. The Apollo has also recently received $2.5 million, as it is being transformed into the Apollo Performing Arts Center.[32]

Increased Property Values for Longtime Owners

Although Harlem was unpopular among many outside of the neighborhood, stunning, ornate brownstones and other residential properties were for sale at quite affordable rates. Average working-class African Americans, and some wealthier ones, bought many of these homes. With Harlem's newfound prominence, the value of these properties has increased by ten or even more times, giving people who stuck it out in the neighborhood when it was not in vogue capital of which they had never dreamed. Some of the residents have sold their homes, cashing out, and moved to more affordable areas, whereas others have remained, some renting out their apartments at the new, much higher, market rates.

Laconia Smedley owns a brownstone, which he purchased in 1980 for $30,000. He estimates the current value of this building at between

$450,000 and $500,000. He had bought another in 1985 for $55,000, which he sold three years ago for $200,000. He said, "Now if I had just been very mercenary, I could've held on to it, and got more money, but I didn't know this was coming; 'cause it seems as though the changes here happened like waving a wand, and all of a sudden, what was ugly became beautiful."[33] Although the changes appeared rapid, Smedley noted that he had learned of the plans to significantly redevelop Harlem through a local politician many years ago.

Smedley, like many of the interviewees, thinks ownership is the key. When asked who are the primary beneficiaries, and who are the losers in Harlem's economically changing landscape, the vast majority said that renters with little economic resources will lose out the most. To the question of whether housing gentrification was good or bad, Smedley answered, "... for those of us who have a stake, it's mostly good, for those who don't have a stake, it's bad." While individually happy to own, Smedley wishes ownership opportunities could open up for less advantaged longtime residents. But at this point, he is left to wonder, "... how much of Harlem is left for people to own?"[34]

With the increased interest in Harlem's real estate, banks and other financial institutions have been providing special low-interest loans for renovations. One can still see a number of boarded-up buildings in the neighborhood, but nowhere near as many as one would have seen even five years ago. Although some cannot afford to take on loan payments, Harlem's community development corporations have been helping, not only to purchase and resell property at affordable rates but also to help those who do not have the resources to renovate their homes to do so. Minnette Coleman told the story of a brownstone that was being renovated on her block. She said, "I was awakened a couple of summers ago, about seven o'clock in the morning, with hammering and screaming and all this noise on a Saturday morning, and I opened the door and I went outside and there were like forty people out there. There's some organization that picks a house to do, and they do it in one day. They paint it. They replanted the backyard, they did the steps, they replaced the windows, and they've got all these people who come in; this is their community service, the company is doing it, and paying for it, and the tenant has to be elderly."[35] This is just an example of the collective effort to renovate property in Harlem.

Overall, the increased services, improved products, renovated properties, reduced crime, the community spirit, increased real estate values, socioeconomically mixed residents, and new jobs are all indicators of progress in Harlem. Many residents can enjoy these benefits. Harlem was a place that several people and institutions wanted to avoid. Now it is a place where they are fighting to get in. Although the neighborhood's turnaround had been a part of a long-term plan, on the surface, Harlem's change appears swift, given where things stood only a decade ago. Even post–September 11, Harlem's real estate rates have continued to rise, and the various development projects are continuing. The development of Harlem is multidimensional, and the neighborhood is clearly in a different place than it had been in recent years.

The Paradox

All of these benefits to Harlem have another, less advantageous side— the paradox of gentrification. Are the jobs coming into the neighborhood leading to the economic empowerment of the community? Are additional services and new residents pricing old residents out of the neighborhood? Is Harlem's unique culture in jeopardy? Are any of the new benefits intended for the longtime residents, who made Harlem what it is today?

We have still not reached a point where benefits to one group fuels the common good. In Harlem, as in many places, changing economies tend to affect people rather differently depending on issues such as class, race, education, and access. Although these residents found positive aspects to the recent changes, far more discussion focused on shortcomings.

Housing

To capture the sense of the residential housing boom in Harlem, I thought it might be interesting to peek at how Harlem is being advertised by one of New York City's most exclusive real estate agencies, the Corcoran Group:

Filled with a spirited bustle—from 116th Street and north to the Harlem River and from the Hudson to the East Rivers—Harlem's rapid renaissance was emerging long before the arrival of Bill Clinton. And aside from the public relations windfall the neighborhood's experienced in recent years, there's no denying the area is hot. Buyers who would never have considered moving here five years ago are clamoring to pick up new townhouses and restored 19th century brownstones for what some say is a song. No doubt about it, these magnificent buildings need extensive renovations—but if backyards, working fireplaces, original moldings and even a driveway for not-so-exorbitant prices is what you're looking for, it's here.[36]

As previously mentioned, some longtime homeowners have realized that they have been sitting on a gold mine. This quote not only indicates the attraction to Harlem, a company such as Corcoran would have never even glanced at Harlem a decade ago, but it also highlights Harlem's unique characteristics. In comparison to the rest of Manhattan, Harlem provides far more humane residential living conditions—space and character.

Although some homeowners have realized benefits, Harlem is still principally a renter's neighborhood. According to the 2000 Census, Central Harlem (District 10) was 93.4 percent renter occupied and 6.4 percent owner occupied. East Harlem (District 11) was 93.6 percent renter occupied and 6.6 percent owner occupied. West Harlem (District 9) was 90.3 percent renter occupied and 9.7 percent owner occupied.[37] Renters have been relatively insecure in this environment of continually rising real estate rates. Rent stabilization continues throughout New York City, but landlords want to benefit. If a landlord can get five times as much rent as he or she is getting currently, then that person may be enticed to force tenants out.

Buildings constructed before February 1947 are subject to rent control program. The program applies to tenants who have been living in an apartment continuously before July 1, 1971. Rent control restricts the rights of owners to evict tenants and limits the amount of rent they can charge. Each apartment in New York City has a Maximum Base Rent (MBR), set by the Rent Guidelines Board, which is adjusted every two years to be consistent with increased operating costs. Landlords may increase rents in a variety of ways. Rents for such apartments can be increased by 7.5 percent each year until the MBR is reached, provided essential services are provided and violations are removed. Landlords also can raise rents if they increase services and provide significant capital improvements or can demonstrate hardship or increased costs in labor or utilities. These are relatively broad categories, which can be finessed to landlord desires. Interpretations of broad policies of this sort provide protections for tenants, but simultaneously do not necessarily stop motivated landlords from finding creative ways of increasing rents or evicting tenants.

Rent stabilization is another housing policy sharing similar principles with rent control. When a rent controlled apartment becomes vacant, it is subject to rent stabilization. Generally, rent stabilization applies to apartments in buildings of six or more units built between February 1, 1947, and January 1, 1974. Rent controlled apartments built before February 1947 and vacated after June 30, 1971, are also candidates for rent stabilization.

As rents in New York began to skyrocket, policy makers discussed the role of luxury housing in rent regulations. Apartments with legal rents over $2,000 per month were deregulated through the Rent Regulation Reform Act of 1993. New York City Local Law 4 of 1994 deregulated apartments at the same $2,000 per month, but went further to include the income of tenants. Those making $250,000 per year or more were deregulated. In 1997, the threshold was lowered to $175,000 per year. Therefore, if high-rent apartments with high-income tenants can be deregulated, then it is in the interest of landlords to rent to high-income tenants, which may partly explain why so much residential housing development focuses on "luxury."

Debates rage on around rent policy throughout the State of New York. Housing advocates, landlords, developers, and politicians have all been weighing in on the status of rent stabilization. During his campaign for a second term in the fall of 2005, Mayor Michael R. Bloomberg pointed to his housing proposals as examples of how he has tried to make New York more affordable to the poor and working class. The New York City Rent Guidelines Board (RGB), consisting of two landlord representatives, two tenant representatives, and five other appointees of the mayor determines how much to raise rents every spring. Although many tenants are supportive of Bloomberg's policies, many have criticized the mayor and Board for raising rents up to 6.5 percent in 2004 and 7.5 percent in 2003, the biggest increase since 1989. In the spring of 2005, the board recommended an increase of 2 to 4.5 percent for one-year lease renewals and 4 to 7 percent for two-year renewals.[38]

Although Harlem has several larger apartment buildings, a good portion of the rental market is in brownstones, with fewer than six rental units. Not subject to the regulations of larger buildings, brownstones, and the degree to which they change hands, significantly impact tenants in those buildings. Many of those purchasing residential brownstones, Harlem's newer residents, are buying for themselves. When less affluent residents had been purchasing brownstones before this current "renaissance," they needed tenants to make their mortgages. Some new residents can afford entire brownstones for themselves. Renters may have lived there before the sale, but if new owners do not want tenants, then tenants must move. Smedley wishes that more African American Harlem residents had taken the opportunity to buy when prices were much lower. But for many low-income residents, ownership was not a possibility. However, there were those who could have bought, but did not. Smedley attributes this lack of pursuing ownership as a "plantation mentality." He maintains that, "The ignorance that comes down from generation to generation, of people not having any desire to get—the government providing them with an income, and they happen to subsidize that income by other means, and if they can't do it legally, of course they are going to do it illegally 'cause they don't have the education, ability to train for some field...." He later elaborated, saying of African Americans, "... after slavery, you became a sharecropper, and after sharecroppers, you became the ultimate consumer."[39] If African Americans do not own, yet they spend, then the retail industry actually benefits from locating in predominantly African American communities. Retailers stand to profit from a community that would rather purchase goods than save to own.

Minnette Coleman thinks the barriers to African American ownership, although a matter of income, is also a question of information. She said, "I mean there are probably people in Harlem who make enough money to go buy, but they don't know how to do it. They don't know what to do." She added that this is similar in the case of business ownership. She noted, "And to set up their own businesses, they have the ideas, but they don't know how to do it, and they also don't know how to get somebody to help them."[40] Without information, residents can miss out, and become vulnerable. In terms of living quarters, uninformed residents, low-income residents, are susceptible to displacement.

Many of the interviewees saw displacement or the prospect of displacement as one of the key weaknesses of the economic changes in the neighborhood. John Bess said, "... people who have stayed through the hard times—through difficult times—may not be able to afford living in Harlem."[41] It is difficult to determine whether or not someone has moved from the neighborhood because of growing gentrification. Indeed, some people may leave the neighborhood simply because they want a change or maybe their lifestyle changed. What's certain is that many residents know or know of people who have recently left the neighborhood or been evicted or been priced out. It appears that those who have left Harlem have gone far away. If they left for economic reasons, this would make sense, because the entire New York City area has experienced increased real estate values in recent years. Prices have reached a plateau or decreased slightly in the immediate wake of September 11, and in the face of a national economy that had already been on the downturn, but they are back on a rising track, partly influenced by supply and demand. With so many people wanting to own property, not only in Harlem, but in New York City in general, it is not surprising that housing costs continue to rise. Rental costs have slightly decreased, partly because of incentives for home ownership, especially low interest rates. However, as only so many ownership opportunities are available in New York City, rental rates will increase again, as will interest rates.

Coleman spoke of how she has gradually seen fewer low-income people. She said, "All of a sudden, pockets of people who are at poverty levels aren't there anymore. A lot of people—the real poor people who used to be on our block, you don't see them, or maybe they moved." She reflected on how the City of New York sold a lot of brownstones that contained renters, and how a number of landlords are taking "steps to get rid of people that they really didn't want in the building."[42]

On the one hand, it appears that Manhattan's economy benefits from gentrification. After all, it looks cleaner, less depressing. However, if all of Manhattan Island is gentrified, other ripple effects could hurt New York's economy. For example, civil servants provide essential services. If no one can afford to live in the city, hiring for those positions, especially the lower paying ones, will become increasingly difficult. Harlem resident and artist Cynthia Simmons said, "I think the inflated real estate values may be good for landlords, but I think ultimately, it's not good; it is going to displace too many people in Manhattan in general." She continued, "Manhattan is going to have a very hard, the five boroughs—they will have a very hard time filling certain jobs that are important to the running of any community, just because what they pay is not enough money for you to live there. So I don't have to commute to be a sanitation worker. Maybe I might commute to Wall Street to make megabucks, but forty thousand dollars? Why would I commute for that?"[43]

John Bess spoke of the experiences of young people associated with his organization, "Lots of young people have been told that their parents have been bought out of their apartments, or they can't afford it. Unfortunately, I hear a great deal of young people, and see on our roster, young people who are moving out to Queens and the Bronx or moving down South because they can't afford escalating rents. Harlem only has a homeownership rate of about six percent, which is still horrendous and drastic. Even that's gonna change very soon."[44]

It would appear that the solution to inaccessible and unaffordable housing would be to build more. Walking the streets of Harlem, one can see the various construction projects underway. Some of it may lead to housing that is affordable for working people. But affordability does not appear to be the direction of the Harlem's housing market. The insecurity that some residents may feel is very much grounded in the reality that the target audience for recent housing developments is not low income or even lower middle class. Harlem small business owner, Reggie James said, "I know I would be scared to death if I was a lower middle class person making maybe around $30,000 and looking at all this development. These brownstones that were given away at one point—then you could pick them up for $60,000 to $80,000 a shell that is now half a million to a million dollars. They have to be scared to death. And they are hardly building any middle class housing."[45]

Much of Harlem is still low income. Tyletha Samuels, a lifelong Harlem resident, said, "And now they're building affordable homes, but it's not affordable for low income people, because affordable homes is $40,000 and up, and the low income person doesn't even make $20,000 to $25,000." She continued, "I see a lot of my friends doing construction work … a benefit would have been them being able to get them apartments instead of working to build those apartments for other people."[46]

Residential real estate rates have gone up so quickly in Harlem that even some of the professionals who moved into the neighborhood during the 1990s could not afford to move in at this time. Deborah Faison, who moved to Harlem in 1991, and is the director of a nonprofit organization, the Harlem Venture Group, said, "I think you have to be in an upper income bracket to move to Harlem. And if you're not, and you're renting, and your lease is going to expire, you're probably going to have to move. I know a number of people—individuals and professionals, who really were forced to leave Harlem. I couldn't move to Harlem now."[47]

If Harlem is following the direction of the rest of Manhattan, Faison's comment speaks to a real estate market that excludes the poor, the working class, and the middle class, leaving room only for the upper middle and upper classes. From looking at Harlem today, it does not appear that such a sweeping demographic change would occur. But many less-advantaged people are able to continue living in the neighborhood because of longtime rent stabilized apartments and public housing. This is where policy becomes so essential—if rent stabilization laws continue to whither, as they have been in recent years, and if public housing units decrease, Harlem will no longer be a place accessible to low income and working class people, regardless of race or ethnicity.

Lorraine Gilbert, a longtime real estate broker in the neighborhood, said of the rising residential real estate rates, "I think the weakness is that the price has escalated so much that when you're talking a million just about for a brownstone, then that wipes out a lot of people, Black and White." She continued, "Senior citizens and people that have been here for many years won't be able to afford, and they will have no choice but to sell."[48] The lack of options is part of what paralyzes residents. Once the services have arrived in their neighborhood, they might very well be able to stay, but in a very limited sense. If they move, it's all over—they can no longer afford to stay in their community even if they have lived there for thirty, forty, fifty, or more years.

This speaks to the continued need for a comprehensive approach to development—if low-income people are going to face difficulties in access to affordable housing, another particular effort will be required to enhance affordability. Buildings where a certain percentage of units are set aside for low-income people, tax credits, jobs, or any number of other mechanisms can make the difference between remaining in the neighborhood and being displaced. But New York City, as is the case in many instances, requires more. Jobs must pay more, set asides aren't enough, tax credits give back only so much, and on. Staving off displacement will be daunting in Harlem's and New York City's future, but little progress will be made without the desire of policy makers, landlords, developers, and businesses. If no one cares enough to ensure benefits for low-income people, it is very likely that we will witness displacement, and even further impoverishment, as the cost of living outpaces the amount of money coming in.

Gilbert thinks that greed has sent prices far beyond where some might have imagined they would go. She has worked with affordable housing developers to renovate homes and sell them at reasonable rates. She worked with the Abyssinian Development Corporation and other local developers to renovate and sell thirty-five three- and four-family houses at between $350,000 and $450,000. She said, "They're beautiful houses; in fact, the income from those houses is enough for an owner to maintain the duplex rent-free because he has two or three other units to support his monthly mortgage."[49] Because brownstones are multifamily units, middle-income people can afford to buy and rent out two or three units to tenants. This rental income pays for the mortgage and beyond.

Although these rates are still out of reach for low-income people, some private developers have been renovating homes to be sold at far higher rates, buying property from elderly residents at low rates, and reselling them for "thousands and thousands." She also spoke of developers who have worked with nonprofit organizations, received homes from the Department of Housing and Urban Development (HUD) to be redeveloped, borrowed money from HUD for renovation, and pocketed the money without doing the renovations.[50]

Vicky Gholson says it is not just the big developers exacerbating displacement. She thinks the movement of various immigrant groups into Harlem has pushed out longtime African American residents. According the Gholson, the rental buildings in Harlem have a tendency of reflecting the ethnicity of superintendents. She said, "If you look at who the supers are of tenement buildings, you'll note in short order, within a five-year period of time, the population of the tenement building will change. As the people, African Americans, you know, migrated from the South, when we came, and we began to get those jobs as supers, our people began to become the residents of those buildings; that's why we have people now who have been living for thirty-five, forty, fifty, going on sixty years in the same apartment." This population of renters, according to Gholson, is not getting its due, as the neighborhood changes. The renters, Gholson said, "... who have been living in those apartments for over forty or fifty years have contributed over five hundred thousand dollars into their communities, into those apartments."[51]

The fact that those residents don't receive anything back for all of that investment is a part of the uglier side of Harlem's new renaissance. Gholson says she knows of several people being displaced. "I know people who have been displaced," she said. She continued, "Yes, I know people, with the mayor's policies changing, you know that the in rem qualifications changed, so you can go in rem in a year, as opposed to three or four or five, which was the case before—the safety net to be able to capture people who have fallen behind in their taxes—all of that was changed in the past ten years."[52]

But displacement, through Gholson's eyes, has many dimensions. Displacement began decades ago, with the drug trade. She said, "People are being forced out. People were forced out first with the drug trafficking; they were forced out second with the drug trafficking and the police corruption; then they were forced out with the immigration." When the drug market in Harlem was at its height, according to Gholson, people had no choice but to leave in some instances. She said, "People were forced out by drug dealers, who made it absolutely impossible to fight for your property—for you to go to a meeting at the precinct council, and by the time you got home, they identified that you were at the meeting."[53]

Gholson speaks of a different kind of displacement than what seems to concern so many residents in today's Harlem. No studies have been able to accurately assess the effect of gentrification on mobility among longtime residents. A couple of recent studies,[54] however, maintain that gentrification leads to some displacement, but, for the most part, it encourages low-income residents to stay. Because residents of all types may move for any number of reasons, it would be rather painstaking to accurately determine the precise motivations for leaving in every case. Does this mean Harlem residents' fears are unfounded?

Harlem's extensive public housing, and New York City's rent control laws would suggest that quite a number of low-income residents could remain in the neighborhood to enjoy the various resources entering the area. However, rent stabilization policy has been under constant pressure from landlords in recent years, and public housing may be policy now, but its existence is not guaranteed. No one knows how policy will change, and no one knows for sure how more affluent residents will receive public housing. Chicago's Gold Coast community, a relatively wealthy enclave that happens to contain the well-known Cabrini-Green public housing complex, has continually advocated for the public development's removal. In the Fort Green section of Brooklyn, a good portion of the extensive public housing development in the neighborhood is being converted into condominiums, displacing about half of the residents, sending them to public housing in the far less convenient Coney Island neighborhood. The Department of Housing and Urban Development's Hope VI initiative is revamping the standard towering and dreary public housing structures, and turning them into low-rise, more spread out developments. However, in order to do that, residents are being temporarily displaced, relying on Section 8 housing vouchers (accepted by very few private developments) to find affordable housing.

This is all to say that Harlem brings no guaranteed living situations, public or private.

To be displaced or not displaced, however, is not by any means the only issue at work; residents may leave nongentrified areas because of the lack of services or limited safety. Most of the interviewed residents are happy about additional services, which is clearly an incentive. However, for low-income residents in particular, options have diminished significantly. The family that has lived in the same rental apartment for twenty-five years simply cannot move within Harlem unless it possesses significant resources. If the landlord in that building might evict that family, it is left out in the cold. Families are vulnerable, tenuously holding on, in many cases.

The concept of a mixed economic community was cited as one of the benefits of Harlem's changes. However, few effective models of mixed economic communities exist. Traditionally, low-income residents become pushed out. The presence of a newer, more affluent population might actually lead to better services. However, some of those services might not be accessible to low-income people, and more affluent neighbors may not actually invest in the public services that low-income people need in order to better their lives, most notably, schools. In many gentrified neighborhoods, residents with disposable income often send their children to private schools. A predominantly White, upper-middle-class urban neighborhood with a public high school containing almost exclusively low-income and working class people of color is a common sight in quite a number of New York City neighborhoods that are much further along in their gentrification, such as the Upper West Side.

But, after a long period of abandonment and deterioration, Harlem needed an infusion. Part of what makes Harlem's situation, and those of other gentrifying neighborhoods, so complex is that they simply were not receiving the funding or attention that was required. Before the Empowerment Zone legislation, few major federal policies were attending to low-income urban neighborhoods. Given Harlem's state during the early 1990s, it was not surprising that the neighborhood became one of the six areas around the country to receive the Empowerment Zone designation. As others mentioned, the seeds for today's economic changes in Harlem had been planted decades ago. Harlem became unlivable for many people in very real ways. Those who stuck it out and stayed endured significant hardships in some instances. But many of those with choices opted to leave—the beginnings of a certain type of displacement that is curiously tied to current economic development efforts. Was that displacement orchestrated in order to make way for Harlem's revitalization? It is difficult to accurately determine a web of conspiracy complete with drugs and crime. However, the lack of concern for low-income urban neighborhoods that enabled drugs and crime to flourish cannot be denied. Once the conditions had gotten so out of hand, the federal government responded with funds. It took the unrest in 1992 in Los Angeles to encourage the discussions that would ultimately lead to the Empowerment Zones.[55]

The place-based focus of this federal policy is important. Bringing services and jobs and safety to particular disadvantaged geographical areas is an essential part of enhancing communities. However, if the quality of life of the people themselves is not simultaneously taken into account and given equal weight, we will only be left with gentrified neighborhoods. A neighborhood may look nicer as a result of strictly place-based approaches, but it also may be terribly overpriced and generally insecure for low-income people.

LIMITED AFRICAN AMERICAN OWNERSHIP

Although new businesses have come to Harlem, ownership still rests primarily in the hands of people who do not reflect the dominant racial and ethnic demographic. The original Harlem Renaissance symbolized the advancement of a people—African Americans and all people of African descent. Although this current renaissance focuses on economics, it does not appear that it is fostering economic empowerment for existing Harlem residents. Higher African American business ownership would be one, albeit limited, form of economic empowerment for existing residents. So, if the policy is to attract new businesses that bring jobs, then do longtime residents only get access to the jobs? Do they receive some co-ownership? Do they collectively enjoy some of the profits?

According to Mary Baker, Harlem's recent economic changes are very much tied to race, and a history of powerful Whites ensuring that people of African descent do not become more empowered. She believes that Whites are threatened by any prospect of Black empowerment. She said, "The White man doesn't care much for you period, because he doesn't want you to get equal with him. Because if you do, what will he have? Because he knows if he gives you the opportunity, you're going to excel him. Because, number one, we're used to hardship, and we can take it." She is critical across the board of the state of urban development in the neighborhood. "No matter what's coming in, the White man's behind it; it's still not colored," she declared.[56]

As she has seen the various Black-owned businesses in her neighborhood close shop, while new business, not owned by persons of African descent, move in, she has grown increasingly displeased. In reference to Old Navy, the Gap, Pathmark, and other new establishments, she responded sharply, "That's nothing to rave about, because what is it bringing in!?" She recalled a local Black-owned drugstore that was at 152nd Street and St. Nicholas Avenue that was recently put out of business, "He was there for over fifty years, but all of a sudden, they just wiped him out."[57]

Limited ownership among African Americans has been a long-standing area of concern. But, as Baker indicates, even in some of the hardest of times, Black-owned businesses were still present. Now, when Harlem is supposedly making its ascent, Black ownership is declining. A part of the stated economic promise of the Empowerment Zone and other economic development projects has been job creation.

Laconia Smedley provided his take on this issue, "People are getting jobs in these businesses, but so far as them having a stake in the business, that's different because there's no ownership there."[58] Some of the few accessible ownership options for local residents came through street vending and very small establishments. Overall, the community's power will always be limited if residents are not positioned to control their future, and make decisions about and share in the benefits of local economics.

Many small business opportunities were limited in order to make way for the retail industry receiving incentives through the Empowerment Zone. The street vendors on 125th Street, who, on the one hand, crowded the sidewalks, but, on the other, contributed to the vibrancy and color of Harlem, were removed, and given the option to move to another site with far less foot traffic. For people with limited means to afford space and other aspects of business infrastructure, street sales became an accessible opportunity for self-employment. Therefore, the apparent infusion of new resources limited opportunities for residents.

The process by which the vendors were removed from 125th Street was highly contentious. Harlem's established leadership did not support the vendors, and, in fact, advocated for their removal. C. Virginia Fields, now the Borough President of Manhattan, while on City Council, stood on the steps of City Hall in September 1994, and demanded that Giuliani remove the vendors. Shortly afterward, the New York City Police Department removed the vendors. This battle had been brewing since the 1970s, as business owners on the street advocated for their low overhead competitors' departure.[59] Ironically, the small businesses that sought to push out the street vendors, are themselves, facing intense competition from new businesses.

Most of the 125th Street vendors were from various parts of Africa. In the new space at 116th Street and Malcolm X Boulevard, some of the vendors were around before the removal from 125th Street, but many of them are new to Harlem. Managed by the Harlem Business Outreach Center, this partially enclosed market sells many of the various African jewelry, sculptures, pieces of cloth, and other works of art that once spread across 125th Street. Personally, I have never seen the new market crowded, however, the vendors note that business is not bad on some weekends.

One vendor from Gambia, a "longtime" United States' resident, located his business on 125th Street before the policy change. In comparing his new location to his old one, he said, "I like it here better. Here we have no problem." The idea of being secure in a space without wondering what will happen is appealing to this vendor. He gave no opinion on the process of his removal from 125th Street. According to him, he was just following orders. "I have no choice," he said. He continued, "They say that nobody can sell here no more. So, I say okay, yeah. And the government say I have to follow that. So I cannot say no. I cannot say yes. Anything they say, I have to say okay."[60]

As immigrants, these vendors experience Harlem differently than African Americans. They have voluntarily, although potentially fleeing unlivable conditions, come to the United States to earn a living for themselves, and their families, both in the United States and in their home countries. As evident in the comments of this particular vendor, he is happy to be in a space to sell his goods. He is not interested in criticizing the government. Whether his new situation could be better or not, he is going to follow the rules. The insecurity of the immigrant experience in the United States, especially with stricter regulations around deportation and immigration status, makes the idea of fighting the U.S. government around any issue an intimidating proposition.

This particular vendor doesn't appear to want to do or say anything that will jeopardize his business. Nevertheless, he is happy with Harlem's changes overall. However, he, like the majority of the vendors in the market, does not live in Harlem. They live in less expensive neighborhoods in New Jersey and the Bronx. What is also interesting about many of the vendors is that some of them have never even heard of the UMEZ. The one interviewed vendor who knew something about the UMEZ, an "East African" man, expressed his frustration with the volume of paperwork required for application for Empowerment Zone funds. He recounted how he and his wife took time to fill out several forms and received no answer. He said, "No answer until you ask." But he kept asking, and had not received an answer at the point when he was interviewed. He does not have high expectations because of his feelings about "American capitalism." He said, "The capitalism of America is like a flat water. I mean, those who are exposed to those people who matter, they get the financial help." What upsets him about the Empowerment Zone is the fact that it is government money. He added, "This is government money, they are supposed to help poor people, and I don't think they help poor people."[61]

Although Harlem's Business Improvement District had favored the movement of vendors from 125th Street, because of the competition brought on by businesspersons who carry little overhead, even incorporated Black-owned businesses have held mixed feelings about Harlem's changes. They feel that the Empowerment Zone in particular, has focused too heavily on large and outside businesses. It includes technical assistance for small businesses, however, some have maintained that it is not enough. Competition has gotten too tough and real estate rates have risen too high for a number of small Harlem businesses.

A proprietor of a thirty-two-year-old small Black-owned business in Harlem, Dee Soloman, discussed the Empowerment Zone as it relates to small businesses: "The Empowerment Zone has been concentrating on bringing the larger corporations into Harlem, I guess for economic development, which is not a bad thing. I don't have a problem with that. The problem that I do have with it is that it has affected the small businesses in Harlem, which the Empowerment Zone has not really, I feel— have concentrated on keeping the small business in Harlem. They have done a couple things for small business, but I just don't feel that it has been enough to say that we are really wanted in our own community."

Soloman continued, "I don't feel that we have come to a time when we are really wanted in our own community. We feel almost like we are being driven out of our community—someplace else. And I know this because it has been said to me. It has been said to me by landlords, by corporations, that now is their time to make money in Harlem, and in order to do that, being a small business, we cannot afford to pay the type ... and to keep up the type of business that they would like for us to keep up."[62]

The sentiment of not feeling wanted was a relatively common theme among a few interviewees—the sense that although the recent economic changes may have some merit, the recent developments, they feel, are not intended to improve the well-being of longtime residents, community organizations, or small businesses. Herein lies the contradiction in many urban development efforts that exacerbate inequity. In the case of small businesses, the Empowerment Zone did not address financial incentives for small businesses to stay and grow. The small businesses already in Harlem did not require any prodding to do work in the community; they had already been doing it for years. And, while some small businesses have been owned by African Americans, many have not. But some question why corporations should receive money to make more money in Harlem. Soloman said, "... these corporations are getting a lot of tax abatements; they're getting other considerations that, of course, we're not getting. The other thing is that the Empowerment Zone then comes along and says (to small businesses) we're going to give you technical assistance. Well, I had their technical assistance, and it does not work. It's just somebody paying somebody some money to come in, give you a whole bunch of words, with about forty people sitting in a room, and we all have different problems. So how you going to give me technical assistance when I've been in business for thirty years, and somebody who hasn't even opened up a store yet, or who has only been here two years."[63]

Improving the capacity of local small businesses is a good idea. However, it is important to assess the effectiveness of technical assistance services. Simultaneously, the challenge facing many small businesses, especially in high priced areas such as New York City, is the cost of doing business. It would seem that a combination of technical and financial assistance would be the most effective approach for small business development. Ironically, the presence of new corporations has driven up the overall cost of doing business, especially regarding real estate. The same small business owner said, "We cannot afford to write off anything because we don't have that kind of money that we can say, 'Okay, so we're paying a six thousand dollar rent and we'll get a write-off of four thousand dollars'; it doesn't work that way for small businesses.

So, this is one of the changes that the Empowerment Zone has brought about in Harlem—by bringing in the corporations, by making the rents go up higher."[64]

Rising real estate rates have led to residential displacement, but it has affected small businesses as well. The challenges around business development in Harlem take on multiple dimensions. Outside of soaring costs and increased competition from larger businesses, consumer behavior plays a critical role. For example, many Harlem residents have traditionally worked in Midtown or downtown Manhattan. Many others have worked in other parts of the city or in the suburbs. Jobs have traditionally been concentrated in these areas. With such limited business activity in Harlem, the neighborhood lacked jobs and consumer activity. Residents' money was often spent after work in other areas.

The piecemeal solution to this problem is to bring business back to Harlem. A more comprehensive approach also would incorporate significant affordable housing, substantial support for small, especially Black-owned businesses, and other decisions that would enhance the well-being of existing, longtime residents, small businesses, and community-based organizations. Some of those businesses may charge too much, but additional support would enable them to stay in business while charging less. Development is about choices.

Another important layer to the issue of the retail industry in relation to residents and small businesses is the attraction of brand names. Consumer behavior tends to gravitate toward familiarity. Those businesses that have been able to cultivate an attractive brand, and a steady following, have leveraged customer loyalty into "mega" business. Indeed, many of the businesses locating in Harlem, Old Navy, the Gap, Pathmark, Starbucks, HMV, and others are chains—megastores. These are some of the retailers that Harlem residents have patronized in other neighborhoods for many years.

Small business in Harlem, and elsewhere, must all face this challenge, and figure out how to market their uniqueness as an asset in comparison to stores that sell the same mass-manufactured products throughout the country and world. For Black-owned small businesses, the challenges can be even greater. In a world where people of African descent have been associated with inferiority, Black business owners must work even harder to convince investors and consumers, including those who are Black, that they can be successful. Many have argued that the Black community has not been supportive enough of itself. For example, not allowing money to circulate in its own community by spending outside of predominantly Black neighborhoods, and refusing to patronize Black-owned establishments, which often are small businesses. Overall, this is a complicated issue that has something to do with race, something to do with resources, something to do with brands, and these issues are all interrelated. Black-owned small businesses have less access to capital, and some businesses may not be patronized because of the race of the owner, and some businesses can't compete because they are not readily recognizable.

The Empowerment Zone's approach to tax abatements for the hiring of local employees inherently limits opportunities for small businesses, and provides an additional advantage for large corporations, which are likely not owned by local residents. Deborah Faison said, "The tax credits for businesses, for example, are aimed at employees; and a lot of the small businesses didn't have employees, or had only one or two employees. So they're not really to benefit from all that."[65] As stated earlier, the Empowerment Zone sought to increase the number of jobs in the neighborhood. With limited resources, the legislation reflected the choice to attempt to attract jobs to the community. Small businesses inherently cannot compete for such advantages because they don't offer jobs. However, corporations that don't need additional funds, got money to locate in an area where some of them are making more money than they would in other places.

The Zone's approach to small businesses is technical assistance, which is indeed needed. Without the necessary skills and information, small businesses will have a hard time competing—surviving. However, simultaneously providing technical assistance and bringing in large businesses does not improve the outlook for small businesses. Faison said, "A mom and pop office supply is not going to survive in an environment of Staples and Office Max, no matter how much technical assistance …" She feels that the program that is in place, "… was under funded, and I think it really lacked the commitment needed to really do the job. I think there were good intentions … nobody really understood the depth of the issues."[66]

Gholson agrees that small businesses did not get their fair share from the Empowerment Zone. She maintained, "You have mom and pop businesses from day one, where we're seated, who have applied for funding. They haven't received it. Their numbers don't match the criteria." The interview with Gholson took place in a local restaurant called Sheryl's Café at 151st Street and Amsterdam Avenue. It is quite a nice establishment with plenty of tables. I was struck by the extremely low prices—a remnant of Harlem's past. But, the restaurant was rather empty by lunchtime. On the day of the interview, the owner expressed her concern about the restaurant's future; Gholson informed me that she wanted to sell. I was recently informed that the owner is being evicted from the space. The prices rose too high for them to stay in business. I also have personally noticed that many of the newer restaurants in Harlem have prices that are beginning to rival downtown establishments, which have prices about three or even four times as much as a place like Sheryl's.

Gail Aska suggested that some of the newer small businesses that appear to be Black-owned actually are controlled by others. She said, "A lot of the businesses that have come are actually fronts, making it seem as if it is a black-owned business, when it may not be—when behind the scenes, it's owned by a white individual or an Asian individual or whatever...." As previously discussed, redlining has historically blocked Harlem residents from loans for businesses or mortgages. Although some suggest this situation has improved markedly, especially through the Community Reinvestment Act, many small entrepreneurs are having trouble financing their businesses. Aska continued, "But I have heard stories of people trying to get into the business—their own businesses, and run into road blocks in terms of financing through the banks. It's like unheard of. You just can't afford it. You can't afford the interest rates and all kinds of things. So I don't think necessarily that the residents of the community have gained through this resurgence of Harlem."[67]

Reggie James, president and CEO of Nujapple Marketing, develops and markets bold and colorful maps of Harlem, entitled "Harlem, USA." He has recently completed a new version that reflects the altered landscape of the neighborhood. The mission of his company is to "promote and celebrate the cultural, business, spiritual community of Harlem." According to James, "50 percent of the businesses have changed" on his new map, versus his old one, which had been developed in 1987.[68] The long-standing family businesses, such as funeral homes, have remained; however, various other types of businesses have closed shop.

But James feels the presence of the larger businesses in the neighborhood is healthy. "It makes Harlem more viable," he noted. Small Black-owned businesses, according to James, can coexist with the new larger establishments. "There are a lot of good small business owners," he said. The various small businesses have recently created a new association to address their need—for example, Harlem & Company, of which James is a member. James is banking on the potential for a variety of types of businesses to collectively make up a thriving commercial community. For James, it is a matter of providing a variety of complementary options in one area. Shopping, eating, seeing movies, and attending cultural events are often interrelated—people tend to engage in these activities in tandem. James said, "We have to have all of those services available, and variety." James just wants to make sure that Black-owned small businesses can take part in all of this potential activity. "Hopefully, we'll find ways that we could be a part of that, and it's not just folks moving their businesses up here, and taking the money right out of the area," James declared. He wants the Empowerment Zone to do more to ensure the health of small business.[69]

Unlike some other interviewees, James feels the Empowerment Zone has been helpful to his business. He earns revenue by charging businesses and other institutions for space on the map. The UMEZ underwrote map space for about forty Harlem cultural institutions, and placed an ad themselves. James also feels that their technical assistance has been helpful to his business.

But when asked whether or not the larger new businesses are forging community partnerships, and making a special effort to reach out to residents, James was not encouraged. He did stress the importance of recognizing the number of new small businesses entering the neighborhood. These institutions, unlike their larger counterparts, are seeing themselves as a part of the community. James said, "I see more coming from the smaller businesses that are moving in here because of trying to get involved with the community and being a part of the business organizations in the community."[70] As others have noted, the larger businesses should do more, especially because Harlem residents are giving them so much business. "Black people are good business," James noted. "We spend a lot of money, and they are just realizing that."[71]

EMPLOYMENT

Businesses receiving tax credits through the Empowerment Zone are required to hire locally. Therefore, assuming that businesses are generally adhering to these requirements, places such as Old Navy, Starbucks, HMV Records, Pathmark, and other new businesses have brought new jobs into the neighborhood. Quite a number of construction projects have been created by development underway, and those new initiatives, as previously noted, will bring in a few thousand jobs combined.

Residents have been dismayed by the fact that the vast majority of new jobs going to locals have been entry level. Opportunities for advancement appear unclear at this time. Moreover, the number of jobs that have entered the neighborhood do not nearly address the need. The UMEZ has lessened its investment in workforce development, but it has recently supported some training and development initiatives. UMEZ recently invested $6.9 million in its Workforce Development Initiative, which sponsors five career centers that have placed 3,195 residents in jobs.[72] Actually, John Bess's organization, the Valley, has received $150,000 for a school-to-work initiative.[73]

CHANGING CULTURE

Walking the streets of Harlem, one can feel that the African American, African, and Caribbean cultures that made the neighborhood so unique still remain very strongly. However, the new corporations, particularly on 125th Street, do not appear vastly different than similar branches of Starbucks or the Gap in other places. It is through Harlem's unique culture that resources for the community have been and can be generated. The Harlem community could probably do even more to exploit the tourism industry to its advantage. Bess suggested, "I don't think Harlem has sufficiently exploited tourism marketing."[74]

Harlem may not have lost its culture, but if the economic, as well as demographic, changes do not embrace the culture, Harlem will lose not only a culture but also a competitive advantage. No neighborhood should be blindly averse to change or forced to cement itself in time; however, Harlem has taken on a unique role in forging an identity and a degree of pride for people of African descent. The preservation of Harlem's culture is, therefore, an essential element in understanding the significance of where the neighborhood is today, and in which direction it may be headed. Approaching the business side without adequately addressing the cultural aspect creates tension and resentment.

Businesses and culture are closely tied. The street vendors, who once lined the sidewalks of 125th Street often sold goods that reflected various cultures throughout the African diaspora. As previously mentioned, megastores with well-known brand names had already enjoyed some degree of consumer loyalty from African Americans. Harlem resident, Cynthia Simmons said of these issues, "I'm not somebody who shops in the Gap or … the merchants that have come just aren't the merchants that I patronize, and the stuff that I want is not on 125th, and where they moved those guys on 116th Street, they didn't get enough traffic, so the true craftsmen aren't there now."[75]

She was referring to the street vendors, who were moved to a part of 116th Street that did not receive enough patrons to keep some of the original vendors. Many of the vendors were artists, selling their own carvings, clothing, and other hand-crafted items. Many of them were African immigrants. Although crowds on 125th Street were sometimes suffocating when the vendors were there in full force, people from all over the country and world could come and purchase something that reflected the culture of Harlem and the African diaspora. Smedley said, "… you have people who have the mom and pop type stores, who can be chased out of business if you put a big record company there, which they have. What's going to happen to the African fella, who's on 125th Street; I don't even know if he's still there or not. He had a store there for many years, Record Shack, right? … His store being there was cultural to us, 'cause he supplied us with a certain kind of thing there—it's the records and certain kinds of records you want to get; you could have them and get them. And the feeling of knitting together, or a closeness, can get lost when you have big enterprises … It loses some of its flavor, its customs, and its color."

Virtually an institution in Harlem, Record Shack, on 125th Street, and across from the Apollo Theater, is still in business. However, it has confronted the realities of rising rents. In an *Amsterdam News* article, Record Shack's owner said, "Last year, my rent was $2,000 per month. Now my landlord, the United House of Prayer for All People, wants to raise it up to $9,000."[76] Owned by South African Sikhulu Shange Record Shack has been very much tailored to its local clientele, with its collection of vinyl records, and including a specialized selection of titles or African, Motown, and Caribbean music that one might not find in more popular chain music stores. The customized, small-shop appeal of a store such as Record Shack is facing competition with the UMEZ-attracted HMV Records across the street. Shange bought the shop in 1979. The life of Record Shack significantly predated his purchase, as it has been around since the 1940s.

Cynthia Simmons has enjoyed the presence of smaller establishments in the neighborhood. She said, "… those little things that really made the community unique and distinctive—we're starting to lose those, and I don't know how we hold on to that." She attributes some of the cultural shifts in Harlem to a certain racial arrogance, "When big business comes—when White comes—when Whites come into a community, they sort of still want to insist upon everybody in the pot coming out as a White man, and it's really a ridiculous concept."[77]

Smedley continued on similar lines, "… there's something lost when you lose something quaint, and something you relate to. All the lights—it's cheap looking to me. I don't mean the structure itself, but it's just simply gaudy; you know it doesn't have the character that 125th Street had before, and I'm not the only one that feels that way."[78] Smedley wishes that spaces for small businesses could be set aside, but he is skeptical of such prospects because, "they attempted that with the Mart (Mart 125), and of course, they chased the people out after they promised they would not do it."[79]

Cynthia Simmons maintained, "I resented the fact that they had to give people Empowerment Zone money to serve a clientele that they already had, because everybody who's shopping in those stores is going downtown to shop in them, so why did we have to give you a tax break for you to come and service a clientele that you already had? Case in point, Blockbuster came before the Empowerment Zone money, so they didn't get it (Zone). The year that they were open, that store did more business than any other store in Manhattan."[80] According to Simmons, a certain cultural aspect of Harlem business, embodied in the street vendors, was sacrificed in exchange for larger businesses that did not even require financial incentives to locate in Harlem, since they were going to profit anyway.

An anonymous developer, although largely supportive of some of the recent commercial developments, said, "They're trying to make Harlem into what the rest of the world is, which is national credit, big bucks, more of the same retail. And they are losing some of the local flavor, not necessarily by subtraction, but I think by making it less of a priority." This person continued, "There's been less of a focus on existing assets, or existing community folks, who have ideas about new retail or commercial ideas."[81] As a non–Harlem resident, who develops property in the neighborhood, this developer does not have the more personal feelings of the residents. But it does not necessarily take a resident to identify the degree to which recent commercial developments have diverged from Harlem's unique culture and identity.

SENSE OF COMMON GOOD

What some residents saw as a benefit—an emerging mixed economy, others saw as a drawback, particularly those who are low income. The presence of new residents with resources may bring attention to needed services. However, conflicts of interest emerge between old residents and new, as well as wealthier residents and less fortunate ones. Tyletha Samuels saw little hope for residents to unify and ensure fair treatment because residents' personal interests have become so divergent. She said, "I don't know how you would organize around that. I just don't see it, due to the fact that the people that's moving in … if society wasn't getting like it was today in Harlem, then I could see you organizing, if it was back then where everybody was on public assistance … but now you got a mixture. You can't fight the businessman just 'cause you ain't got no money."

It does not have to be an automatic that only low-income people will be concerned with issues such as poverty and access. It does appear that Harlem residents of the past had a greater sense of unity among themselves—many of them are low income, and some others not. However, a number of interviewees suggested that newer residents are generally not identifying with the neighborhood or respecting older residents.

The irony, according to Samuels, is that, as others have noted, much of the activity in Harlem appears to target newer residents, "It seems like they're building and making things accessible to the people that's coming in, that's moving in, like I said, middle class people, not low income people. 'Cause they're moving into our community and moving us out."[82] If, indeed, new residents are moving in, thinking that the neighborhood will soon be comprised primarily of their peers, then it is not surprising that they are not embracing older residents. They could, however, enter the neighborhood with a different mindset—one that stresses a common good among neighbors. They have the option.

PRICING

Rumblings in the community have suggested that some of the new retail establishments on 125th Street have been charging more for the products in Harlem than in other neighborhoods. Given that Harlem residents and African Americans in general, have often paid more for their cars, homes, and other items than Whites, overcharging would not represent a historical departure.

But, according to Tyletha Samuels, it does not even make sense for stores to charge the same prices in wealthier areas, as they would in Harlem. She likes the fact that various stores have come to the neighborhood, but much is still inaccessible to low-income people. She said, "I don't have to go all the way downtown to buy what's downtown, like stores are downtown, now I don't have to go downtown; they're up here—since I like to shop. But as far as me benefiting from it, that's the only benefit I see. The prices are so ridiculous; I figured if they come up in Harlem, maybe the prices would be cheaper, since it's more expensive downtown, but that's not the case."[83]

Gail Aska noticed that newer stores in Harlem are charging higher prices for goods that sell downtown for less. She said, "I have found their prices have tended to be higher than they are at the same type of store downtown, so I have been offended by that." She continued, "For my son, he is a teenager now; he's been a teenager for a while now. He started out in that teenage era enjoying Old Navy clothes; he has since changed his mind. There's no doubt that in terms of buying at the Old Navy that's on 125th was somewhat differently priced that the Old Navy that was on 19th and 6th."[84]

My research assistants investigated pricing at Old Navy, selecting particular items at three different stores: the one in Harlem, the one to which Aska referred in Chelsea, and another store in Brooklyn. For the most part, we did not find vast differences in the prices. In fact, we saw no variation in price in the items we selected. Our research of Old Navy prices was conducted approximately two years after the interview with Aska.[85]

URBAN PLANNING

Some interviewees made reference to a certain limited overall logic to the recent economic development strategies. With the Empowerment Zone, for example, many of the businesses are retail establishments. Some interviewees questioned whether this choice was consistent with the community's needs. Others suggested that the economic development strategy never appeared to be logically tied to the overall socioeconomic and geographical needs of the neighborhood.

Bess maintained, "… I think there should be a body of people who can do an economic analysis of what does this mean for this economic project to be here. Do we need more teachers? More schools? Do we need more minutes of sanitation support? How do we align it with other possibilities of making sure that in mapping that geographically, that a church is there, that a hospital is there, that child care is there, that the essential services for families with children are near each other, and that Harlem becomes another kind of marketplace."[86]

Design is an essential element of urban planning. Gholson suggested that the design of the new businesses on 125th Street and new housing developments are out of sync with the neighborhood. She said, "When we look at the rehabilitation of housing that's taking place ... if we look at the new development, new structures that are being designed, they don't have a Harlem flavor. Harlem USA, although it might be a fantastic concept, has two blatant inconsistencies: it looks like a strip mall out of the suburbs plopped onto 125th Street, number one, and number two, you don't have black independent entrepreneurs on that site."[87]

Gholson speaks to both design and a certain respect for the neighborhood. As with the discussion of culture, the new developments, according to residents, don't seem to fit. Had residents' ideas been more seriously considered, many believe, development would have been more sensitive to the preexisting culture and style of the neighborhood. Recognizing the whole is an essential component in urban planning—visualizing the big picture and attending to how each decision about one aspect impacts each other aspect.

WILLIAM JEFFERSON CLINTON

Bill Clinton's decision to locate his office on 125th Street made national news. He was given a hero's welcome—a well-attended, star-studded celebration—a celebration that would suggest Clinton's presence would bring dignity and resources to the neighborhood. Although many residents attended the celebration, it does not appear that many have high expectations about the significance and potential impact of his presence. To Gail Aska, the meaning of Clinton's presence depends on what he does. She thinks he could use his power and influence to ensure a more equitable form of development. In fact, in his speech at the celebration, Clinton suggested that he did not want his presence to lead to displacement of longtime residents.

Aska said of Clinton, "If he were to get behind the issues of the Empowerment Zone and really see that this concept had become ... if it became anything at all, and would speak out about the fact that it hasn't serviced the residents of Harlem, as he had hoped, or as we thought he had hoped. And as it should be, that his being here would be beneficial because it would bring the publicity to it—maybe push a couple of people to tighten up a little. But standing back and reviewing it, I also became somewhat upset that people were talking about it in a way that this was just going to turn us totally around, and I don't believe that. But it definitely disturbs me to know that there is now and probably going to be so much effort put into making this more of a tourist attraction because he's here.... all the improvements, all the little fine tuning of the neighborhood should really have been done already, and done because of the residents that are here, not just because a former president is coming."

She continued, "So now there's a reason to think about fixing those streets, you know, putting better light on the corner and whatever, because you have a former president that's coming, and his wife is going to be dropping in, and so on. Terrific! But these are things that should be done anyway." Some of the local restaurants, she said, "are just thrilled because they think, 'Now that the president's here, oh he'll be in for lunch a couple of times a week and then people will want to come in and see where he sat at, and we're going to make a bundle.' Maybe you will. What's in it for the rest of us? Because your menu is probably going to change, and will that person be able to afford the changes in menu prices?"[88]

Urban development for whom? Is a question posed by many people around the country in circumstances where gentrification is taking place. Aska's remarks speak to the political realities of inequality. The location of Clinton's office in Harlem was newsworthy. Of course, the office was his second choice. Nevertheless, Aska's point is that the neighborhood is being fixed up for other people. Issues around recognizing the common good and relative desire to improve the conditions of low-income people are essential factors in the pursuit of equitable development. If the interests of low-income people are not held as a priority, urban development will often result in displacement or disinvestment or some other means by which those without resources to begin with miss out.

Clinton's presence in Harlem, to Lorraine Gilbert has made Harlem more attractive to a number of more affluent African Americans, who once shunned the idea of living in the neighborhood. She said, "I guess they say to themselves that if it's good enough for Clinton, here I am Black, then it's good enough for me." She recalled the days when it was more difficult for her to sell property in the neighborhood. She said, "People who were here and never would buy when the houses were forty or fifty thousand, they are trying to come late. They wait until the house is a half a million, then they're hollering and saying, "Well I can't afford anything because all the whites are buying up everything. When I tried to sell you a house for forty or fifty thousand, you said, 'I'm not buying a house on that block!'"[89] Although Clinton has attracted attention, the option of ownership is too late for some. Harlem has become fashionable, but some people would not invest in the neighborhood when given the opportunity. In the end, Clinton's presence has made some difference in the sense that it elevated Harlem's already rising desirability. A key aspect of this altered point of view on the neighborhood is the presence of new services, as has been stated by many interviewees. However, low-income people are still priced out. Even if they stay in the neighborhood, their position could be tenuous, as the path of other New York neighborhoods has demonstrated. Without incorporating this eye toward equity in the overall scheme of development strategies, low-income people will continue to be left out.

Clinton brings unlimited connections to resources. Through his foundation, he can develop various programs that can address Harlem's social concerns. The foundation has not been in Harlem for long, but Clinton has begun to address some local issues. Regarding small businesses, Clinton's foundation organized technical assistance teams, drawn from a management consulting firm, Booz Allen and Hamilton, the National Black MBA Association, and students from the Stern School of Business at NYU, to stabilize small businesses. Clinton has also worked with the Harlem Children's Zone and the Robin Hood Foundation to raise awareness among low-income people regarding the availability of the earned-income tax credit, a thirty-year-old program, which was expanded in 1993. In terms of Harlem's public schools, Clinton spawned an effort to enhance economic literacy among students (with Carver Federal Savings Bank), and partnered with VH-1 to promote music education.[90]

According to Clyde Williams of the William Jefferson Clinton Foundation, small business development is critical to the future of Harlem. "If you help small businesses grow, you stabilize a community," said Williams. The foundation is actually pursuing a small business development strategy, which provides advice for small businesses through the consulting firm, Booz Allen Hamilton, and the New York

University Stern School of Business. The Foundation decided to take this direction as a result of a meeting between President Clinton and various community leaders. Clyde Williams is satisfied with the direction the Foundation is taking. According to Williams, this approach builds upon the commercial progress in the neighborhood. He is pleased that "now people can get services in the community." The foundation's effort intends to enhance the sustainability of small businesses in the community. Owners of all businesses benefiting from this program "have to live in Harlem," according to Williams.

Social issues such as education seem to have been lost in the various discussions about Harlem's "new renaissance." Clinton has not shied away from this direction, including assistance to small businesses. However, even with Clinton's influence and power, it remains to be seen whether or not technical assistance will make the difference between staying or going for small businesses. Nor can we assume that economic literacy will enable residents to make their rent payments, or a few programs will address the scope of challenges confronting public schools. Clinton is only one person and his foundation is one institution. The most significant obstacles to be overcome, for Harlem's less advantaged residents, are shaped by market forces—forces that no one person, no matter how influential, can stop. Nevertheless, this is not to stay that people should not try. It has been the residents and community organizations that have been cleaning up the neighborhood, working to end the local drug trade, attempting to improve schools, lower infant mortality, fight environmental racism, and improve access to housing.

Not every potentially influential institution, such as Clinton's foundation, cares enough to address local issues; Clinton, at least, has made some effort, within a short tenure in the neighborhood, to pay attention to the fact that most Harlem residents, despite all of the changes, are still facing limited access and poverty, somewhat exacerbated by recent developments. The skepticism of some residents around Clinton is certainly warranted, given that the Harlem community in the decades before the recent wave of development, had been ignored and abandoned. As previously noted, many longtime residents do not feel the changes are for them. Therefore, anyone's effort to bring money, resources, jobs, services, or housing to Harlem is viewed with a critical eye. Many residents want to be shown that Clinton's presence will improve social conditions, that new businesses will bring economic development, and that all of the apparent local improvements will benefit longtime residents. Harlem's history does not suggest that, especially low-income residents will benefit, nor does the history of other New York City neighborhoods that have been experiencing significant development over a longer period, such as Park Slope, Chelsea, or the Upper West Side.

With respect to Clinton, residents don't agree; some are quite pleased that he decided to bring his foundation to the neighborhood, as evidenced by the attendance at his welcoming rally. A national, and probably international, news item, Clinton's uptown sojourn is part of what separates Harlem from other neighborhoods. Clinton's arrival only adds another notch to Harlem's lengthy lore. None of the other gentrified New York City neighborhoods are as well known as Harlem, nor are they as massive. Harlem is probably the most well-known neighborhood in America. Everything in the neighborhood is on a different scale. Had Clinton ended up on 57th Street in Manhattan, it is unlikely that any of us would be discussing what he will do for the neighborhood or the meaning of his presence to the neighborhood. And even though Clinton has been challenged to do something for the community, and has likely challenged himself around the same idea, Harlem is not the kind of neighborhood that can change overnight.

Youth Perspective

If Harlem's youth are able to afford to have the option of staying in the area in their adult years, they will be charged with the task of local community building. Having grown up in the neighborhood, Harlem teens, in particular, have lived and observed the noticeable changes in their surroundings; they also may be around to deal with their consequences. Harlem youth bring a unique perspective to the table. They did not witness Harlem's heyday and lament its decline. They were born into a Harlem in transition. They are not as wedded to tradition; they like brand names and anything that is new and fresh and tailored to people like them. But they are simultaneously aware of inequality, and maintain an interest in seeing a better neighborhood. They do not all agree on how to get there, but they have been thinking about and analyzing Harlem—the Harlem that is their lives.

The Wadleigh School in Harlem hosts a comprehensive after school program for high school aged youth in the neighborhood. This "Robeson" program, which takes place from 5:00 p.m. to 7:00 p.m. on Tuesdays and Thursdays, brings the youth together to discuss a variety of topics. They attend high schools in various parts of the city. One of my research assistants, Cynthia Jones and I conducted a focus group with some of the youth in the program.[91] They were asked similar questions about the economic changes in the neighborhood, but the youth perspective is worth particular attention, as they are keen to particular dimensions of the issues. Because they had grown up in Harlem, these youth have had the benefit of watching Harlem's development throughout the period in which real estate has been refurbished, prices have ballooned, and the Empowerment Zone has come to fruition. Although many of the youth agree with their parents' and grandparents' generations about a certain neglect of resident needs, their thinking about issues such as crime and consumer behavior are noteworthy, and sometimes divergent from the thoughts of their elders.

The youth seem to share similar opinions with adults with respect to residential and commercial real estate. One youth, Tamika, said, of the various local redevelopment projects, "Some of the stuff I don't see beneficial to us, like when I say us, I mean like minorities, like African Americans, like a lot of the old brownstones and stuff that were … they fixing up now, but they raising the price on the building and most people like minorities and stuff can't afford those houses. So that's why a lot of Caucasian people and Indians and all kinds of other people are moving into Harlem 'cause we can't afford them brownstones they building; they not making them for us; they making them for people with more money than us."[92]

This quote raises a number of issues around class, race, and the politics of Harlem's new renaissance. She referred to "minorities," but clarified that she meant African Americans. She associated an inability to afford renovated brownstones with the experiences of existing African American Harlem residents. She indicated that Caucasians could afford higher real estate prices, but she said that a number of other racial and ethnic groups could afford to move into Harlem as well.

Another focus group participant, Angel said, "Harlem is gaining a lot of respect." To him, issues around policing and crime are most salient. For example, he noticed the increased police presence in the neighborhood. He thinks crime is coming down, but he questioned whether police officers were respecting longtime residents. He spoke of his observations of the reduction in crime, "I used to live in the other part of Harlem, like 135th, that's where I used to live at; now I live at close to 125th, 129th, so like I see changes—it's not that much people, you know, not that much gang members, you know, outside like it used to be."[93]

A central characteristic of the drug trade was the persistent presence of gangs that managed local sales. Residents were often terrorized by such groupings, making their departure a welcome change for many residents. But the youth seem particularly keen to these issues, as the drug trade often particularly touched them and their peers in very direct, sometimes brutally violent, ways. But Angel is unsure of where all of these people went; and he thinks the cops are responsible for moving people out of the neighborhood. He said, "More cops, like, you know, trying to take everybody out of Harlem—that's what I see. That's the only change that I see, and they taking people out from Harlem, you know. I'm seeing less people than what I used to see from my project window since I was little. I see less people." When asked where he thought people were going, he responded, "They in jail. I don't know where. I don't know. Everybody getting locked up."

Many of the youth, like their elders, questioned the planning logic in Harlem's economic changes. One youth said, "One thing I think about, like they building buildings in the wrong places, 'cause there's an open space—117th and 8th Avenue that's been there since I was a baby. They haven't put nothing in it—nothing there. What do they use it for?" As the youth continued, she also questioned the commitment of developers to the needs of residents—the needs of people who could benefit from resources targeted to them. She said, "They should put a shelter there or something; do something with it; try and clean it up … why can't you make it into a community center where kids could go, or why you can't make it into a shelter, where people … where it's not so much of a higher rent, where some families could afford it."[94]

The youth have a sense of justice; they can see that changes are rapidly occurring, but they don't seem to buy that the changes will benefit residents. This particular young person has concrete recommendations for alternatives that, she believes, would uphold some sense of a common good that puts people before profits. These youth have a sense that they have been wronged—that the world does not work in their favor because of race and class. This same youth completed her commentary by pointing out how negative perceptions have worked against her and her community, "… they don't never want to do nothing to help us, then they want to know why we are the way we are sometimes. So you can't put a label on us, 'cause we try to take it off, but it's stuck. You done crazy glued it to us and then we just get comfortable with it; so don't complain when we get comfortable because you helped put it there…. it's just like you stapled it to our forehead, so now we go through, like we the bad people, when it should be vice versa."[95]

The youth are all too aware of the stigma associated with being a young, urban African American or Latino. This youth, like many of the adults, pointed to a mentality in her community—a mentality that reinforces negative stereotypes. This could be similar to the "colonial" mentality discussed in some other interviews, in which a historically disenfranchised population internalizes an inferiority complex and expects to gain very little in life. Some of the adult interviewees noted that the community was aware of the changes taking place, but did not take advantage of them—did not seek out the knowledge that would help them own a home, profit from some form of enterprise, or obtain employment.

The youth also appear to be awfully aware of the class differences within the neighborhood—the more affluent areas versus the less affluent ones: Sugar Hill, on the one hand, and the Valley, on the other. One youth referred to "the mountain" on which Sugar Hill rests. They can tell which parts of Harlem appear more desirable, and subsequently, more positioned for redevelopment and renovation.

Some of the youth never understood the logic of living in downtown Manhattan, when one could live in Harlem for half the price, and remain conveniently located. This is what made Harlem a sensible place to live, in their eyes. One youth asked, "Why am I gonna pay $1,300 a month on a studio that's facing Central Park when I can go right there to Harlem, when it's convenient to everything, and pay maybe like $700?"[96]

Non-Harlem residents, they believe, have just figured out that Harlem is convenient and cheaper, but at the expense of existing Harlem residents. One young person said, "They don't want us to be convenient no more because they don't want us to feel relaxed no more, 'cause when you in Harlem, you don't have to walk that far to get to a train station, catch the bus—you got the train, or you got the … now we got a cab service; you just call and they come get you in front of your house."[97] They can see that Harlem already had many conveniences—many assets—an exceptional foundation from which to build.

Like their elders, the youth can see the plight of small businesses. One youth said, "A lot of old places that was in Harlem, like old barber shops from like '60s and '70s, and stuff, they getting, you know, put out of business and taken down because they can't afford to pay that rent … I know, 'cause like on a 100th, what is that, 18th and 7th, it's this old man barber shop, and I could—you know, don't nobody really be in there but his old friends … and it's like they got old restaurants and stuff like that, and old folks own them, and it's like when they put these new buildings up, got some more complexes, got these little mini malls inside your building where you don't really have to leave your building for nothing, and they can't pay the rent on them 'cause some of them can't afford to pay $1,200 for a space that's not even that big."[98]

The energy level of our conversation rose when we moved to the relationship between consumerism and small Black-owned businesses. To some of the youth in the room, the small businesses will fold because the newer businesses understand the wants of consumers and have a brand name to which people have become accustomed. These youth did not have a problem with the presence of newer businesses, because they are bringing products that residents already purchase in other areas, especially youth. While some of the adults saw no need for Old Navy or Footlocker, some of the youth very much welcome these establishments. One youth said of these stores, "They know what the kids like now; it's all about the sneakers, the clothes, the shirts, stuff like that."

But a smaller group of students stood hard and fast by the need to develop, maintain, grow, and support small Black-owned businesses. One young woman was particularly firm in her opinion around the need for Black people to create and operate their own businesses. If the community wants fashion, then Black businesses should create and market fashion to the community. She said, "We don't need to go to Old Navy, if we knew how to sew or do whatever; we could have our own." She continued, "I think that successful Black and minority, or any type of minority, can come to a community and start they own businesses instead of us putting the money into big corporations they not giving us anything."[99]

But although many of the youth want certain name brand clothes, they are skeptical of corporate intentions. In other words, they do not think these various retail corporations are meeting consumer desires because they care about the community. One youth said, "They using black people, not even black, minority—they taking the money, 'cause they know that black people—we not saying all of us, but we love clothing, sneakers, and stuff like that. They not worried about that; they worried about they sneakers and they clothes, and how much they ... and they know what sells in Harlem."[100]

A certain cynicism ran through the whole group, from those who were in favor to the presence of new businesses to those who were opposed. None of the youth seemed to believe that new businesses were going to help the community. Many feel they are meeting consumer desires for fashion, they do not think they are bringing in many sustainable jobs, and they do not expect them to do very much in terms of community development. With respect to Magic Johnson's Theatre, for example, the youth realize that the presence of the theatre is a new convenience, but they do not seem to feel that the theatre is about helping the community. One youth said, "These owners today are not trying to give back to the community. I think what they're trying to do is just make a profit off the Black and Latinos here. He didn't set up the theatre to give back. He knows that everybody—that Black people are gonna go there; he knows he's gonna make money off us. That's why he put it on 125th Street, like the most richest place there in Harlem, and the other stores."[101]

According to one youth, it's not the job of large corporations to give back to communities. That aim rests with the nonprofit sector. The youth said, "Most of these economic places is not to give back to the community. I'm sorry; they do college things every now and then, but that's not what's up. That's why you have, like Countee Cullen, the Schomburg, where you go in there and learn about your history. You got P.A.L., that's like a predominantly Black center; you got the Valley. You got mad centers out there, just people don't want to go."[102] This person suggests that nonprofits are responsible for helping the community, and that the community bears the burden of taking advantage of all of the services that already exist.

One youth did reply, noting that the big companies have community programs, saying, "Most of these places have funds. They do scholarships, stuff like that, but sometimes you gotta go out and you gotta find them 'cause they not always gon' be broadcast."[103] Although some noted the community programs of such corporations, no one thought the businesses shared any sort of primary goal of helping existing Harlem residents. The call for personal initiative is also interesting in this quote, suggesting that it is up to the residents themselves to learn more about the businesses. Overall, the young people were fairly critical of their fellow Harlem residents.

One focus group participant thinks the community is never satisfied and should not complain at this stage in the game. This person said, "The way I see it, like people don't really know, like people don't know what they want—'cause like when two fifth didn't use to have nothing, everybody used to be like, 'Oh downtown got everything, dah, dah, dah,' but then when they threw the Modell's and the Old Navy and they threw the HMV up here, then people was like, 'Oh, they taking money out of Harlem.'"[104] This youth is happy to see the new businesses in Harlem because, "you don't have to go all the way downtown" to buy clothes or see the movies or buy records. But she would like to see more jobs for young people. For most jobs, she said, "... you gotta be eighteen; eighteen be grown ... we sixteen, so let us work now."

Many of the youth maintain that residents should not complain, because the businesses are meeting a demand. One youth said, "I feel that it's just like with the stores and stuff; it's like a fashion. I'm saying if Beverly Hills could have it, why can't Harlem have it? We could have what they have. If they could be all high classy with furs and the minks, why can't we be high class with the furs and the minks?"[105] With youth in particular, another participant noted, "All the kids want to wear brand name stuff." And parents, according to another youth, "don't want your kids looking like bums. Everybody wanna go out looking nice." Taking these quotes into account, the sentiment suggests that new businesses are meeting a consumer demand for high quality—quality that Harlem residents deserve. It also suggests that Harlem residents are particular about brand names that connote quality. A certain material dimension pervades these remarks as well—good living being equated with not just name brands but luxury goods. The new establishments in Harlem are not exactly bringing "furs and minks," but these voices suggest a desire for certain external symbols of good living.

One youth piped up, arguing that the community's priorities are out of whack. This person said, "We are more concerned about what we wear, then we go home, we can't afford more than a ninety-nine cent bag of chips for dinner." A respondent countered, "I'm never gon' have on no cheap stuff 'cause I gon' work too hard for it."[106] The reward for hard work, according to this particular youth is, in fact, quality fashion. After all, fashion is what everyone can see, interacting with others on a daily basis. Not everyone is going to see one's home, know what one eats, or know the state of one's bank account. This is a fairly practical way of thinking.

It is important to note how often words like "hungry" and "work hard" surfaced over the course of the focus group. These youth are motivated and driven to succeed. They know that some Harlem residents will lose out over the course of the neighborhood's metamorphosis, but they are determined to be the ones who win. They know that they will likely search for jobs outside of the neighborhood, and seek out funding for college, and they know that they may need multiple jobs to live at the level that they desire. But the desire to work toward their goals was firm and unmistakable.

Adult interviewees also varied in their thoughts about the benefits of the presence of new businesses in Harlem, as well as the relative responsibilities of residents. Youth, in fact, seem to be more critical of their fellow residents of all ages, and of politicians as well. One youth said, "Maybe one of these stupid-ass politicians will come through and help us—give us some money or something." It should also be noted, that Bill Clinton was singled out as a good politician, who "Knows what Black people need right now."[107]

The convenience issue seems to be a recurring theme among many interviewees of all ages—residents like the added conveniences but do not appreciate the negative consequences. The youth in the focus group were a bit less empathetic around the negative consequences of the businesses, as most of them felt the businesses are meeting their desires for certain fashions. Nevertheless, the negative consequences of the changing commercial base would be lessened with greater attention to comprehensive approaches that prioritize equity. The presence of businesses means only so much without jobs, but the jobs mean only so much without training and opportunities for advancement; and even then, the convenience goes only so far if it drives up property values. It appears that a series of back up plans, influenced by various scenarios, tested by residents, could help in this respect. For example, if residents had an opportunity to play out what would happen on the arrival of new businesses. In playing out such scenarios in advance, it may be easier to predict the impact, positively and otherwise. Exercises of this sort could highlight the importance of comprehensive approaches, but also reveal true intentions—whether or not those with decision-making power have the will to find the resources and energy to forge equitable development strategies.

The Role of Corporations and Developers

Corporations and developers will have to be central to new development strategies that benefit low-income people. Although they may be in business to make money, they can pursue approaches that enable them to make some money while being socially responsible. But entry-level jobs and "affordable" housing that is out of reach for those with a low income can only go so far. If the concept of corporate social responsibility is truly going to be tested, it must be able to demonstrate that such pursuits don't only look good but actually make tangible improvements in the lives of low-income and other less-advantaged populations.

Jobs are crucial for communities such as Harlem, with high unemployment rates, and a spatial mismatch between where jobs are located and where the unemployed reside. Urban sprawl throughout recent decades moved jobs into the outer-ring suburbs, far from the majority of people in the most need of employment—low-income inner-city residents.[108] The advent of aggressive community development strategies, such as the process by which the Empowerment Zone was created, provided incentives for businesses to consider setting up shop in inner city communities. Of course, these new businesses could still import their workers from other communities, but the trade-off for financial incentives to locate in the inner city is to provide local jobs. But should this be the only expectation of corporations?

"Harlem USA has taken an active role in making sure that it reaches out to the community, and that's HMV, Modell's, the Magic Johnson Theater, New York Sports Club, and Old Navy—they've taken an active role in trying to connect to the community and work with the community and offer funds and stuff to some community based organizations that are uptown. I don't get a sense that all these other stores have any connection to the community. And I think that's going to become a problem. I think that, again, if they're smart, they will, to force the group relations, they will establish that, but right now it's very few stores or complexes that are progressive and see themselves as community partners and are connecting with community organizations, institutions, churches, synagogues, or mosques."[109]

As Bess suggests, community involvement is to the advantage of a business or developer. Healthy relations with the community open doors for future projects, and build consumer relations. The demand for greater corporate accountability and responsibility rests in the context of a continually expanding gap in wealth and access to information.

Accounting scandals involving nonretail, but corporations just the same, have heightened public skepticism of corporate aims. Are they out to simply make money at all costs? Corporations are not all the same, but their existence is predicated on the profit motive. Therefore, expectations for truly altruistic goals are often quite low.

Nevertheless, we must rethink these expectations. As the gatekeepers of so many needed resources, corporations are positioned to provide an infusion of resources, services and jobs into low-income urban communities. In the case of Harlem, it is not enough that major retail establishments have located in the neighborhood. Nor is it enough that real estate developers have refurbished residential and commercial properties. If our society is interested in improving the lives of low-income people, especially at a time when joblessness is significant and the economy is tenuous, then it is important to hold major institutions with resources accountable to higher expectations. One key aspect in imagining greater equity in development is recognizing the whole. But once it is recognized, how can it be done, and where are the resources? Large corporations and developers doing business in Harlem should engage in true partnerships with the community.

A partnership constitutes a deeper relationship—one where all parties involved recognize the interdependency among themselves and collectively forge mutually beneficial activities. The hurdle facing partnerships between communities and major institutions is power. Corporations can make decisions without community involvement, for example. But the reality is that corporations can't survive without consumers. Historically, Harlem residents have contemplated or attempted economic boycotts of particular business to highlight the interdependency among corporations and people.

An anonymous executive in a Harlem Community Development Corporation gave high marks to some of the new retail establishments, "Pathmark, Old Navy, Gap, those kinds of businesses have been very good corporate citizens. They sponsor little leagues, they sponsor fundraisers; they're good corporate citizens." But residents are not satisfied across-the-board with the state of corporate/community partnerships. The executive continued, "I think the way it's been received by the mainstream community is very good. I think there are some elements of the community on the margin, who are real radical, very radical, and really see this as an opportunity to go back to the days of marching and getting in people's faces and calling them all racists...."[110]

It appears that discontent with the new corporations extends beyond the very radical, as interviewees run across the political spectrum. As previously mentioned, some see the new retail presence as too far of a cultural departure, many others think the stores just aren't doing enough, and others think the stores got too much of a sweet deal to locate in the neighborhood. The opinions are wide-ranging, but they emanate from a set of expectations that is shaped by a history of failed development initiatives. It is one thing to set policy that brings in retail and says, "get on board or get off." It is another to recognize the totality of experiences in making decisions. The historical feelings of betrayal in the community, and the sources of those thoughts should be addressed in combination with the concrete attempts to stimulate jobs and attract improved services.

Although Harlem's new retail industry has not satisfied everyone, some corporate/community partnerships have emerged. The anonymous executive gave an example, "Old Navy does this whole thing with Frederick Douglass Academy, where it really has a partnership with them and has a deep commitment to doing everything from hiring the kids in the summers at the stores to making the school t-shirts for free, and giving them to them and giving every family a fifty dollar certificate at the beginning of the school year towards clothing." This kind of partnership, according to the executive, ultimately benefits the business, "it's good for business because people become very loyal to their brand and certainly they are seeing the results of that because the store in Harlem is doing very very well."[111]

The degree to which corporate partnerships of this sort actually improve local conditions is uncertain. They may make a difference in the lives of a handful of people, but it is unlikely that they move the Harlem community much closer to overall community empowerment. According to the anonymous executive, the most important thing that retail corporations can do is hire locally. This person said, "The responsibility of business in the community, I think first and foremost, it is to reflect the values of the community—to have a level of sensitivity about the community and the context in which you're operating, and I think the issue of a commitment to hire locally is the most important thing they can do. And that is why I support having local businesses commit to a number, commit to a goal of hiring locally, commit to training managers—that if you're going to open a supermarket, you're not just committing on hiring cashiers, but that you want to have your management team also come from the community and have career ladders that allow for community people to move up and monitor those things."[112]

This perspective is consistent with that of most residents—jobs are critical, but not enough without training, opportunities for advancement, and a commitment to hiring managers as well as entry-level workers. Although the CDC executive and residents agree philosophically, the resident interviewees generally did not give high marks to the retail corporations' hiring practices.

Communities need services and jobs in any community development model; corporations can make some of that happen. Banks also play an essential role—communities need the support and cooperation of banks to finance large- and small-scale projects and enable ownership opportunities for residents. As previously discussed, banks have not always been friendly to Harlem residents, as they had redlined, refused to make loans, in Harlem and many other inner-city African American neighborhoods. The anonymous CDC director said of the current state of bank/community relations, "The banking community has been, I think, very committed overall. Banks like Chase, Deutsche Bank, Citicorp have come a long way—have commitments, both in terms of the grant making that they do in the community to qualified community-based organizations that are doing charitable work, and also in terms of the lending, are putting private capital into the community, in terms of construction lending, mortgage loans, bridge loans, permanent financing on projects … But we can't fool ourselves—that is the result, primarily, I think, of the Community Reinvestment Act (CRA) and the implication of that. The implications of not being an investor and a lender in low- to moderate-income communities is that you will be penalized as a financial institution, and the banks certainly do not want the regulators to penalize them or give them unsatisfactory ratings under the CRA standards. So they have been very, very aggressive."[113]

This form of bank/community partnership, facilitated by federal policy through the CRA, created an incentive for banks to take a more socially responsible approach to urban communities. Therefore, policy created an interdependency between banks and urban communities that had not existed. Before the CRA, banks were regularly redlining without any accountability. Partnerships are enhanced when incentives are clear. The CRA is an example of the critical role that government can play in stimulating greater responsibility among major institutions and industries. It is critical in looking to the future and potential of any form of corporate/community partnership to recognize where communities can have power and influence in such relationships, and where communities do not have the optimum amount of leverage, where can government intervene to create it.

Absent of a widespread spirit of common good, some of which is still necessary in order to forge truly equitable development strategies, corporations and other major institutions tend to require incentives in order to develop programs and initiatives that benefit low-income people. Corporations have the resources, but their missions as institutions are not automatically geared toward sharing. However, when a consumer base can demonstrate its power to influence corporations, and when policy creates regulations to ensure that corporations meet the needs of that base, corporations are pushed to recognize interdependency. But this does not often occur automatically. The involvement of policy makers and the action of communities are critical drivers in enforcing corporate accountability.

Nevertheless, in the grand scheme of things, a few corporate community partnerships, enhanced bank lending programs, and affordable housing projects are going to do only so much toward eliminating poverty and noticeably curtailing the negative effects of gentrification. This would take a far greater and more comprehensive investment in addressing the broader social needs of the community.

5

MAKING URBAN DEVELOPMENT WORK

It would be fantastic if every block in Harlem could look like Convent Avenue between 141st and 145th—stately, sparkling brownstones. Peering through these windows, one can see pristinely and artistically decorated homes. Parallel to Convent is Hamilton Terrace, which is even more gorgeous; the block has remained integrated, with some of the most valuable properties in all of Harlem. So, why not make the rest of Harlem as lovely as this apparent paradise perched on a hill? One only need move one block in any direction from this enclave to feel Harlem's poverty and intensity. Yes, let's renovate those abandoned buildings on neighboring streets, and this is being done. But the residents question, for whom? Proposed resident solutions center on fairness and equity. They know Harlem's potential, and want the neighborhood to improve, but in an accessible fashion.

Although most residents who were interviewed shared a variety of views about changes in the neighborhood, they transcended problem-identification, and proposed a variety of solutions. Their perspectives were largely balanced in terms of the responsibility of outsiders, developers, and businesses as well as that of preexisting longtime residents.

Like residents' assessment of the state of Harlem's changes, their recommendations for improvement also speak to the importance of recognizing the extensive array of interconnected issues that must be addressed in order to make urban development more beneficial to communities. One decision impacts something else. That same decision could have negative ripple effects in various other areas. Determining how to address a particular aspect of development, although adequately focusing on other aspects to ensure the benefit of low-income people, remains a formidable challenge facing urban policy.

RESIDENT-DRIVEN DECISIONS

The first thought when one suggests a resident-driven decision-making body might be, doesn't the neighborhood have a Community Board? Like all New York City neighborhoods, Harlem does have a Community Board, in fact it has three—one for each of the three districts that make up the areas of East, West, and Central Harlem. But Gail Aska is skeptical of the ability of Community Boards to adequately reflect resident needs and interests. She said, "I think that the residents of Harlem need to make that decision to be a part of, whatever, whether you call it a board, or a committee of being able to scrutinize people for this, be able to do the investigation themselves of their own fellow neighbor." She continued, "I'm proposing something completely new, and the only reason I say that is right now, I cannot honestly say that I am on top of actually what the three community boards are doing. So because I cannot tell you they've tried this and it didn't work or whatever, I would be totally considering something totally new with a different feel. And the reason I say it's different is because, unfortunately, I don't think residents in any community ever really get to be the final say, and that's what I am suggesting."[1]

Given that so few residents could recall being solicited before the coming of the Empowerment Zone, and other economic development initiatives, it does appear there may be some gaps in local communication. Indeed, the will to communicate to a broader section of residents may not be present. Even though some interviewed residents actually participated in the preplanning for the Empowerment Zone, few interviewed residents could identify any neighbor or colleague who was actually involved in that process.

In reference to the beginnings of Harlem's recent development, including the Empowerment Zone, Minnette Coleman said, "When they started, there was not a lot of community support for it. When they started moving the small businesses and folding on 125th Street, the first thing we saw were businesses closing, and we're like why is this happening? The rent started going up because they could legally raise the rent to a certain rate and they had, you know, we're like this is a sign, you see, but nobody's explaining what's going on, and all of a sudden, the big storm moves in. There were some in the community who were involved, but I don't think enough to make a big deal."[2] A more extensive and inclusive process for soliciting resident input had been missing.

THE IMPROVED ROLE OF CORPORATIONS AND DEVELOPERS

As previously mentioned, corporations and real estate developers are involved in an extensive array of projects in Harlem's present and future. Residents wonder about how to make decisions around those projects consistent with community needs and priorities—how to involve those resources in improving the overall health of the neighborhood. Most interviewed residents do not think it is enough for corporations to provide jobs; they believe that new corporations in Harlem should adopt a higher degree of institutional citizenship, including in depth participation in community improvement. From many residents' perspective, an inherent responsibility, beyond employment, comes with doing business in the neighborhood. They envision an exchange—if residents are going to patronize the various new establishments, then the establishments should contribute to their community of consumers. Many feel this is especially true given the various monetary perks, through the Empowerment Zone, given to these businesses. They wonder how businesses can benefit from their patronage, yet get paid to do so.

Some residents are rather skeptical about the businesses entering the neighborhood because their presence may be more geared toward newer residents—a community to come rather than a community that has been in Harlem for decades. Real estate developers, driven by profits, are focusing on luxury, rather than affordable housing, creating a climate in which individual landlords are finding various ways in which to evict old tenants, and bring in new ones paying above-market rents. The following are some ideas drawn from the interviews about how urban development initiatives could become more equitable.

THE ROLE OF COMMUNITY IN POLICY

Involving all residents in shaping local policy in a neighborhood the size of Harlem would likely be daunting and unwieldy. However, selecting among a few residents presents its own set of challenges as well. After all, who really represents the community in a neighborhood historically fraught with internal political tension and often controlled by a small group of elites? Nevertheless, the vast majority of interviewees generally feel out of the loop when it comes to major policy decisions affecting their neighborhood.

The UMEZ was developed through a process that solicited feedback from community residents in 1995. The results of this discussion informed the development of a proposal to the Federal government, which was ultimately successful. Approximately three hundred residents were involved in ten different focus groups designed to propose how the Empowerment Zone could add value to the neighborhood. Resident advisory groups are generally limited in their power, as they only provide input, rather than actually develop policy. Obviously, no process will please everyone. Decisiveness, almost inherently, creates resentment, disappointment, and mistrust. However, if people feel sufficiently involved in decision-making processes, they at least know they had an opportunity. Most interviewees said they were not aware of these ongoing meetings. However, even those who did know or were actually involved wish they had more involvement in the actual development of the plan.

Vicky Gholson was a part of this initial dialogue. At first she was rather optimistic about the process, and its invitation to people of all walks of life to engage in discussion about the neighborhood's development. She said, "The Empowerment Zone was another opportunity for a true and honest collaboration to be demonstrated across the section—everyday people and entrepreneurs coming together with their paid representatives out of the elected officials and politicians to merge and bring all those visions and plans and dreams and hopes of what ought to be, which was evidenced in the working groups that took place over a two-year period of time. But then that becomes a little bit jaded when you have black professionals upstairs working and white professionals on another floor, rewriting the script. And then the disparity in terms of what is sent to Washington as the final proposal, and how much was left out." She continued, "So those agreements that were made in terms of what the priorities were from a residential perspective were thrown out each time there was another head of operation, or each time there was another development on the board of trustees."[3]

When asked how she got connected to the process, Gholson said, "I was called by elected officials, community organizations, a couple of business people, to say that this thing is ready to go down, and they're looking for people to come together in areas of transportation, ecology, telecommunications, and information technology, entrepreneurial efforts, etc. And I think it was pretty much word of mouth, and heavily political identification. And then people came together in about ten different groups and thrashed out ideas on the table and this should happen. It was a rich experience."[4]

Gholson mentioned that seniors in the community had warned her that the process was not genuine—that the politicians would take it over and discount many of the residents' ideas. In some specific ways, Gholson believes this actually came to pass. One particular example involved a communications research lab. Gholson, who holds a doctorate in communications, believes she was called to the table for that reason. She and some of her colleagues pushed for this lab. She noted, "The communications research lab, was proposed and accepted in Washington, as part of the designation. We applied the first round of funding, and since, no funding, no nod."[5] According to Gholson, this was an instance where residents put a particular idea on the table, and were given the impression that the idea would come to fruition. However, they were ultimately required to apply for funding from the Empowerment Zone to implement the idea. This funding was never received, and the lab was never created.

Gholson mentioned other ideas that were unfulfilled. She said, "Being able to bring academicians, community professionals, retirees, give formidable experience to the many colleges and high schools in the area, where they can apply their skills and get something out of it … that was all cut off and what wasn't cut off was taken and duplicated in a watered-down fashion …"[6] When asked when she first realized that the Empowerment Zone was not going to genuinely reflect the ideas of the working groups, Gholson said, "When we reviewed the organizational structure." She strongly suggested the restructuring of the decision-making channels and funding approval process. The existing structure, she maintained, is not efficient. She said, "There's no way anything can get done. The Empowerment Zone funding that was given to the South Bronx—they have their board. Upper Manhattan has their board—then you have representatives on another board where city, state, and federal is represented, and then on top of that board is the final approval. I mean, it's—Stevie Wonder can see the problem with that! What's been cut off that was so extremely important was the organization of the working groups."[7] She feels the working group should continue in order to provide an ongoing feedback mechanism that could influence UMEZ's decision making.

The UMEZ has three bodies for decision making: the New York Empowerment Zone, the Board of Directors, and the staff. The New York Empowerment Zone includes the Congressman representing the Harlem aspect of the UMEZ, Charlie Rangel, and the one representing the Bronx aspect, Jose Serrano. It also includes the governor of the State of New York, the mayor of the city of New York, and the president and CEO of the UMEZ (a staff person), who is now Ken Knuckles. This Board is the highest level of decision making; however, the particular decisions around the governance of the UMEZ itself, and the investments that the UMEZ chooses to pursue are made by the UMEZ Board of Directors. This Board includes over twenty members, many of whom are influential professionals who represent the communities included in the UMEZ. The UMEZ has fourteen staff members. The staff ultimately carries out the decisions of the UMEZ Board of Directors.[8]

Decisions must be made, and people will always be unhappy with decisive behavior because everyone's views cannot be reflected in the end. In all fairness to those who drafted the policies nationally and for New York, there is no easy way to draw the line and sift out what is important from what won't work. Consensus, when it comes to broad social policy at the level of the Empowerment Zones, is virtually impossible to achieve. Having stated this, decisions should strive, as much as possible, to reflect both the needs and views of a community. Gholson believes enough was not done.

Community engagement is a key component toward the creation of more comprehensive and equitable development strategies because their insights will push policymakers to think about the implication of various directions and the overall interrelationship between various key social issues. Simultaneously, the limitation of resources is a constant barrier to development that can truly take account of various concerns from housing to employment to education to economic development, and beyond. As a result, it is essential that nongovernmental major institutions and industries contribute resources to fill in gaps. The resource question will constantly hover over any development process.

Nevertheless, dialogue is a key element in the process by which proposals are developed, conclusions are drawn, and decisions are made. According to scholar and business consultant, Daniel Yankelovich, our complex society, more than ever, requires "shared understanding" to solve problems.[9] Dialogue, according to Yankelovich, is not a question of winning or losing arguments, it is more about achieving mutual understanding, despite conflicts of interest. Successful dialogue, he maintains, can only be achieved when people participate as equals. He said, "Dialogue becomes possible only after trust has been built and the higher-ranking people have, for the occasion, removed their badges of authority and are participating as true equals."[10]

Negative ripple effects cannot be transformed into positive ones without the level of dialogue that Yankelovich suggests. Without this kind of a process, it is difficult to set policy that meets resident needs. And, if resident needs are not a priority, failure to try to take account of resident opinions could be a missed opportunity to collectively develop mutually beneficial strategies. Town meetings that descend into gripe sessions (because residents can sense the limited influence of their voices) are not dialogue. Actually sitting down at the table, with the genuine desire to listen to the community is a more productive approach.

Many of the interviewees are generally dissatisfied, and feel that if their input had been solicited or taken seriously, development might have taken some different turns. Some critical needs that are considered common concerns by several residents would be more sufficiently addressed with more significant community input. These views are not only of those who did not have any access to the process. They are also not only the views of renters. Deborah Faison also attended some of the early meetings associated with the Empowerment Zone. She noted, "I went to a few publicly held meetings where basically I was just told what the plan is. This is: we have this money, we have these tax breaks; I think the program was planned ahead of time. I think that again, part of the problem is that we don't have confidence about the input of people within the community." When a public Request for Proposals around training for small businesses was issued, Faison and her colleagues applied. "And we were accepted," she said. "And we were very happy about that, but the initial plan that we submitted was not accepted. It ended up being redesigned for us. We put in the classroom training piece, and we wanted to do something earlier that was a lot more complicated."[11] As discussed in Chapter 2, the UMEZ's Business Resource and Investment Service (BRISC) provides various types of assistance to small businesses.

From her experiences as a resident and as someone providing resources and advice to small local businesses for a living, Faison had particular insights about the needs of her constituency. However, her suggestions were altered to fit a design that she believes, was already constructed. She wanted ongoing one-to-one assistance for small businesses. She said, "We wanted to involve most of the large consulting companies and see if they could make a contribution, not by giving money necessarily, but by allowing us to use their employees a certain number of hours every month to help develop these businesses."[12] The consulting firm, Booz Allen Hamilton, as indicated in Chapter 1, is now playing a role, along with Clinton and others, in developing small businesses.

Community input, according to Faison, is critical because it broadens policy makers' understanding of the problems they hope to address. Money is always a necessary factor in urban development, but without an in-depth understanding of the issues at hand, money stands the risk, political will aside, of being wasted. Faison maintained, regarding decision making within the Empowerment Zone, "I think it's getting to understand the problem and taking ownership of it, really. You know, I think that if you say to an entrepreneur, we can't approve you because you don't have professional—you don't meet the professional standards, and that's the end of it, I think that that is just showing a lack of commitment to addressing the problem."[13] The idea of the economic changes in Harlem benefiting those who already have skills, access, or property is a recurring theme among interviewees. Small business owners who cannot benefit because of their lack of skill is one example. If the available technical assistance does not bring them to that acceptable level, then it is difficult for many local entrepreneurs to benefit. Faison explicitly pointed to a lack of commitment. This may be the case, especially as so many people who live and work and do business in Harlem seem to have multiple suggestions, based on experience, about what could be done in a manner in which existing residents would benefit.

Harlem native Abdul Salaam would like to see the Empowerment Zone become more accessible to residents. He said, "I think that if there is a way for the Empowerment Zone to be even more accessible, I'm not saying it's not accessible, but for it to be even more accessible, and what way that is, I don't know. You know, there's a newsletter, so that exists. There could possibly—there are community wide meetings, you know, where people are invited to come. There are letters—mailing letters out."[14] Salaam was not as critical of the Zone as some others, but he still wants to see improved communications between the Zone and residents. He also suggested a cable television show, which should be well publicized in the community. Access is the primary issue in Salaam's view; he sees the potential in the Empowerment Zone, "but the potential can only be realized if something with power makes the kind of power it has accessible to those with less power."[15]

Salaam says that he has been invited to various meetings about Harlem's development. He said, "I've been invited to a number of different meetings, but if I'm in the middle of a project, I can't go, so I don't go. If I don't go, there's a certain amount of information that's not made accessible to me."[16] It seems that outreach has been and continues to be done, but residents like Salaam question whether it is done in a manner that is accessible. Can residents find the time to attend meetings?

One such meeting, organized by local Senator David Patterson, took place in June 2000 at the Schomburg Center for Research in Black Culture. Representatives of UMEZ, banks, New York City's Housing Preservation and Development (HPD), and the public housing authority attended. The seven hundred residents and interested parties attending this meeting expressed anger, particularly regarding the affordability of housing, often heckling the speakers.[17] Clearly, some residents found the time to attend this particular meeting. It appears that many residents are looking for avenues to express their dismay over the state of the neighborhood. As previously mentioned, some do not feel that the development is intended for them.

Some Resident Recommendations

Interviewees mentioned a number of recommendations for some more equitable version of urban economic development for Harlem. Not everyone agrees, but it is clear that residents have been thinking practically about improving their neighborhood. Following are some ideas that emerged from the interviews.

First Priority for Residents and Those Demonstrating Commitment

Many interviewees bemoaned the absence of benefits for longtime residency in the neighborhood. Gail Aska suggested that residents should, "have a priority in acquiring property, acquiring real estate, choice locations ..."[18] Aska continued on this line of thinking with respect to businesses. According to Aska, the right to do business in Harlem should be gauged by a person's or organization's demonstrated commitment to the neighborhood. She said, "I think that the fact that they would have been here for X amount of years shows their devotion, shows their commitment to the community, their willingness to help build it, their willingness to raise families, so I think that, therefore, I think that an investment that they've made qualifies them to help kind of weed out the people who can make a similar investment." For Aska, unregulated market forces where those who happen to have the money and the will can buy in, ignores the kind of priority that she thinks residents should be accorded because they stuck it out and demonstrated a commitment to the area.

Stabilization Fund

John Bess recommended a stabilization fund to enhance the prospects for small businesses that have been in Harlem. This would help small local businesses "anchor themselves and be secure and competitively market and sustain themselves."[19] He emphasized the need for stronger technical assistance for small, particularly, Black-owned, businesses. He recommended financial consulting to help businesses with their books and help them understand various codes and potential violations. He maintained that these types of small businesses need more effective guidance in understanding the long term—investing in improvements that will benefit in the end.[20]

Lower Prices

Although it may appear to some that the act of corporations entering and doing business in Harlem is a socially responsible act in itself, many residents want more. Some don't feel that the newer stores are the right stores for existing residents, largely due to pricing. "Make stuff more affordable ... if they're gonna try to help the community, help the people that's already here," said Tyletha Samuels. She continued, "All them high-priced stores that they have downtown, they moving them up here, but yet and still them high prices is coming right along with it.

Make a Bargain World. Make more Bargain Worlds, make more Woolworth's."[21] She continued on this train of thought, "... bring something that I can afford. Bring retail prices, like they do in Chinatown ... they open up a store in Chinatown, those are the cheapest places ..."[22]

Sectoral Business Development

Although uncertain if this would be the right timing, Bess suggested that Harlem could be another Silicon Alley. He lamented the fact that Harlem had not attracted a larger percentage of the high-tech industry. He suggested that, through this industry, residents could have been trained and employed. Harlem's existing approach to development stimulates jobs, but does not build longer-term career opportunities for a critical mass of residents. Bess's suggestion of an industry-specific approach might be a more viable long-term option for the community. Technology would not have to be the only possibility. The neighborhood could make a strong pitch to a couple of different industries, outside of retail, with greater potential for advancement and career development. Various training programs could be developed around the specific industries, enabling residents to not only obtain jobs but also develop sustainable economic opportunities.

Deliberately Building or Setting Aside Housing for Low-Income People

It is difficult to imagine any way to protect low-income residents from displacement that does not include some form of guarantees—fixed spaces for low-income people.

Smedley suggested, "... have more housing built in the area, and they are doing that, and they're calling that affordable housing. But my thought is, when they say affordable housing ... those would be running into thirteen, fourteen, fifteen, sixteen hundred dollars, so that would not be for people in the area, who just have a minimum income."[23] He went on to note that policy already has addressed such issues for seniors through the Senior Citizen Rent Increase Program, which allows seniors to stay in their apartments if they are below a certain income. He suggests something be arranged for low-income people in general: "... in some of the housing, you could have a two tier thing, where you have the people who can afford to pay their rents and the twenty percent ... of people who don't have a certain income, and you can't charge them over a certain amount, or you at least start them at a lower amount."[24] He also suggested that housing could be built over the various new businesses in the neighborhood.

Unfortunately, not everyone knows the law; some try to exploit this fact. The New York City Department for the Aging administers the Senior Citizen Rent Increase Exemption Program (SCRIE). This program provides exemption from rent increases for seniors. In order to qualify for the program, seniors (heads of household) must be sixty-two years of age or older, have an annual income of $20,000 or less, spend at least one-third of net monthly income on rent, and reside in a rent-controlled or rent-stabilized apartment.[25]

Bess recommends the development of mixed housing that would, by design, allow spaces for low-income and higher-income residents. This mix, according to Bess, would have ripple effects on Harlem's other social concerns. By living together, mixed economic communities can forge a shared interest in schools, for example. Bess said of mixed communities, "… you can have communities where everyone has an interest in that school, an interest in that faith base … interested in all those streets, interested in elected officials, interested in the city surfaces."[26]

This appeared to be an area in which quite a number of residents were in agreement. They were not directly prompted to answer whether or not units should be set aside. This was a confluence of independent thinking. Gail Aska made some similar commentary, but with an entitlement thrust—suggesting that low-income existing residents deserve to have housing set aside for them, and that this is the least that developers and landlords and policymakers could do given how much they have already taken from the neighborhood. She said, "If you're going to come in and drain people of their monies and stuff, you need to also give them something back in terms of making that community or neighborhood somewhat better…. I think this should be some kind of mandate. I think that some of the housing that was built when Section 8 was really running high, there were developments that were mandated that a certain percentage of those apartments go to low-income people or people on welfare … And I think it should be something as simple as that—you're going to come in, you're taking pieces of the pie every week, every day for that matter, then you should be mandated to give something back."[27] According to Aska, this "mandate" extends beyond housing, "I think it should be given back to projects that are going to rebuild. We do have a shortage of children's programs. Children's programs were cut so tremendously over the past years; you need centers for them to go to after school, encouragement of kids reading again, putting back into the library system ... all kinds of things—exposure to the arts."[28]

PLANNING FOR RESIDENT OWNERSHIP

Smedley suggested to "... have it planned where people would not be renters ... but actually owning their buildings."[29] Although lower rents would help a significant number of residents, ownership would enhance their independence and investment in the future of the neighborhood. When Smedley discussed the composition of his block association, he said, "... you have mostly owners, and I would say it's about ... ten to one in favor of owners."[30] It is through that association that Smedley and his neighbors addressed the drugs and crime on the block, gotten street lights and potholes fixed, pushed to get the garbage collected on time, and many other issues. Homeownership can have ripple effects into the overall civic engagement of residents, which can improve conditions in communities.

Well-Paying Jobs with Training and Advancement Opportunities

In general, the Fairway supermarket in West Harlem got much higher marks than the Pathmark from interviewees. Ironically, Fairway was not attracted to Harlem through Empowerment Zone financial incentives; it set up shop before the creation of the Zone. Cynthia Simmons praised Fairway for its employment practices, "I've been in the HMV store, and they seemed fine, but I didn't see the kind of stuff that I saw in Fairway, like in Fairway, when people come to work there ... if they're bright, if they have any interest, you may see them on the cash register to begin with; in three months, you may see them behind the counter ... it's interesting to see some guys from the community become experts about something, even if it is food service ... because that means there are other kinds of jobs, you know—all these little gourmet shops, they pay much better, but you see people move up in Fairway."[31]

Minnette Coleman provided some similar praise for Fairway, suggesting its approach as model behavior that other local businesses should consider. For Coleman, having a job or not, is only one aspect of the kind of economic development that will help residents. Like Simmons, Coleman sees Fairway as a career path for residents. She said of Fairway, "The manager is from the neighborhood. In fact, he used to be a security guard at the seventy-something street store (Broadway between 74th and 75th). Most of the clerks, most of the people are from the neighborhood."[32]

Negative perceptions have been a critical barrier in the hiring process. As the youth had mentioned, the preconceived notions that some people develop have blocked opportunities for local residents. A Harlem-based C-Town supermarket has a class action suit filed against it because the store refused to hire Black people based on the notion that Blacks steal. According to Coleman, stores such as this one and others should have a recruiter, who is responsible for helping them to hire locally.[33]

Greater Attention to Nonprofits and Social Services

A few interviewees noted the lack of attention to nonprofit organizations through the Empowerment Zone and other recent economic development efforts. Bess stressed the need to infuse "support dollars to help faith-based institutions stay here in Harlem and stay here in New York City." Indeed, large corporations received the most substantial financial incentives from the UMEZ.

The list of Harlem's social challenges remains far and wide, from education to housing to AIDS and HIV to drugs to an overall lack of access to services, and beyond. Communities such as Harlem are increasingly looking to nonprofit organizations to address issues of this sort. Moreover, nonprofit organizations are also most likely to address various aspects of human development—support, encouragement, advice—issues that complete the picture, and position communities for greater self-sufficiency. Although some of the newer retail businesses have provided support to some nonprofits, this appears less deliberate or extensive than the overall effort to provide financial incentives for corporations.

UMEZ has provided some direct support to nonprofits, but comparatively, the numbers are quite small. The employment approach was clearly designed around the private sector. Indeed, corporate jobs were a missing link in Harlem, but nonprofit and government jobs have been essential throughout the neighborhood's history. Before the creation of the 1995 UMEZ, 43 percent of Harlem's jobs were concentrated in nonprofits and government.[34] To Charlie Rangel, this suggested a limitation. Another perspective could have suggested that these jobs contributed not only to Harlem's economy, but to its social condition. According to Rangel, $1 billion in retail sales were being lost to the Harlem community, thus the strategy to attract retail companies. The retail industry has brought jobs and services, but is this approach balanced with a more targeted effort to directly address persisting socio-economic needs in the community?

In terms of nonprofit organizations, UMEZ has, as previously noted, provided support to various arts institutions. It has supported other types of nonprofits as well, including Harlem Dowling, the neighborhood's oldest nonprofit. BRISC provides nonprofit workshops and supports the tuition of nonprofit executives who wish to attend Columbia University's Institute for Nonprofit Management at the University's School of Business.[35] Some of BRISC's nonprofit workshops have addressed topics such as financial management, strategic planning, and grant writing.[36]

Despite the efforts to support nonprofits through the UMEZ, some residents want to see more of the profits from retail corporations feeding into the issues facing the community. Lorraine Gilbert suggests that businesses be required to provide "a percentage of their profit towards economic development or taking kids and training them, all types of different scenarios to help those in the community, 'cause we're not Midtown Manhattan."[37] This particular suggestion raises a number of issues in terms of an influx of new resources entering a low-income community. The complexities of the realities of low-income people extend far beyond any isolated issue, whether it is jobs or services or any other issue. Although Harlem might have some new jobs and better services, communities still need better schools and better health care—basic concerns. Unless corporate resources and new residents' income go toward improving social services, then low-income long-time residents will not experience the elevation in quality of life that urban development could stimulate.

Nowadays, in most low-income communities, nonprofit organizations take on a significant load in terms of providing social services or holding public systems accountable to community needs. Business development and real estate development absent of attention to the broader array of social concerns facing low-income communities go only so far.

Greater Assistance for Small Businesses and Street Vendors

As with nonprofit organizations, many interviewees suggested additional support for small businesses from tailored and effective technical assistance to assistance with real estate costs to help with advertising. Dee Soloman, a small business owner, spoke of an advertising initiative in the Magic Johnson Theater, which enables local establishments to advertise at the movies. While the idea was good, she thought, the fees to advertise were beyond the means of the typical Harlem small business. "… I don't know how they pay those fees; I really don't know. And then I realized also, it wasn't the little stores that were advertising in the movie houses; most of them were larger stores …" Her recommendation was to provide a "cut rate" for such advertising costs for longtime small businesses.[38]

Cynthia Simmons recommended a commercial space set aside for longtime small businesses. She said, "… maybe there could be a commercial space—a big commercial space—that all of these people could put into, and have their little shops, almost like a little mall…. that's something that I think people always ought to address when things gentrify, because so many times the people who have provided a service to a community for forever are the first ones to go under, because they don't have the kind of contract for services and goods that you get by buying in bulk."[39]

According to Gholson, many innovative ideas to protect small businesses were discussed in the Empowerment Zone working groups. One was to give small businesses and community residents the first right of refusal around which types of businesses should enter the community, and which companies will do business with newer establishment.[40] Apparently, this idea remained at the level of discussion, as various small businesses, the street vendors, and the Mart 125 vendors have been faced with their vulnerability rather than their power to decide.

The removal of street vendors from 125th Street, and their subsequent placement at a market on 116th Street caused quite an uproar in the community, which still resonates. It appears that it was more symbolic, representing the removal of the old to make way for the new. Many residents think that situation could have been handled better. Gail Aska said, "… they could have come up with a better solution. It could have been maybe alternate days—those who had licenses or whatever could have, by alphabetical order or whatever, today is your day, tomorrow is somebody else, and there wouldn't have been as many on the street; there could have been numbers attached to it or whatever …"[41]

Whatever could have been decided with respect to the street vendors, the overall opportunities for independent business people of limited means have been gradually dismantled in Harlem. Aska makes a very logical point regarding the vendors; crowding on the street was one of the given reasons for why the independent business people were removed. However, if crowding was the only issue, maybe Aska's recommendation might have been considered. Independent vendors don't appear to be a part of the plan—inconsistent with a focus on established retail businesses whether outdoors or in. The Mart 125 vendors, as previously mentioned, were not crowding streets while indoors, but they were also displaced. When Harlem USA was originally designed, it was supposed to include spaces for small, independent vendors, but when it was developed, those spaces were not there.

Landlords Taking Responsibility for Affordable Housing

As new residents buy up units that once were multifamily, and make them single-family homes, fewer rentals will be available for low- and moderate-income residents, who can't afford to own. Smedley sees it as his responsibility to provide affordable housing. He said of his property, "I've tried to maintain this building as a place for rental, just to say I would like to keep some people in the neighborhood, who are decent people, who are working people. So that's one way—landlords could, who are Blacks or Whites, whoever, who own buildings and they realize that people have to have a place to stay—try to accommodate them."[42]

CORPORATE COMMUNICATION
WITH RESIDENTS BEFORE ARRIVING

Given the popular sentiment in Harlem that businesses are not logically tailored to resident needs or desires, many interviewees suggested that businesses communicate with residents before arriving in the neighborhood. Smedley said, "I think that companies could do something, but they need to talk to the people in the community to find out what the people need, and say we'll do this, and not always look at the bottom line."[43] He noted that residents are generally not informed about zoning, and the plans for future business activity. He recommended that residents be notified as to the nature and number of new businesses coming in, so that they can have an opportunity to share their perspectives on the neighborhood's priorities, and how those businesses could address them.

Some of the new businesses in Harlem have learned how to target the existing population after the fact. For example, Cynthia Simmons said of the music store, HMV, "HMV had to realize that they needed more jazz. That was something they assumed was not a big seller up here."[44] Fairway, according Coleman, "catered to people being adventurous and coming to Harlem to buy food from a warehouse. But now they cater to Haitian, Dominican, and Puerto Rican flavors ... Other businesses don't do that."[45] It was through listening to the local community that they figured out the diversity among residents and their cultures. Coleman argues that businesses tend to overlook these concerns, and "just impose their ideas on the neighborhood."[46]

Robert Roach thinks corporations should do a great deal more research on the community before and after locating in the neighborhood. He said that corporations should "have employees who live in the neighborhood, or at least have some fact finding meetings through the churches, communicating with community organizations, attending some of their meetings, because there is a customer base here, who utilize some of their products, but what you have in a lot of instances in corporate America—people in authoritative positions who don't even know anything about the neighborhood, because they never experienced it."[47] As previously mentioned, the movement toward corporate social responsibility has heightened awareness about mutually beneficial partnerships with communities. However, the perspectives of residents in Harlem suggest that a great deal of work has yet to be done in this respect.

Although nonprofit organizations, for example, institutions of higher education, are corporations, and although they are unique institutions, colleges and universities must think about some of the same dynamics that confront large corporations when it comes to community relations.[48] Columbia University and the City University of New York are two major institutions of higher education in Harlem. Roach recommends more sharing with the community, particularly regarding Columbia. He said to me, "Take back to your employer, Columbia, to be a little bit kinder to the community, and share some of the educational tools they have. I think that's one of the premier universities in the world, and I think they could do a lot more for the community."[49]

Given the oft-surfacing idea that longtime Harlem residents can only truly benefit from the changes in the neighborhood with more knowledge and skills, it does appear that the local universities could be essential in assisting Harlem residents and community organizations. Columbia has been developing a number of initiatives to work with the community,[50] but this work could be expanded and improved. Hopefully, those of us at Columbia will do a better job in the coming years.

More Logical, Holistic Planning

Many interviewees, although happy to see increased services in some areas, felt that attention to other areas was lacking—too much of one thing. For example, Cynthia Simmons thinks the array of local restaurants could be more diverse in terms of types of food and style, "... we have more restaurants; they're all sort of basically the same thing. I would like to have some different kinds of food, and I would like more people who would deliver. You know, 'cause the joke uptown is if you want delivery, you know, you got Chinese for Chinese."[51]

As Reggie James looks at Harlem's services from a business perspective, he sees a need for more health food stores and restaurants, a need for more men's clothing stores, especially finer boutiques. Service businesses, like his, which he calls a "design firm" are also lacking in his eyes. The planning around business development, according to James, has been too limited, focused on a particular type of retail. He also noted the need for "more technology companies." The UMEZ tried to build something in this respect, a "technology zone," but according to James, this effort "went down because it did not have substance."[52]

Coleman complains of the saturation of business ventures on one street—125th Street. She noted, "There are tons of restaurants and little spots that are opening up, but nobody wants to take a chance on a street that's not a premier street, you know. Just walking down 125th Street will make you sick, because this is where they put everything here, and we'll be safe because we'll all be together. Then you get to 145th Street, and there's nothing. I keep thinking, if you want to do something, put a big bookstore up here."[53] Coleman lives near to 145th Street. Not only is her point interesting in that so much of Harlem's development is concentrated in one spot, but also in the fact that a large, chain bookstore has not been included in the plans. Actually, the UMEZ opted to invest in an independent Black-owned bookstore, located in the Harlem USA complex on 125th Street. This establishment, Hue Man, given residents' comments, would represent some degree of progress as it simultaneously supports a Black-owned business and it brings a bookstore to Harlem.

Overall, residents are not short on opinions or proposals; their suggestions generally make sense. Some suggestions, such as a stabilization fund and higher paying jobs may take more time or money than others, such as greater resident input. But the suggestions are consistent with some of the concepts with which communities have been grappling in other areas, as will be discussed later in this book.

As important as it is to emphasize the responsibility of policy makers, businesses, and developers in the process of urban development, it is more likely that we will see the kind of change recommended by residents when the community is informed and engaged. After all, it was the community's drive that got policy makers to pay attention to the lack of services and jobs in the neighborhood. It will likely take the community to round out Harlem's development. And it will likely take the community to figure out how to make new resources in the community work to their advantage.

GETTING TOURISM REVENUE TO RESIDENTS

As previously mentioned, the increased attention on Harlem has made the neighborhood one of the primary tourist destinations in New York City. However, the degree to which residents are sharing in the resources that tourists bring to the area is questionable. We know from the experience with developing countries, which have used tourism as a means of economic development, that a booming tourist industry will not automatically end poverty. It can bring jobs and other resources, but who actually profits is not necessarily indigenous and rarely low income. In many developing countries where tourism is a major aspect of the local economy, hotels are often owned by people who do not reflect local demographics, for example. It is not uncommon to find tourist industries that are primarily run and operated by outsiders.

The many tourist buses that enter Harlem daily, often bringing residents to churches, are, in many instances, owned and operated outside of the neighborhood. Reggie James recommends that "the tour companies that come up here—they need to have partners with our Black tour companies that are in Harlem, and things like that. We need to demand that those types of things are being addressed."[54] It is interesting that some of Manhattan's tourist companies are bringing visitors to Harlem. The New York Conventions and Visitors Bureau has tended to focus its attention below 96th Street. To this day, maps of Manhattan in taxicabs do not even include Harlem. Now that Harlem is more fashionable among tourists, maybe this will change. But not that long ago, Harlem did not receive this sort of attention; now this has changed. However, as in the case of housing and business, longtime Harlemites are not necessarily reaping the benefits of their neighborhood's "renaissance."

The Harlem Churches for Community Improvement (HCCI) has worked with a nonprofit organization created by Columbia University students, the Alliance for Community Enhancement (ACE) to create a tourist guide.[55] Some of the proceeds from the guide go to local churches. This is one example of an effort that explicitly seeks to secure tourist revenues for Harlem. Among first time visitors to Harlem, the primary way in which they learn about Harlem and its landmarks is through tourist guides. This is also true for all international visitors to the neighborhood.[56] The ACE/HCCI guide fills a clear void, as tourist guides are not generally produced and marketed in Harlem. The guide also provides an extensive overview of Harlem churches, and seeks to educate tourists about church culture and etiquette. One issue with tourism anywhere in the world is that visitors do not always know how to behave in a manner that is respectful of indigenous cultures.

Leveraging Resources to Residents' Advantage

Knowledge and skills among longtime residents may not end gentrification, however, they might make the difference in someone being displaced or not. As Robert Roach said, "If you don't hone or sharpen your skills, you're gonna get left. You cannot do the same thing every day of your life and expect to excel."[57] He prioritizes getting involved and getting informed for Harlem residents. He continued, "very interesting what you can accomplish once you document it. And most people in the neighborhood never document it. They would have problems with their apartment that the city would manage, and they would call and never get anything done. And I would say, well what complaint number did you get? They didn't know what I was talking about. Then I'd say, okay, let's write a letter."[58] Roach brings a certain sense of entitlement and assertiveness that one might find among many professionals like him. He is taking it on himself to help others in the neighborhood keep abreast of policies that shape their lives and take informed action to avoid being abused or cheated.

Information and active engagement can make the difference in whether or not some residents will actually secure financial benefits for themselves. As people like Lee Farrow of Community Pride at the Rheedlan Center for Children and Families (now the Harlem Children's Zone) help residents turn old city owned buildings into low-income cooperatives continue their work, they demonstrate to residents that knowledge of laws and regulations, and skills around management and finance can help residents navigate a scenario that will not naturally work in their favor. Cynthia Simmons reflected on when she first moved to Harlem, "Lots of people in Harlem own, and that is not readily apparent because so many buildings were abandoned, and if there was one intelligent person in the building, who had a little time … one person who would take it upon themselves to go downtown and find out what it took for tenants to get control of the building and oversee that transition … I think there is a percentage of people who won't get displaced—the old timers are really aware on my block, of what's going on, so they're just not gon' move."[59]

But, as has been stated, many Harlem residents have lost out or gotten taken advantage of because they were not as informed or active as they could have been. Minnette Coleman reflected on the sewage system at the State Park on the far west end of Harlem—the Riverbank State Park. She said, "My biggest pet peeve in Harlem is the State Park. It's built on top of the sewer system between what is 145th and 139th Streets. Great park! Stinks like hell sometimes! Now, there is a rumor that it was supposed to have been built at 72nd Street, but the residents got together and said, 'Oh, no, no, no! We're not having it!'" When the idea of bringing it to Harlem surfaced, according to Coleman, "Only a few people knew what was going on."[60]

The park is over the North River wastewater treatment plant, which is on the Hudson River, just off of the Westside Highway, from 137th Street to 145th Street. The park itself includes three swimming pools, a well-utilized athletic center, sports fields, and even a restaurant. However, it is the only New York State park facility built on top of a water pollution control plant. The odor is noticeable, however, the city has recently invested $55 million to improve odor control by funneling air through activated carbon filters.[61]

More affluent communities, such as the one near 72nd Street, tend to be given more opportunities for input from policy makers and developers in situations such as these. But, in the grand scheme of things, many such communities tend to be more on top of affairs affecting their personal vested interests, and more organized around their collective interests. This is often the result of education, access, and a general understanding about how decisions are made, since they themselves are often involved in some form of decision making around business, law, real estate, and so on. These are worlds separate and apart from the existence of your average low-income or working-class person. This is not to say that low-income communities are not organized in any way. On the contrary, many of the improvements in Harlem were stimulated by their engagement. However, lack of knowledge and skills will limit any group's opportunity to shape policy and change on a regular basis.

Abdul Salaam believes that many residents simply did not take advantage of opportunities before them even though they knew changes were on the way. He said, "Yeah, but we've seen that shit coming. You know what I mean? We saw it coming back in the seventies. The problem with that is ignorance and the inability of African American people on certain levels to pool their resources in order to fight those particular demons—self-ownership part of that—you know whatever residuals of the plantation mentality, you know what I'm saying, that we as a people still have to stop us from doing that. And I have no excuse for that. On the flipside, you know a building that, five years ago, was a quarter million dollars, that is now eight hundred thousand—give me a fucking break. You know what I mean?"[62]

"Change is a good thing," according to Reggie James. He continued, "When there's growth and progress, there's always going to be some people that get hurt, and I think everyone that comes up here, from the tourist to the traveler to the corporation to our own elected officials—we have to hold everyone accountable. And make sure that we just don't get left out in the cold—out of the mix with no housing, with no ownership, because we own so little of Harlem. I just hope we keep holding people accountable."[63] Change is inevitable, but how to create a situation where residents can benefit through some set of formal decision-making channels is a persistent obstacle. Holding the more influential figures, making decisions about Harlem's future is essential, but it is difficult to imagine an added degree of resident engagement being embraced by policymakers and other key decision makers, absent of some recognition of the benefits of such widespread participation.

According to an anonymous CDC executive, positioning residents to take advantage of resources coming into their area is "a challenge." However, the executive suggested that a variety of initiatives of which residents should be aware are in place. The person said, "I think there are a number of policy and program opportunities for residents—everything from home ownership, where local residents are able to become first-time home buyers through a matching down payment program that some of the banks are working on. So if you are a local resident wanting to buy a home in Harlem, you can get a three to one match for your saving from up to five thousand dollars. That's a huge opportunity to build your assets, but you got to be positioned to do that, so you got to have a decent credit rating; you've got to have done some level of financial literacy."[64]

The same degree of challenge comes with small business ownership. One cannot merely become a successful businessperson without education. Moreover, competition limits the amount of realistic business opportunities, meaning that anyone running a business must be awfully savvy in order to succeed. The African American community, although filled with entrepreneurs throughout its history, has still not, according to Faison, reached a level at which the community generally expects to be in charge, running all of the businesses in its community. The lack of opportunity is a significant factor, but Faison suggests the community's mindset is important to consider as well. She said, "Entrepreneurship and business ownership has been alien to our culture for many, many years, even though it was not always."[65]

Even those of any race or ethnicity who venture to create businesses rely upon extensive social, intellectual, and capital resources for success. Faison suggests that policy makers closely examine successful businesses before deciding on programs to improve residents' potential to start or manage small businesses. She said, "Most people who are running large corporations have some formal education in business, either in business school or by real practical experience working with someone that they know in their family, or they came up through the ranks, and that took time to develop a skill base to run a large corporation—a successful corporation, by and large." She continued, "People who run corporations have more than mentors; they have a whole team of people behind them that advise them on a regular basis, from a board level. But they also have access to highly qualified professionals like accountants and attorneys and technical advisors who design their computer systems and they have that access by just picking up their telephone—because they are backed—they have stockholders' money to pay for those services. Entrepreneurs in communities like Harlem need that also." Given these realities, the technical assistance through classroom training, provided for small businesses through the Empowerment Zone "by itself is not enough."[66]

In this respect, for residents to take action that will lead to improved businesses owned by community representatives, they must seek out highly qualified advisors, who can be on call on a relatively regular basis. Certainly, current and aspiring business owners can seek out information, but even the most successful require a wide range of advisors. In a specialized society, it is difficult for any person to be a true generalist with a wide variety of skills.

Whether we are addressing jobs, home ownership, small business ownership, or any other way by which an individual can attain greater control over one's life, it is difficult to imagine advancement when people do not already possess resources, knowledge, and access. Deborah Faison said, "It seems that the design of the programs, like the Upper Manhattan Empowerment Zone, are such that you sort of have to be in a strong position already to participate, and so the people who don't have that position either are not already financially strong, or don't have access to a lot of other resources to complement what they might get from the Empowerment Zone."[67]

Any form of equitable development should include educational and training efforts to provide skills and knowledge. The banks can provide people resources, but, in order to get a match, one still must have money from the start. When looking at low-income inner-city areas, we must realize that we are often faced with starting from scratch—developing strategies that can work for people who have little or nothing.

Looking back over the course of her long life, Mary Baker is not only discouraged by what Whites are doing, she shares a similar degree of concern about what African Americans are not doing. The Black community, in her eyes, once held a greater sense of common good—cooperation with one another. Some of this is a function of general societal change, and some of it because of changes within the African American community. "We have to learn to stick together. We have to learn to trust one another," said Baker. She is saddened by the behavior of Black people with money in particular. She said, "I was just looking here on TV, looking at all of the people who make big money, you know. What they buy? ... five or six automobiles, houses for three or four million dollars that they never live in, for what? Because they thought that what the white man had with his luxury is what's important in life." She continued, "And that's our weakness, because we think the almighty dollar is everything, which it's not."[68]

This sentiment, according to Baker, is a departure from the African American culture that she has known. She said, "We always have to have somebody; we're going to pull somebody along with us. Whether they appreciate it or not, this is the way we were brought up. And I find that, New York really hasn't grown anywhere, because when I first came here,

I didn't have locked doors. I slept with my door open. We could sleep on the roof. And we shared what we had. Today, they're not sharing."[69]

In analyzing the array of factors that must be taken into account in order to make urban development more beneficial to less advantaged residents, evidently will and desire are essential ingredients. Although mutually beneficial arrangements that can simultaneously help business and communities are possible, it can only go so far. When we look at the individual level with any race, those possessing resources must hold some concern for those without. As previously stated, Harlem's changes are not neatly cast in Black and White, to the point at which Whites gain and Blacks do not. Many of the newer, more affluent Harlem residents are African American. Both a sense of common good within the African American community, and one between African Americans and others will be essential. Moreover, African Americans may be the vast majority in Central Harlem, but they are not in East Harlem. Additionally, Central Harlem is likely to diversify.

Overall, Harlem's transition is still in relatively early stages. Although many plans have been made, as long as everything is not built and finalized, residents have an opportunity to influence the process. The Empowerment Zone still has a few years remaining, and residents, as Smedley suggested, should organize to convene a meeting with the Zone to make their concerns and recommendations known.[70] Moreover, Harlem's development will not cease once UMEZ funds are discontinued.

However, none of this will organically emerge, nor will it occur without tension, struggle, and conflict. So many stars must be aligned in order for urban development to become more beneficial to longtime residents, and particularly those in lower income brackets, with limited wealth. Businesses stand to make money, but they need residents' patronage in order to do so. This interdependency is the community's leverage. Policy makers may have different conceptions of how the neighborhood should develop, but they rely on residents to hold (and maintain) office. Moreover, their legitimacy as representatives of a population relies on the nature and character of their relationships with those residents. The community can leverage these dynamics that are inherent in democratic societies.

A comprehensive approach that takes account of the mosaic of issues shaping the community's existence and future and prioritizes the needs and interests of longtime residents is what can ease anxieties among Harlem's residents and reduce the real threats to their livelihoods. In order to travel down this path, businesses, developers, and policymakers must feel the need to do so. Therefore, resident knowledge and engagement is yet another critical piece of all that must be in place in order for development to become more equitable.

Standing somewhere in between the residents themselves and the major institutions that ultimately make the larger-scale decisions about the neighborhood's future are community based nonprofit organizations. In any community, they range in size from the most grassroots neighborhood associations and startup initiatives to expansive social service agencies, community development corporations, and churches. These organizations have, in fact, been the lifeblood of Harlem's economy throughout much of the twentieth century. They not only address the various social issues in the neighborhood; they also provide jobs and bring resources into the community. As they interface with residents around the health and well being of the area and its population, and pave the way for various development projects of all types, they have critical insights into Harlem's state and future. They will likely play an essential role in the next steps of the neighborhood's development.

6

CBO'S PERSPECTIVES AND PROPOSED SOLUTIONS

It is difficult to separate the perspectives of community-based organizations and those of residents. Indeed, many of those interviewed work in community-based nonprofit organizations and are lifelong Harlem residents. Nevertheless, community-based organizations have a particular vantage point, because their work often focuses on improving the conditions in the neighborhood or on the people in the neighborhood. The distinction is important, as community development can take a place-based or a people-based approach. One can gather from the perspectives of some of the residents that the place-based approach is getting more attention, in some ways, at the expense of people—the longtime residents of Harlem.

Cdcs on Economic Development

Community Development Corporations (Cdcs), as previously mentioned, have played a significant role in the physical development of Harlem throughout the years, although many Cdcs have been criticized for taking an approach that is too limited and too place based and

169

housing oriented. CDCs have been integral to recent economic development in the neighborhood.

Karen Phillips, the former Executive Director of the Abyssinian Development Corporation (Sheena Wright is the current director), sees many positives in Harlem's economic changes. Her former organization is one of the historically more recent but well-known CDCs in Harlem. They have redeveloped and refurbished properties throughout the neighborhood and helped attract Pathmark to Harlem. As a longtime executive director and resident, Phillips is familiar with the community's conditions. She maintains that property redevelopment was needed in the neighborhood because Harlem was fraught with abandoned buildings and vacant land.

The new businesses in Harlem, according to Phillips, are largely positive as well. These businesses have, she noted, "… done a lot of active outreach to hire from the community and partner with a lot of community-based organizations."[1] They also "bring goods and products that respond to the needs of the community."[2] This perspective is similar to those of many of the other interviewed residents in its praise for the services entering the neighborhood. However, she paints a more positive picture regarding partnerships with community organizations and local hiring. Furthermore, others seemed to be much more skeptical as to the appropriateness of new services to community needs.

But Phillips indicated that she is quite familiar with the disgruntled feelings among many residents and small business owners. In terms of small businesses, these views, according to Phillips, are very logically based on the fear of additional competition.

She does share the recommendation to "diversify the types of businesses that are coming in, for instance, to get more office space and not just rely on retail for the business sector."[3] She also recommends provisions for affordable housing to curtail displacement. But, ultimately, from Phillips's point of view, it is up to residents to determine how they will survive in the midst of economic changes. She said, "People have got to be prepared." She continued, "… if you're paralyzed by the fear that somebody's going to move you out, then are you really doing what you need to do to make sure you can stay, and figure it out."[4]

As previously discussed, strategies to enable resident ownership are essential for surviving gentrifying conditions. However, the average Harlem resident does not have the knowledge and skills necessary to make this happen. Residents must recognize their assets, feel entitled to ownership and control in their neighborhood, and get the information and know-how to make this happen.

An anonymous executive in a CDC suggested that much of the economic change in Harlem was precipitated by resident "civic engagement." However, a number of residents, this person suggested, are still out of the loop. The executive said, "… many of the economic changes that have taken place in Harlem were actually rooted in community initiatives. If you look at the Pathmark supermarket, for example, which was really probably seen as the sort of metaphor for Harlem's revitalization and that one sort of marquis project that everyone points to as a turning point—that grew out of a complete community initiative around the need to have a supermarket that was led by a woman called Alice Carnegay, who regrettably is no longer with us, but Mrs. Carnegay was fed up with buying all her groceries at the bodegas and those small six thousand square foot mini marts that did not offer her and the people who lived in public housing over in East Harlem what they needed, and that was back in the eighties. And after a half dozen false starts, getting the banks interested, finding a supermarket chain that would be interested, and then them backing out, and the city getting the land, and backing out of giving the land and back and all the quagmire of negotiations; it wasn't until 1997 that construction was started on the project."[5]

The irony of Harlem's development is that community building activities among residents attracted new resources into and attention to the neighborhood; however, some longtime residents may not significantly benefit from their own work to improve the community. Of course, not every resident is actively engaged in neighborhood improvement efforts, and not everyone agrees on the approaches to be taken. But although resident participation has always existed in Harlem, some of the more recent local efforts constitute a change in the social fabric of the neighborhood. As Harlem declined, and drugs and crime were rampant, communication and cooperation among residents was stifled. This fear and lack of trust among residents had implications for community organizing, limiting its practice and potential. "… for a very long time, Harlem residents really did not talk to each other and did not engage, and I'm making some generalizations, but did not engage in a lot of organized activities in a constructive way to really demand accountability from the public sector or the private sector and their institutions."[6]

Although many residents increased their participation in the community, and their resolve to improve local socioeconomic conditions, the vast majority of resident interviewees for this project felt their input was either not solicited or ignored. It appears that a combination of factors created this situation. On the one hand, many residents were not solicited; on the other, many simply did not know what was going on. Is it the responsibility of businesses, government officials, and real estate developers to more actively and extensively seek out residents, or is it the residents' responsibility to be more involved, and by doing so, stay abreast of the various projects-in-the-making? In the case of new retail businesses, for example, various community meetings were held, but only certain residents were involved. The answer is a combination. It would be nice if powerful institutions automatically prioritized low-income people, but that is unlikely. But when those institutions and individuals are pressured to recognize their real interdependency with common, everyday people, they are more likely to respond to resident needs. Residents can only be positioned to push for that level of change when they are informed and engaged.

The anonymous CDC executive, and most interviewees, agree that it is essential for businesses entering a new community to communicate with residents before setting up shop. But this person suggests that such efforts were made prior to the certain retail establishments' location in the neighborhood. The executive praised the Gap and Old Navy for their efforts before arriving in Harlem, "… before those stores were even under construction, they had people out from headquarters out in San Francisco coming to community board meetings, going to all the churches, meeting with the civic clubs, getting people's input about different aspects of their business, sharing their vision …"[7] It appears that if residents do not go to church or attend community board meetings, they may miss out on critical information. However, given the residents' commentary, it does not appear that residents were really in the position to decide *whether or not* the Gap or Old Navy should come to Harlem.

Overall, the CDCs have played an essential role in stimulating economic and real estate development in Harlem. The full landscape of community organizations in Harlem are expected to take on a healthy share of all that must be done. All of the organizations do not agree, and their levels of effectiveness vary, however, each follows a perspective on how Harlem should be improved. But in the grand scheme of things, CDCs are a small piece in this overall collection of community-based nonprofit organizations, large and small, old and new.

The Abyssinian Development Corporation's (ADC) rehabilitation and revitalization efforts at the Ennis Francis Houses on Adam Clayton Powell Jr. Boulevard provide an example of a comprehensive approach for what can be done to help lower-income residents face community change. In 2004, ADC was assigned to manage the residential building that had been "effectively abandoned" by owners and in which conditions were "dangerous to life, health, or safety."[8] ADC helped to make specific improvements, including repairs to sewer lines, lighting systems, and restoration of the community space. Throughout these efforts, Ennis Francis tenants also have been introduced to ADC's Family Services, educational initiatives, and programs. These low-income residents, living in a poorly managed, neglected building, benefited greatly from ADC's management as the CDC not only improved living conditions but also increased residents' sense of security in the face of a tightened real estate market and provided an important connection to ADC programs and resources. This project serves as an equitable community improvement model, providing overall development to low-income residents.

OTHER CBO PERSPECTIVES

The bulk of Harlem's community based organizations run the gamut from social service providers to arts organizations to community organizers. Harlem's social needs have been so extensive over recent years that these organizations have become vital aspects of Harlem's overall existence. As real estate rates continue to rise in the area, space has become one of the primary negative ways in which these organizations have been impacted by recent changes. Churches also fall into this category. Harlem has become known for its many churches; in fact, some of the larger churches have benefited from tourism, as tourists pile in on Sundays to get a taste of the lively oratory and energetic singing for which the African American church has become known.[9]

Churches, according to an anonymous source, have been essential in developing a spirit of activity among Harlem residents, "The churches like in Abyssinian or the churches through HCCI, for instance, have played a very very vital role in organizing people. So you see more block associations. You see more tenant associations. You see more civil society forums, where people are organized and come together to talk about community-wide issues."[10]

HCCI has been emphasizing "equitable development" in their community development efforts. This organization, located in the northern part of Central Harlem, has been focusing on developing affordable housing. At the point of my interview with HCCI's Director, Lucille McEwan, which took place at the legendary Londell's restaurant at 139th Street and Frederick Douglass Boulevard, HCCI was in charge of thirteen hundred units of occupied affordable housing units.

According to McEwan, "Equitable development is about getting at deeper roots." One concern of HCCI's has been the limited knowledge of certain aspects of economics in the community. As a result, HCCI has been holding financial literacy classes, particularly in some proximity to tax season.

As the former General Counsel of the UMEZ, McEwan has an intimate familiarity with the workings of the effort. She, like most who were interviewed for this book, is "glad to see the new services and improvements in the community." She is simultaneously "sad about gentrification issues." She thinks the original design of the UMEZ was "ideal and very flexible." However, she sees various limitations. When the key political offices, the mayor of New York City and the governor of the state of New York, changed to Rudolph Giuliani and George Pataki, according to McEwan, the interest in the UMEZ moved toward "contractual obligation." City and state matching funds are required to implement UMEZ objectives. As a result, who sits in the key political offices does matter in shaping the direction of the effort.

As indicated by others in these pages, McEwan does not think $250 million is enough to "change the entire community." She feels the UMEZ has been meeting the goals of the project, but not "the hopes and dreams of everyone." McEwan sees "the development of two separate communities"—one that is well educated and professional, and the other that is low income. Of the professionals, McEwan noted that they "are not integrated into service provision and what goes on in the community." And, in terms of low-income residents, McEwan said, "Low-income people don't feel nice places in the community are for them." Indeed, this dynamic has been raised by other interviewees, and characterizes the paradox of the kind of economic development taking place in Harlem.

Acknowledging the significance of churches to the neighborhood, UMEZ has developed an initiative to ensure that local houses of worship are well kept. The churches, like the various cultural institutions, are key ingredients in tourism to the neighborhood, outside of their social and spiritual significance to residents. In 2001/2002, UMEZ provided $1,080,000 to various local churches, largely for physical restoration.[11]

Deborah Faison is the director of a nonprofit organization, the Harlem Venture Group, which provides financing for local entrepreneurs; she is also a Harlem resident. She, like some other interviewees, maintains that nonprofit organizations have not received enough attention through the Empowerment Zone. She said, "Lots of nonprofit organizations are suffering, and I think that part of the plan should have included that corporations that came in had to either sponsor a not-for-profit organization or do something really tangible and significant that you could put your hands on and say, well Sprint is here, but now this is being paid for that wasn't being paid for before. This school now has more resources than they had before, or you know, they should adopt—they should absolutely adopt some of the institutions of the communities that they move into, especially if it's needed and it's part of an economic development program."[12]

Corporate social responsibility can take many forms; Faison's suggestions stress direct corporate accountability for the health of the community-based institutions that directly address Harlem's primary social needs. She makes recommendations that suggest a corporation's responsibilities extend beyond merely hiring locally. One can infer from Faison's comments that corporations are institutional citizens, and if they should choose to locate in any community, they must give back. In a community that has been traditionally disadvantaged, such as Harlem, the responsibilities naturally increase because of the high need. As previously mentioned, the Harlem community has been giving enormously to many of the new businesses through their repeated patronage, in some instances, far exceeding sales expectations. Many Harlem residents and community organizations wonder, where is the reciprocity?

The real estate and displacement issues that have affected residents in general, according Faison, have also impacted nonprofit organizations significantly. She said, "And the rent is still going higher and higher and higher. I mean, the Harlem Venture Group rent went from $350 to $1,000 in just a few short years, even though we did occupy a little bit more space, but certainly not in proportion to the rate that our rent increased. And, you know, that's why we have to move out of our office. And that's happened to a number of businesses."[13]

In this regard, small for-profit businesses and nonprofit organizations are in a similar predicament. Without the resources, neither of these types of businesses will be able to afford Harlem. Gholson maintained that the lack of attention to nonprofits is one of the key mistakes in the Empowerment Zone and the overall economically changing landscape. She said, "There's a whole red line that's been taking place for years, which is never talked about, with the not-for-profits." She continued, "Not being able to get the construction or mortgage loans with the banking institutions while all the hoopla is going on about how much we're doing. When in actuality, they're dictating that if you're not involved in housing—if you're involved in education, if you're involved in culture, if you're involved in the mental health and spiritual awareness of a community or neighborhood, we're not funding them."

Therefore, although banks may be meeting their Community Reinvestment Act requirements in some areas, according to Gholson, they are missing the various essential elements of community life. The approach is piecemeal, neglecting the natural interrelationship between key social issues confronting a community. Indeed, the nonprofit sector is where social issues are most likely to be addressed. Gholson added, "And when it comes to the not-for-profits and their development, that's a key place where the Empowerment Zone should have been there."[14] The money through the Empowerment Zone, according to Gholson, could go a longer way.

Abdul Salaam, a Harlem native and director of the dance theater company, Forces of Nature, a twenty-one-year-old nonprofit organization, has seen some arts organizations benefiting from the changes in Harlem. He said, "I do know a number of artists and entrepreneurs and business people who have coalesced and applied to the Empowerment Zone for funding and subsidy in order to create—you know—economic collectives. There's one with Barbara and Dance Theatre of Harlem, and somebody else, you know, where there are five major arts companies that have done that, and certainly ... so, they've benefited."[15] However, in his own efforts to secure funding for his organization, he has felt a bit challenged by the requirements of the Empowerment Zone. He does not feel that organizations of the size of Forces of Nature have much room to benefit because of the requirements. Therefore, as others have noted, it becomes inherently difficult to take advantage of the new resources as a small business, for-profit or nonprofit. He said, "A lot of it is based upon your ability to provide employment, at least within the last eight to ten years, that was something that came up. As a guideline for applying, if you weren't trying to provide employment for larger numbers of people, or putting programs together that weren't talking about employment, that there was no need in even trying to apply."[16]

As with for profits, all nonprofit organizations are not alike. Those that are larger, with bigger budgets, greater capacity, and access, are likely better positioned to take advantage of new resources. The Harlem Children's Zone (a nonprofit), for example, has built a $30 million complex on 125th Street at Madison Avenue. This "community center" will, in its one hundred thousand square feet, provide "comprehensive social, educational and recreational services to the residents of the Harlem Children's Zone." Services including a technology charter school, a dental clinic, a medical clinic, a head start program, and a "baby college" (parenting guidance for those with small children) will take place at the center.[17]

The Harlem Children's Zone, in fact, has been a significant player in redeveloping its neighborhood in Harlem, while ensuring that low-income residents gain access. Their Community Pride initiative has been focusing on community building and community organizing since 1993. It began as a homeless prevention program that could help residents who were being re-housed from local homeless shelters into city-owned buildings. Because the conditions in those buildings were "worse than the shelter conditions," Community Pride decided to "work on one city block in Central Harlem to provide a saturation of services ranging from tenant organizing and block association organizing, social support services, and just neighborhood revitalization activity that would engage people in such a way that they'd want to stay in these homes."[18]

Because of their success on one particular block—119th Street, they decided to apply their strategy to twenty-four blocks in the immediate area, from 116th Street to 123rd Street from Fifth Avenue to Lenox Avenue, which they ultimately called the Harlem Children's Zone. Lee Farrow, director of Community Pride said their "main focus of organizing is apartment by apartment, building by building, block by block." Within about half of their target area, about 60 percent of residential property was owned by New York City. In those city-owned buildings with four or more apartment units, they organized tenant associations to assist them in leveraging existing housing policy that enabled tenants to manage the buildings. Through policies such as the Tenant Interim Lease Program or the Neighborhood Entrepreneurs Program, residents could collectively own and manage these various public buildings.

Tenants now own twelve out of nineteen West 119th Street buildings that were once city-owned as a result of Community Pride. This form of ownership is known as a limited equity cooperative. Farrow outlined the process by which they were able to achieve such accomplishments, "We organized the tenant associations, they managed the property under city supervision, the city renovated the properties, relocated the tenants out of the building, renovated the apartments, made completely brand new apartments, brought the tenants back into the apartments, and they sold the buildings to the tenants as low-income coops at the rate of $250 per family."[19]

The city legislation that allows for cooperative apartment units to be purchased at such low rates emanates from tenant activism in the 1970s. According to Farrow, various South American families squatted in vacant buildings on Amsterdam Avenue and around 110th Street. In partnership with the nearby Cathedral of St. John the Divine, these residents protested to allow them to live in these buildings that were not being used. What is now called the Tenant Interim Lease Program was called Direct Sales, started officially in 1978. This was during the city's fiscal crisis, when many neighborhoods were considered unsafe, and many building owners were burning down their own properties to collect insurance.

During the 1980s, when city property gradually became more desirable, the legislation was revisited. The $250 concept remained, but with the condition that some property be sold at market value. Moreover, when a $250 apartment was sold at market value, the city gets 40 percent of the profits. This 60/40 idea lasted until the end of the 1990s, when the original $250 concept was restored, because it was too difficult to monitor the flow of profits through apartment sales.

Recently, a group of squatters in New York City's Lower East Side had eleven buildings turned over to them, through a nonprofit developer, by the Bloomberg administration. Despite the existence of the $250 law, many squatters had been evicted and treated rather harshly during recent decades. In this August 2002 Lower East Side case, 167 apartments were turned over to the Urban Homesteading Assistance Board at $1 per building. These properties will ultimately be turned over to the squatters. The city currently has three programs through which properties can be turned over to low-income tenants. As of August 2002, eight hundred buildings that the city gained through foreclosure, are now owned by tenants through low-income cooperatives at a monthly maintenance of $500 per month. Apartments must be the tenants' primary residences and they cannot be sold at a profit.[20]

In any of the above instances, it took residents to make the issue of unaffordable housing clear to New York City. Now that these various affordable housing programs are in place, the challenge is to inform and guide low-income communities in making these policies work to their advantage. Community Pride has been working to do this, but the sustainability of resident control of, not only housing, but the various issues of concern to them rests in the availability of decision making avenues. It is the organization of residents that enables them to maintain a voice that ensures that their interests will not be overlooked.

Community Pride established associations on each block of the Children's Zone, which is more significant in New York City than in some other places, given that neighbors are not always acquainted, and, as previously mentioned, given the fear and isolation brought on by Harlem's decline. A democratically elected body of owners and renters governs these block associations.

Overall, Farrow, Community Pride, and the various residents and staff working in the Children's Zone have been able to enhance living conditions and directly engage residents in the process. Residents in this section of Harlem needed additional information and resources in order to become less vulnerable to displacement and have better lives. Community Pride provided that, but in cooperation with residents. Although they focused specifically on housing, they "saturated" the community, addressing a comprehensive array of issues. Additionally, for the long term, they helped the community set up indigenous governance structures that could serve as vehicles through which they can control the decisions affecting their respective blocks.

Some essential resources that have helped Community Pride in its efforts have come from corporations. Farrow mentioned Timberland, Modell's, American Express, and Viacom as examples of corporations that have been assisting their efforts. From these corporations, Farrow noted a total 180 volunteers working in the neighborhood. Viacom has been helping to renovate vacant apartments and paint hallways in the building—activities that the tenants would ordinarily have been required to take on themselves and pay for as well. American Express and Timberland have been working in the elementary schools in the area, helping them to build and refurbish playgrounds. Community Pride also has painted classrooms, installed bookcases, and created horticulture gardens in various local elementary schools.

As Community Pride continues to forge ahead with its community building, Lee Farrow does not give a ringing endorsement to the broader context of development in Harlem. She does not feel that enough residents have been hired; she noted that fewer have been hired than projected. To Farrow, not only are the number of jobs significant, but the type. She said of Pathmark, "And we know that to get any corporation like Pathmark, you're talking about professional jobs at some levels, butcher jobs and that type of thing; that didn't happen."[21] In terms of Old Navy, she stated, "The store that seemingly does the best out of all of them has been Old Navy, but then there's been the rumor that the products are inferior than Old Navy's in downtown Manhattan, and that's something I want to investigate also, because I think that's a real issue. If you have inferior products, and you're not getting the first cuts off the assembly lines ... in addition to that, the prices are one to two to three dollars higher than they are in other stores." She added, "If I had to summarize the Empowerment Zone and what it promised to give the community, I think it's fallen short."[22]

Similar to many of the residents and local entrepreneurs, Farrow believes that small businesses have not been receiving their due. She told a story to capture what she sees as the Empowerment Zone's lack of support for existing small businesses. She mentioned a friend of hers who owns one of a few full-service gas stations in Central Harlem, which is at Frederick Douglass Boulevard and 110th Street. He submitted a proposal to the Empowerment Zone during its early stages to set up a new gas station at Central Park West and 110th Street at their suggestion. He continued to call for an update on the progress of their decision to no avail. After repeated attempts to contact the office, he ended up making an unannounced face-to-face visit. At that point, he was finally told that they had other plans for the area, particularly residential development.

It took assertiveness simply to get a negative response. The Empowerment Zone is faced with making decisions with limited resources and space. However, one would imagine that responsiveness to community requests should be high on the agenda of an initiative that is explicitly designated to serve the interests of residents. In retrospect, Farrow suggested that the process through which the Empowerment Zone, while inclusive of some in the community, was fundamentally flawed. If she could have had the power to do things differently, Farrow said, "There would have been a different kind of community participation, that really was community participation." She continued, "I think that it becomes very, very convoluted whenever things are put into one pot and it's whoever can speak the best, whoever can write the best, whoever knows the people, whoever knows how to get things, and then the promise just sort of dwindled down."[23]

Content and process appear to be the principle areas of concern among residents and community organizations in Harlem. The two concepts are inseparable, as what ultimately gets addressed is a function of who was allowed to influence the process, and how the process unfolds is a function of the priorities of those involved. The governance structures developed by Community Pride have certainly elevated the degree of residents' ability to shape very localized decisions. However, some of the bigger issues that belie the immediate surroundings of these twenty-four blocks will always be of concern. Nevertheless, the enhancement of social bonds within and among these various block associations has spawned a forum through which ideas can be laid on the table, and a broader community agenda can be formed.

Community Pride's office has served not only as a place of business for staff, but as a house of dialogue for local residents. A few days after interviewing Farrow, I facilitated a focus group of residents and Community Pride staff to ascertain their thoughts on Harlem and its future. Overall, this group of about fifteen African Americans (some circulated in and out of the room) was rather dismayed by the economic changes in Harlem. Many of their thoughts resonated with those of the other resident interviewees. They are glad that Community Pride has helped to organize them to address issues of concern, but they raised concerns around the ability of recent changes to improve the lives of low-income residents.

Low-income families, many in the group maintained, are very nervous, particularly with respect to recent housing developments. One man noted, "I think the greatest fear right now is that most of the buildings that are going up—most of them will not provide housing for people who are considered as low-income families, and people are scared because these buildings are coming up, but they don't get to live in them."[24] This man told of his own experience, as a new Harlem renter,

"I started off paying $822 for a very, very small two bedroom apartment. Well, I thought everybody paid $822. I came to find out that I was paying the most rent in the building, because I was the most recent resident. Therefore, because I already signed a one-year lease, at the end of the year, my rent was up to $921, and when I moved from that building, the rent was going to be $981." He indicated that most residents in his building have been there for at least fifteen years, which is why they can afford to stay. They are banking on rent control to keep roofs over their heads. The man said, "There are people who've been there thirty-five years, and those people could live nowhere else; they couldn't afford to pay rent anywhere else."[25] When asked where displaced families go after leaving Harlem, focus group participants threw out a number of locations, most often, New Jersey, Virginia, and North Carolina. A woman said, "These people were born and raised right here. That's what hurts; you were born and raised here, and you're just uprooted."[26]

The group also held negative opinions of the ability of the burgeoning local retail industry to help the community. This group was less positive than other interviewees regarding the conveniences that have come with these new stores. One woman characterized Pathmark as "a load of trouble" for anyone without a car. She additionally noted that the supermarket's bathroom has been out of order for five months. "All they're doing is taking money and nothing's coming back out," she declared.[27] However, this group, like many other interviewees, gave positive marks to Fairway.

The presence of small businesses in the community, to one woman in the group, is and has been more than simply a smaller scale of commerce. Small businesses are an extension of the community. She said, "The larger the institution, the less they want to give. They shun you. The smaller ones, that's who you get the cooperation from; that's who Harlem was built on—the smaller stores, and it's more of a family thing."[28] But others in the group pointed to the limited options for grocery shopping. They spoke of the "inferior products" at many of the smaller local corner stores (or bodegas). For this reason, the 125th Street Pathmark continues to be one of the higher-performing stores in the entire corporation.

Although the larger businesses possess greater resources, and can afford continually rising rents, not all of them are doing well. The Disney Store's performance is not near that of Pathmark or Blockbuster (both of which preceded the Empowerment Zone). The Magic Johnson

Theater, which is in the Harlem USA complex, along with HMV, Old Navy, and others, according to the focus group, is not doing very well. To some of these participants, it is a function of trying to make Harlem something that it is not—something that resembles lower Manhattan, but cannot truly compete at the same level. When it comes to going to the movies, one man noted, "most people want to go out of the neighborhood." Another man added, "When you're with your family, you want to take them downtown—the lights … you got the ESPN Center (Zone), you have different video—there's different things. I mean, if you want to get a quick movie, there goes Magic Johnson, but with the family, let's do something different."[29] With adequate preliminary research, this man noted, those who drafted the UMEZ would probably have made a different decision regarding the theatre.

A woman in the group concurred, and went further to say, "They don't have a clue; they don't even have a clue of what is needed in Harlem." Dismayed over the Apollo Theatre being owned by Time Warner, she said, "The Apollo is not the Apollo anymore … you're still taking away everything that fits with us too."[30] This comment speaks to the perception that not only are new businesses coming in but also that an active effort to dissolve Harlem's cultural institutions is underway. It actually appears as if the Apollo Theatre is on the rise, with its exclusive ongoing production, "Harlem Song," and it's revamping of its television show. Nevertheless, indigenous ownership, as has been the case throughout Harlem's history as an African American neighborhood, continues to be a priority for many longtime residents.

In terms of recommendations, the group called for greater resources to be funneled into enhancing and sustaining existing institutions that have been useful to the community, such as the Apollo or Bargain World, the discount store that recently closed. Too many of the remaining small businesses are "at the mercy of the landlord," according to one man in the group. A woman said, of the new developments, "There's nothing that's tailored to fit the community." This tailoring, according to another woman, never came to fruition partly because of the process. She argued that the community should have been thoroughly surveyed before any decision making. In such a survey, another woman maintained, residents should have been able to answer questions about what types of development or services would be beneficial to Harlem, along with questions about long-range planning.

"We were sold down the river," said one woman. She continued, "With the planning boards, councilmen, community boards, the senators, all of them had a hand in it." A man suggested that the community is continually kept uninformed intentionally. As an example, he mentioned how some know about new housing developments "before they even break ground."[31] Therefore, even if residents want to apply for some of these units, they find that the list is closed before anything is even built. This same person suggested that residents need to form networks and share information as well as attend various meetings taking place in the community. He suggested that churches make more of an effort to inform parishioners.

It is ironic that one of the major recommendations emerging from this focus group was the need for residents to be organized and informed, since this is why the initiative at Community Pride has been created. In many ways, this very discussion was an exercise in informing residents about what is happening in the community and building their resolve to be engaged. Absent of a sweeping political will to ensure that low-income people always benefit, many Harlem residents will continue to be left out of the process and made vulnerable to displacement. However, as Community Pride has demonstrated, mobilizing a community, and providing it with useful information can help residents gain from the changes in their neighborhood. This is not to suggest that policy makers shirk all responsibility; they should be held accountable as well. But, in reality, communities, especially those that are low income, will continue to require an exceptional level of organizing and informing in order to stay afloat as market forces send Harlem down a more exclusive path.

The Empowerment Zone, in its effort to stimulate far-reaching economic impact, seeks to create jobs. However, in doing so, it can limit opportunities for local residents to run thriving organizations, either for-profit or nonprofit. Small businesses and nonprofit organizations are the managerial and ownership opportunities open to a more extensive population, including people at various class levels. Therefore, an apparently noble effort on the part of the Empowerment Zone has a painful side effect that results in limiting community control—providing opportunities for residents, primarily as employees (generally at lower levels), rather than as owners or managers.

In general, the perspectives of community-based organizations are as varied as they are. But the desire to improve the community is a consistent theme across the various types of organizations; they differ around the how. Community Development Corporations play a unique role in this category, however, because urban development is their primary goal. Some of the larger CDCs, in particular, have already been intimately involved in the process of Harlem's current economic changes. Those organizations that have been on the outside might share a different spin on the neighborhood's state of affairs, sounding more like the interviewed residents.

Although residents, community organizations, policymakers, academics, businesses, and developers can all make development proposals, it is crucial to understand the population at hand. Not every group of residents will receive development in the same way. This can be shaped by culture, race or ethnicity, history, the nature of local politics, and so many other factors. But the psychology of a group is one of the critical, less tangible, factors that should be incorporated into any development strategy. This book deals primarily with Black Harlem—Central Harlem—the Harlem that became known for cultures of African descent from the turn of the last century until now. If the history of African Americans and how their thoughts are impacted by such are not addressed in the planning and process of development, efforts will likely not succeed. The way African Americans perceive the world, based on experiences and history, shapes expectations. Therefore, what might work with some other races or ethnicities might not catch on in an African American community.

EXPECTATIONS

Because of historical exploitation and discrimination, African Americans do not have high expectations of the country's major institutions and industries. Although hope has kept African Americans going through the most trying times, a certain cynicism about government, developers, and corporations pervades the community's psyche. It is important to recognize this in thinking about how to forge equitable development strategies.

Interviewees made references to the fact that residents did not take advantage of homeownership and business opportunities. This is not a surprise when a community has been so often burned historically. Why should now be any different than any other time? And, at this time, African Americans have seen a Civil Rights movement influence sweeping legislation designed to improve opportunities for not only

African Americans but also Americans in general. African Americans have watched some of those same gains gradually slip away. The vast majority of predominantly African American communities still face the same array of social, economic, and political barriers, but in a manner in which the concepts of rights and entitlement has been obliterated.

The anger and resentment of some longtime Harlem residents is, therefore, understandable. Many residents already knew that Harlem was convenient and that it had a lovely housing stock; and they knew that eventually, the neighborhood would be slated for "redevelopment." Some got excited when they heard about changes on the way, and others were simply skeptical, presuming that these changes would necessarily be designed with their interests in mind. Given such dynamics, urban development in a place like Harlem becomes inevitably and thoroughly complex.

With so much to think about in order to make urban development work for those with the least resources at their disposal, some may wonder whether it is even worth the effort. It is easier to simply ignore people, forge ahead, let the market freely run its course, and displace people. But, in looking toward a better future, which is focused on a common good, examples of communities that have transcended a standard gentrification model, and yielded tangible benefits to longtime residents, especially those who are low income, could provide guidance in thinking about Harlem's direction.

7

DEVELOPMENT'S NEW DAY?

With this rich and extensive set of recommendations and ideas from those who experience Harlem on a regular basis, we can infer some general sense of factors to consider toward more equitable forms of urban development. As previously discussed, these factors include: avenues for resident ownership, attention to small business needs, affordable housing, employment with advancement and training opportunities, effective partnerships, logical planning, involvement of residents in setting policy, cultural appreciation, informed, involved, and organized residents, and a spirit of common good.

Although a newer population may ultimately populate a changing geographic area, existing residents are still the engine behind a neighborhood's economy and overall livelihood. In a case like Harlem, the population is so large, and the area is so vast, that such a population shift will not happen overnight. Moreover, extensive public housing in the area suggests that many older residents could remain for some time. Businesses new to Harlem still depend on longtime residents to stay afloat. A place like Pathmark, for example, generates revenue because of longtime local patrons. If this population does not feel that businesses and developers are committed to the overall health of the neighborhood, residents can organize and undermine their efforts. Residents have the power, if organized and informed, to push local development in various ways. They are not inanimate recipients of the decisions of outsiders who have recently recognized Harlem's viability. Therefore, businesses and longtime residents are interdependent, making good corporate citizenship smart business sense, and inclusive policy making more effective for the long term. It is in the best interest of Harlem's new corporations to make more extensive investments, beyond low-end jobs, in the overall health of the neighborhood. Harlem needs major institutions and industries that will not only locate in the neighborhood, but address the most pressing social concerns confronting residents, such as education, health, economics, and others.

But the most unwieldy aspect of achieving a broad, multi-issue, participatory approach to urban development is implementation. Although it might sound logical that multiple intersecting issues should be simultaneously tackled in order to pay adequate attention to the plethora of social concerns facing any urban area, it is painfully difficult to actually achieve an effective, yet productive, process through which residents are sufficiently included, and their concerns are adhered to in policy. First of all, residents do not agree across the board. Although consistency emerged among many residents' ideas and recommendations, not everyone affords the same weight to each issue.

Second, coordinating the various opinions of a vast urban population into some coherent policy that generally suits the majority's interest is daunting. Many community-wide planning processes have tended to result in endless lists of the various local concerns. The challenge to democracy in general is ensuring that citizens are educated and rational decision makers. Participation is a competency in itself. To comprehend a neighborhood's landscape is one thing. Being able to translate such into policy is entirely another. In the case of the Empowerment Zone, neighborhoods around the United States played some role, to varying degrees, in influencing the nature and scope of local strategies. However, in all of those situations, resources were limited. No matter how many ideas were taken into account, policy makers were ultimately challenged to arrive at conclusions. Conclusions mean choices, and choices mean exclusion of some ideas at the expense of others. It is important that residents understand how to make strategic choices and recommendations within the parameters of limited resources. Community building initiatives around the country, stressing comprehensive approaches to problem solving, continue to confront the difficulties of simultaneously prioritizing particular issues while maintaining a broad multi-issue approach.

Harlem's residents are right to critique displacement and hold new businesses accountable to a higher level of local economic development than entry-level jobs. They are right to desire greater control over the forces that are moving their neighborhood toward a new "renaissance." However, the problem is not only one of process, and it is not only one of fragmented policy decisions. It is also a question of the overall limitation of resources designated for urban development, whether they originate from the public or private sectors.

The perfect model does not exist, given the shear magnitude of influences over the state of urban America. It will take more than local participatory, comprehensive decision making to make a noticeable dent in the gap in wealth and access that often leaves low-income urban people of color firmly at the bottom. Massive shifts in political will and, likely, collective vocal public demand will be required to alter some of the broader sources of inequality. In the meantime, we can draw some lessons from examples of participatory community building efforts that invite community input and decision making, and comprehensively address various local concerns.

EXAMPLES OF EFFECTIVE URBAN DEVELOPMENT

In terms of attracting business, some would say Harlem is an example that can guide others. However, there is much to be gained from taking a glance at strategies elsewhere. PolicyLink, as previously noted, has been conducting research on "equitable development" strategies over the last few years. Their website's "Gentrification Toolkit" provides more extensive summaries of specific examples that place greater resources in the hands of community residents and enhance community-based decision making around local development.

I already mentioned the legendary example of the Dudley Street Neighborhood Initiative, which, during the 1980s, gained the right of eminent domain, enabling residents, through this nonprofit organization, to make decisions about the development projects that would enter the neighborhood. Any time the idea of "equitable development" surfaces this example is worthy of note. As noted, the development in

Harlem has some merits in terms of services and forging a mixed economy. With the numerous critiques of Harlem's development by some of its longtime residents, it make sense to look to other attempts to foster more equitable forms of development. All communities are not the same, and it would be naïve to suggest that a strategy that works in one city will automatically work in another. Harlem's uniqueness aside, some helpful lessons might be drawn from development efforts in other places.

Market Creek

Market Creek Plaza in San Diego, like the UMEZ efforts in Harlem, focuses on retail development, along with restaurants, a movie theatre, and office space. Also, as with the strategy in Harlem, job development is one of the key drivers in the Market Creek approach. What is unique about Market Creek is its focus on community ownership.

The Plaza, spanning twenty acres, is a partnership between the community and the Jacobs Center for Nonprofit Innovation. The Jacobs Center's shares in the Plaza will ultimately be transferred to a community controlled capital pool. A Community Investment Team was put in place to ensure that the community ultimately takes 100 percent ownership. Over time, the ownership interest will support community-owned vehicles.

A focus on social concerns in the community is another important aspect of this effort. A number of different teams address various issues: an Art and Design Team, a Youth Center Team, a Childcare Center Team, and a Construction Team. Market Creek stresses both business and social services, as the Youth Team is charged with creating a safe space for youth, and the Childcare Center Team is focusing on developing childcare opportunities to enhance residents' ability to take advantage of new economic opportunities. Two thousand adults and over one thousand youth to date have participated in land planning, leasing, marketing, research, advocacy, and ownership design.[1]

Three hundred sixty jobs were created through the effort. As the effort was under construction, hiring minority- and women-owned firms was emphasized. Sixty-nine percent of the construction contracts were awarded to local, minority-owned enterprises, totaling $7.1 million.[2] The anticipated sales revenue of the Plaza is expected to exceed $25 million per year. Residents have designed a locally controlled foundation to grant a portion of the profits from the Plaza back into the neighborhood.[3]

It should never be suggested that any of the efforts listed as good examples or "best practices" are without flaws. Indeed, Harlem's UMEZ is often listed as a good example of urban business development; it is, depending on the angle. If the goal is to attract business to an area that has been previously neglected, then UMEZ and other development efforts in the neighborhood have done a fantastic job. What appears compelling about Market Creek is the attention to community ownership, the comprehensive approach that addresses social issues in conjunction with business, and the awarding of contracts to minority- and women-owned firms, which can have ripple effects in job development, as those firms may be likely to hire their own. Overall, it seems as if this effort is at least attempting to take account of the "who" as much as the "where." It is developing a place, but it is stressing and prioritizing direct benefit to the existing community.

Nashville and Mills

The Mills Corporation builds shopping malls. Historically, they had focused on sprawling suburban malls but eventually decided to create them in urban areas as well. Seeing their effort as a jobs development strategy, Mills did not originally realize that residents would critique their plan because of the limitations of the kinds of jobs that would be provided by a mall. Retail development can bring services and jobs. However, the types of jobs offer salaries that hover around minimum wage. Indeed, these are the jobs that are available to those with limited skills and education. But the longer-term question is, where will the jobs lead? If the goal is to enhance the sustainability of the community, something must be done to train and educate unskilled and semiskilled laborers to enhance their opportunities for advancement.

When the Mills Corporation was challenged to consider these realities, they, in partnership with local community based organizations, and the Rockefeller Foundation, created a training and development center for employees in the mall. The center helps employees build on their existing jobs in order to move to higher levels within the various companies in the mall or elsewhere.

It is important to think about supportive services in development. Simply trying to address every issue at once is not easy, but when one issue, jobs, for example, is the focus, then the various supportive services that can make a job go a longer way should be considered as well. A job in itself is not the panacea if it does not pay enough and if childcare, transportation, and other related issues are not addressed. And the impact of simply having a job can only go so far unless economic sustainability is the longer-term goal. Economic sustainability cannot be achieved unless minimum wage jobs can lead to additional opportunities—opportunities that don't often arise without additional training and education.

Numerous ideas for equitable development have been circulating throughout the world. However, successfully implementing these strategies in a manner that actually improves the lives of significant numbers of low-income people remains elusive. Implementation remains difficult because of the breadth of the context in which urban low-income and working-class residents reside. However, substantial improvement of the livelihoods of such residents requires comprehensive approaches that take account of multiple intersecting issues. It is easier for policy makers and business to envision strategies that can be accordingly comprehensive, when they collaborate with the residents themselves.

THE FIFTH AVENUE COMMITTEE

Community developers and community organizers in the essentially gentrified Park Slope section of Brooklyn make up the Fifth Avenue Committee, which was originally developed in the 1970s in order to redevelop the many vacant housing units in the community. Vacancy is no longer the issue, as the neighborhood has become one of Brooklyn's most desirable and expensive. Now the organization is known for having established an "antidisplacement zone" to prevent low-income people from being evicted. The committee continues to organize at the neighborhood level, but it believes that "government action" and "expanded rent regulation" will be required to stave off potential displacement.[4]

Land Use Plans and Inclusionary Zoning Campaigns

Communities around the country have provided a range of technical and financial assistance to nurture and grow small businesses and local ownership. Methods have included business incubators, stronger antitrust and antichain policies, leasing municipal property to local businesses, and the orientation of land use and zoning to favor local owners.[5] Zoning codes are plans with specific land use rules and have been applied to prevent the growth of chain stores by restricting the size of new retail establishments, limiting "formula" businesses or those that have standard services and methods of operation, and reviving taxes on chain stores.[6] In addition to commercial zoning codes, inclusionary zoning is also a tool to create affordable housing by setting aside units in developments, promoting mixed-income communities. In New York City where the demand for housing has created a tight market, PolicyLink and the Pratt Institute Center for Community and Environmental Development have partnered to promote inclusionary zoning to balance out neighborhoods, create more mixed-income communities, prevent larger-scale development, and ensure greater affordability.[7]

In addition to zoning codes, community land trusts are nonprofit organizations that hold parcels of land on behalf of the larger community and aim to preserve the long-term affordability of the land by removing it from the control of market forces and placing it under the direct control of the local community. Most existing residential urban land trusts are small in scale. However, there is enormous potential to extend the model to the commercial sector as a means to launch community-owned business endeavors.[8]

Land-use plans and inclusionary zoning campaigns are feasible strategies to directly involving citizens in community building and economic cooperation. These strategies are capable of making a substantial contribution to the economic security of low- to middle-income Americans by stabilizing long-term housing costs and ensuring the stable supply of quality resources.[9]

Policy and Method—the Role of Community

Turning back to Gail Aska's suggestion to create a new formation, more thoroughly representative of community voices than traditional Community Boards, policy makers and residents should consider other ways to involve residents in major decisions that will comprehensively impact neighborhoods.

Vicky Gholson lamented the dissolution of the various working groups that informed the development of the Empowerment Zone. Although the process did not capture the perspectives of a broad enough cross-section of residents, and although many were disappointed with the ultimate outcome of the legislation, the working groups were a part of a process that was intended to be influenced by resident perspectives. Continuation of such formations would create an ongoing avenue for resident participation in policy making. It appears clear that such participation could enhance the logic and usefulness of the final drafts of urban planning initiatives.

Worldwide, participatory planning efforts are taking root. It makes sense for a number of reasons—the recipients of policy are more likely to own and accept it when they are solicited up front; moreover, those recipients know their communities, consequently, they have good, informed ideas. A true paradigm shift would be when residents are as much drivers of policy rather than merely recipients. However, even in the most participatory processes, questions around who gets to the table and who truly represents one's constituency rightfully emerge. Nevertheless, any genuine effort to solicit popular participation in shaping policy will likely lead to new ideas, raising overlooked concepts, making innovative recommendations.

The general attitude toward planning is that it should be participatory to be effective, sustainable, and lasting, engaging residents in a democratic process that makes it easier for everyone to see the whole picture. However, according to studies conducted by Michael Hibbard and Susan Lurie for the *Journal of Planning Education and Research,* many stakeholders are systematically excluded from participating in the planning process, creating a distinct contradiction between the dominant mode of practice and the empirical data.[10] Their article explores why participatory planning failed to achieve its potential in a community with a history of local problem solving. They argue that professional staff and decision makers can make a difference in the quality of participation by using existing social networks to help citizens with various viewpoints and backgrounds work toward a common, community-focused, interest.

According to Richard Margerum in his article for the *Journal of Planning Education and Research,* participatory or collaborative planning is an interactive process that builds consensus and fosters implementation involving various stakeholders and public opinion but faces some common obstacles that have confronted the process of consensus building.[11] He identifies a number of obstacles for planning groups, including limited resources, parochialism, operational problems, state agency commitments, member abilities, a lack of strategy, and the fact that frequent reliance on alternative dispute resolution is not always appropriate for collaborative planning. His findings suggest that effective communication, collaboration, and interaction are prerequisites for planning as well as strong member or stakeholder commitment. However, as Hibbard and Lurie suggest, Margerum argues that the model for collaborative planning must be continually refined.

Recently, a few thousand residents of the New York City metropolitan area critiqued and analyzed the plans for redeveloping the site of the World Trade Center (Ground Zero) through a participatory process. The plans crafted by developers and presented to the public, as a result of opening up the conversation, have been entirely rethought. Residents, who experienced the pain of the events of September 11, 2001, pointed to the fact that the plans did not begin with a memorial. They critiqued the limited, commercial focus that reflected the business backgrounds of the plans' original designers.

On July 20, 2002, four thousand people from the New York City area participated in "Listening to the City," a process to solicit resident feedback on the redevelopment of lower Manhattan. This large group divided into subgroups of ten to respond to six proposed plans created by the Lower Manhattan Development Corporation (LMDC). Several interesting ideas emerged from this historic event. In terms of democratic participation, this event was monumental in that it was a formal process, beyond electoral politics, community boards, and traditional town hall meetings, which sought resident perspectives. The effort also was nongovernmental, as it was sponsored by a nonprofit organization in collaboration with private developers. The Regional Plan Association, in conjunction with almost one hundred organizations formed the Civic Alliance to Rebuild Downtown New York, a coalition dedicated to assisting in and influencing the planning of the redevelopment of downtown Manhattan.

Rarely are private developers held accountable to the public in such a manner. It is clear that the developers were relatively out of touch with the ideas of residents. Many of the plans that developers had put forward did not resonate with residents. For example, residents wanted more affordable housing, diverse types of businesses, and cultural activities.[12] Therefore, without resident participation, it is very likely that the developers would have traveled an entirely different path, underscoring the significance of soliciting popular input. This is not to suggest that every proposed idea was dismissed. Residents took a balanced view, as they not only criticized; they supported such ideas as a memorial promenade from the site of Ground Zero to Battery Park, and the footprints of the Twin Towers kept intact.[13]

However, as with the resident meetings around the UMEZ, the question of participation versus actual decision making arose. Soliciting advice or feedback from residents is not a new idea in itself, however, actually incorporating resident perspectives in decision making or involving residents directly in decision making is far more complex. Shared governance among residents, policy makers, and business is the new frontier. Because of this lack of precedent around shared governance, many New Yorkers, and Americans in general, do not have faith in democracy. Only one third of participants in "Listening to the City" were "confident" that their perspectives would actually be incorporated into the final development plans.[14]

Undoubtedly, the development of downtown Manhattan will not happen as quickly as the LMDC would like. Time is always an issue where participation is concerned. Not only is it likely that once a process is opened to a broader public, the resulting strategies will take longer, but it takes time to bring people to the table as well. It takes even more time to involve others earlier in the process, or keep people involved in the governance and maintenance of the implementation of strategies. On the surface, participation at this level might appear inefficient. This all depends on long-term goals. If people are expected to comply when they feel they have not been solicited, which is the case with many longtime residents in Harlem, they will find ways to rebel through protest, voting, or other means. In other words, they will not own the policies that have been set. If the long-term goal is to solicit popular investment in policies, then it makes sense to involve a broader population in decision making.

Who's participating? This is another central question to pose around shared governance. Taking a glance at the demographics of the participants in "Listening to the City," it is clear that the group was predominantly White and significantly upper income. Sixty-two percent of those participating in the event make $50,000 or more per year. Only 7 percent were African American, and 10 percent Hispanic. The entire group was drawn from the vast New York City Metropolitan Area, which is 20 percent African American and 20 percent Hispanic.[15] Therefore, participation in the event, which was heavily publicized, was not representative of even half of the Black and Hispanic populations in the New York City region. Granted, downtown Manhattan teems with bankers and brokers, often White and wealthy; however, many African Americans and Hispanics were impacted by September 11, 2001.

Historically oppressed groups are less likely to have faith in such participatory processes because policy has often not worked in their favor. The African American community, in particular, has tended to create its own, less institutionalized, means of impacting policy, such as social movements. But it appears that if processes are going to be developed to engage the African American community in shaping policy through institutional channels, a special effort must be made to solicit participation. Additionally, it appears more likely that such participatory processes will improve in incorporating resident voices, when residents are involved in shaping the process itself.

Indeed, process is as essential as content, since the direct involvement of residents in decision making not only increases a collective sense of ownership, it leads to policies and approaches that are more consistent with residents' needs. As Aska noted, we need new formations that are more representative of the interests and concerns of residents, particularly those who are low income. Although American democracy has developed a system of representation, it is limited in its ability to genuinely incorporate community voices in a productive and informed fashion.

Such a variety of extensive democratic practices would not come without its challenges. As numerous community building strategies and innovative collaborations have demonstrated, the continuous involvement of numerous diverse parties in decision-making requires incredible patience and takes time. It may be inefficient in the eyes of many, but in the end community residents' involvement can lead to more informed decisions in the end, and a greater sense of connection with a neighborhood's future. In such formations, participants may jockey for power, and the most informed and privileged residents may dominate. Mini fiefdoms are scattered about any neighborhood, and they may collide in collective decision-making processes.

In the end, a spirit of common good is key to success, and this may be close to unachievable in a society that promotes individual gain over collective interests. A new way of thinking will be required to effectively develop this degree of widespread participation and control. Many people, especially those who are low income or disenfranchised, are unaccustomed to making key policy decisions in collaboration with government and business. Why should communities even seek participation in such formations if they always end up drawing the short stick? As some residents noted, communities like Harlem need priority and the final say in major development decisions. Such community-based power would ensure that community benefit is a priority. This would require extensive training, especially as such communities have not historically had a say at this level. But if we are interested in forging a truly democratic society, where citizens are not only participating, but controlling, this is the kind of hard work that must be pursued.

The Empowerment Zone was a landmark piece of legislation. The kinds of seemingly intractable social issues that it is designed to address require decades of work and significant resources. And the legislation should be viewed in this context. It has certainly produced jobs in urban areas where there were few jobs, and it has brought a certain degree of hope to some residents. First of all, the Empowerment Zone's funding may sound like a great deal of money, but it is not. If the political will to improve urban conditions for low income and disenfranchised people is genuine, the Empowerment Zone should be expanded. It should include more cities, and each city should receive a greater allocation. Pools of private funding could complement these investments. The Empowerment Zone/Enterprise Community (EZ/EC) Funding Consortium attempted to do this, by bringing various private foundations together to provide additional financial and technical support to each city with an EZ or EC grant. The level of funding was not enough, and the initiative was never able to become sustainable. However, it is important to reiterate that the amount of funding does not matter if the goals of the development strategies are not in the interest of longtime residents.

It is not enough to say that retail conveniences have improved access for residents if the price of those conveniences may be displacement. Numerous guidelines or safeguards to protect residents from the side effects of economic development should be in place. Again, communities should be positioned to craft such guidelines. For example, corporations entering urban neighborhoods like Harlem should be accountable to a coalition of residents, representing different parts of the area and ensuring a significant low-income presence. That coalition would determine which businesses would enter and how business is conducted. It also could evaluate businesses' contributions to the neighborhood. This group could actually develop indicators for corporate social responsibility beyond producing local jobs.

The presence of local jobs should not be underestimated; this can have a critical long-term impact on some residents. In the case of young people, for example, a first job can be awfully elusive. This is especially the case for young people of color. The first job is experience, and experience leads to other jobs. However, residents should be in the position to assess the quality of jobs, whether or not jobs provide opportunities for advancement, whether or not training is tied to the jobs. They also should be able to evaluate the degree of a corporation's institutional citizenship. How does the company treat customers? Does the company make grants in the neighborhood? Does the company work to improve public schools? Does the company pollute the environment? Does the company's presence in the neighborhood positively contribute to the quality of life of residents? These additional questions should be posed in order to create a more holistic sense of a corporation's accountability to a neighborhood. Without any residential authority over corporate behavior, there is no space to ensure that residents will benefit.

One might suggest that if communities are doing all of the work government should be doing, doesn't this let a lot of people off of the hook? Government accountability can be viewed from multiple angles. Informed and organized communities can make government better. Participation in the democratic process can shape the direction of candidates and policy. However, all politicians should be held accountable once they are in office. External formations have always been the true engines of change. Historically, most major policy shifts had been sparked by social movements on all ends of the political spectrum. If communities are not organized to affect local policy then it is very possible that local policy will not work in their favor.

Another important factor to keep in mind is that the majority position can sometimes oppress others. This is a reality when discussing any broad decision-making body. However, the best decision making is informed. Education is essential in this respect. Community based decision-making bodies should be committed to learning, as a means of quality control, and a way to avoid choices at the expense of others. Any decision has consequences, but education can minimize the negative effects of such choices.

In Harlem, for example, the presence of businesses makes the neighborhood more desirable. As the neighborhood's desirability climbed over recent years, so did real estate values. In order to make policy that helps residents, the complex array of interrelated issues should be taken into account. Policy around commerce must be made in conjunction with policy around residential real estate in this instance. Not only are business and real estate intertwined, but so are education, health, the environment, transportation, and a variety of other issues. For example, if new businesses help to raise real estate prices that displace longtime residents and attract new, more affluent ones, do the new residents send their children to public schools? If they don't send them to local public schools, do they have an investment in the quality of the schools?

In other words, all policy decisions have ripple effects. Sweeping urban policy such as the Empowerment Zones help in some ways, but they may hurt in some others, regardless of intent. The real estate issue in Harlem is of continuous concern. In many ways, the sometimes, majestic housing stock in the neighborhood attracted a great deal of the recent interest in the neighborhood. As real estate prices rise in Harlem, and throughout New York City, rent control laws have been loosened. It would be difficult to avoid displacement in any low-income urban areas without tight rent control laws. Housing codes are often on the books but not enforced strongly enough. Therefore, landlords have been able to harass residents out of apartments or illegally evict their tenants. Absent a true popular spirit of common good, residents will continue to be displaced in neighborhoods such as Harlem if policies are not designed to protect low-income tenants.

Finally, ownership could position residents with greater control over their livelihoods. It is important to promote and draw lessons from the creative work of the Harlem Children's Zone's Community Pride and various approaches around the country like the Dudley Street Neighborhood Initiative's use of eminent domain to the residents' advantage, and the work in Market Creek. Not every area is the same, but what can be learned in order to help residents in gentrifying areas benefit from the resources coming in and secure greater control over their own choices? All of the aforementioned efforts could not have happened without funding. Therefore, pools of funding to develop cooperatives, community land trusts, and other, what has become known as Resident Ownership Mechanisms is of utmost importance. Foundations, wealthy individuals, corporations, and other sources of private funds can support these kinds of efforts.

RESEARCH DIRECTIONS

As a national movement to make institutions of higher education more accountable to the needs of society develops, more people are coming to the realization that research should not be insulated within academia. The development of the kinds of policy suggestions made by Harlem residents and by various nonprofit organizations can be aided by data. Researchers should turn their attention to issues of urban development, as the majority of the global population has become urbanized. What affects urban areas ultimately affects everyone.

Although gentrification has become a widespread, global phenomenon, little research has been conducted on these concerns. Moreover, much of the existing scholarly literature has not been solution-based, recommending strategies that will enable residents to benefit from new resources entering their community. Most of the research taking a more practical thrust has been conducted by nonprofit organizations, such as PolicyLink and the National Community Building Network. We would all benefit from more joint research between scholars and nonprofit organizations on urban development.

Research seeking to highlight case studies in which communities are employing equitable development strategies will continue to be useful and necessary, as would research on effective corporate/community partnerships that stimulate more equitable urban development. In conducting this research, corporate/community partnerships that truly led to an improvement of residents' livelihoods were hard to find. Indeed, jobs and philanthropic initiatives were present, along with greater financing from banks. But the sum total of these initiatives has not led to any substantial access or advantage for a broad cross-section of Harlem residents. Most of the innovative efforts that have tangibly improved the livelihoods of residents have been developed by nonprofit organizations.

Getting an accurate handle of gentrification-induced residential displacement is daunting. Anecdotal data, as can be found in this book, provides a general sense of what is happening. But accurately determining why people move from their residences requires a combination of quantitative research on who is leaving, and qualitative research on why. It does not appear that any research has effectively employed this method in any substantial manner. Commercial displacement may be a bit easier to gauge, as there are fewer establishments, and it is easier to contact merchants regarding their reasons for leaving. This research has also not been substantially conducted. Stories emerging from this book's interviews referred to various instances where longtime small entrepreneurs have been forced out due to increased rents or competition from larger corporations, however, there has been no systematic study of this form of displacement.

This book focused specifically on Harlem, partly because of its size, symbolism, and uniqueness; little research has compared how different neighborhoods across the country and world address extensive urban development. Numerous factors shape how urban development unfolds in various areas—a neighborhood's history, proximity to other resources, relationship to a metropolitan region, density, transportation services, demographics, housing stock, nature of commercial activity, and other issues, all help shape the nature and character of development. Comparative research would help highlight the relative significance of a variety of factors in determining whether or not urban development will lead to gentrification, what steps should be taken to avoid significant displacement, and other social concerns.

INSTITUTIONS, INDUSTRIES, AND COMMUNITY PARTNERSHIPS

Greater equity for low-income people in urban neighborhoods requires a *two-pronged approach* that focuses on both the community level and the institutional level. At the *community level*, residents must be better positioned to take advantage of opportunities and advocate on their own behalf. The community development and community building field often promotes greater "community capacity." Organizations such as PolicyLink have been exploring effective "community equity mechanisms"—processes by which low-income communities can use resources toward their own benefit. These efforts have been addressed particularly in the context of neighborhoods undergoing significant economic change, especially when new resources threaten to displace residents, alter their power, and change social and cultural priorities, as in Harlem.

If communities were armed with greater knowledge, skill, and access, they could take advantage of existing economic opportunities, such as the limited equity coops implemented by the Community Pride initiative. Cooperatives, community land trusts, and other forms of collective resident ownership strategies can stave off overwhelming displacement and place community residents in the position to make decisions about the nature of economic development in their neighborhoods.

Communities will never be able to implement these innovative strategies without skills and knowledge. These strategies cannot work without some facility with banking, the law, policy, real estate, technology—the many areas in which low-income communities have been left in the dark. When communities do not have such knowledge, they are vulnerable to outside interests. Institutions of higher education and intermediary nonprofit organizations, like the Abyssinian Development

Corporation and other Community Development Corporations, can play an essential role in training residents and smaller community-based organizations around these types of skills.

The idea of empowerment has many dimensions. Knowledge and skills make a difference; however, low-income communities must believe they are entitled to resources, knowledge, and overall local control. The African American community has faced several hundred years of disempowerment. This has affected the sense of expectation and entitlement among African Americans throughout the United States. The Harlem Renaissance represented a period when African Americans were asserting their pride as a community. The twentieth century is filled with instances of African Americans displaying pride and recognizing power. This has, indeed, altered some aspects of the access and freedoms available to all people of African descent, as well as other people of color and women of all colors. However, poverty and disempowerment remain quite prominent in the African American community despite the enormous individual successes of a handful of famous African Americans.

It is important to distinguish between collective economic development strategies and individual economic strategies. During the Black Power movement in the late 1960s and early 1970s, many activists stressed the limitations of the creation, enhancement, and expansion of a few highly successful African Americans. The presence of African American multimillionaires, in itself, does not represent progress for the majority of African Americans or make life easier for low-income African Americans. Unless those individuals make their wealth and access available to low-income African Americans, progress is not collective. If African Americans were a country, they would have the ninth largest gross national product in the world. The money in the community exists; however, an effective coordinated approach to widely disperse resources across the Black community does not. An increasing effort to promote "Black Philanthropy" is an important trend to watch in this respect, as numerous organizations, including the Twenty-First Century Foundation, and others, are designing the future of what it will take to funnel resources within the Black community in a manner that addresses the priorities of Black people.

The persistent disempowerment of African Americans is a problem of race and class. Traditional economic development strategies have tended to focus on the individual more than the community.

Small business development in neighborhoods such as Harlem is critical; however, unless these businesses can enhance the quality of life for greater numbers of low-income people, these strategies will have little impact.

Protest, community organizing, and advocacy have been essential components of the African American experience. Because of the persistence of institutionalized racism, African Americans have been forced to continually employ a variety of strategies from civil disobedience to violent rebellion in order to achieve policies that address the continuous barriers facing the community. We have not reached a point at which protest is unnecessary. However, protest should be recognized in the context of a variety of strategies. When communities are organized, communicating with each other—achieving "social capital," they are better positioned to mobilize and protest when necessary. When communities have greater knowledge and skills collectively, they feel more entitled. Therefore, if they do not get what they believe is their birthright, they will fight to get it. Greater community capacity, greater knowledge, greater skills, a sense of collective destiny, and the desire to protest when necessary are all important ingredients in community empowerment. Too often, they have been treated separately, as if they are unrelated, or at odds with each other.

As important as it is to enhance the community level, and better position communities to control their life circumstances, it is also essential to recognize and engage the *institutional level*. Although our major institutions and industries have replicated and exacerbated social and economic and political inequality, those same institutions and industries still hold the power, knowledge, and resources. Moreover, they still depend on people for their survival. The retail corporations in Harlem need local residents to buy their goods. The community level and the institutional level should be recognized for their natural interrelation. If Harlem residents are knowledgeable, skilled, and organized, they are positioned to hold new local corporations accountable.

Conflicts of interest are real. This is why protest is inevitable. However, many of our major institutions and industries have been able to operate absent of significant popular criticism. When those institutions and industries are made to recognize that they cannot afford damaged reputations or lost business, they are more likely to behave in a socially responsible manner. We can look at government through this lens as well. Many urban policies have not benefited low-income urban residents.

Elected officials need votes and healthy reputations. Oftentimes, policies are made absent of significant popular opposition due to lack of knowledge, lack of organization, or even lack of resources on the community side. It is important for communities to stay abreast of policy developments and push for government accountability to the needs of low-income people. Enhancing skills, knowledge, and access at the community level and holding major institutions and industries accountable are essential strategies on the path to greater community empowerment.

Community partnerships are where the community level and the institutional level come together. Low-income communities and major institutions/industries aren't necessarily inherently at odds. Because of the interdependency between our major institutions and industries and communities, mutually beneficial partnerships are possible. Some of the hope for the future lies in the ability of everyday citizens working in conjunction with our most powerful institutions and industries in developing policies and practices that promote a common good. Conflicts of interest will continue to limit the fruition of such partnerships. However, conflict is a necessary aspect of any healthy partnership. If community residents and banks, government officials, businesses, institutions of higher education, and real estate developers can collectively craft strategies that promote a common good, the future of Harlem and other communities will be characterized by the combination of new businesses and redeveloped housing along with lessened poverty and increased opportunity.

These are the components that can bring communities closer to urban development that fosters equity. Development is necessary, and critical to the future of urban communities. But the challenge to the future is not to abandon all existing approaches or start completely from scratch. The long-term challenge is to do better, focusing on people in addition to place.

I founded Marga Incorporated, a consulting firm, based on the belief that existing resources can be leveraged to address social issues. Our mission is to maximize existing resources for societal gain through the development of strategies that include partnerships. We work with foundations, universities, nonprofit organizations, government, and corporations in designing the kinds of strategic plans that will make practical use of the resources of institutions and industries in a manner that simultaneously fulfills the mission of institutions and industries and addresses community priorities. Direct communication between community residents and these institutions/industries is critical to the development and success of any of these plans.

Much of our work begins with an assessment—an inventory of sorts—of existing resources, institutions, and initiatives. Looking at the Harlem community, it is hard to miss the proximity of the neighborhood to major institutions and industries of various sorts. The potential to tap into the vast nearby resources is enormous. Our work with the Morningside Area Alliance is an attempt to create a strategy to apply the resources of the various hospitals, universities, and other heavily resourced institutions concentrated in the lower part of District 9, known as Morningside Heights. Tapping into educational resources, health-related resources, and other social resources could round out the development underway in Harlem, and provide the missing pieces that would improve the life chances of residents. These institutions also happen to be economic engines, with the employment, procurement, and real estate development dimensions that they bring to the table. A coordinated effort can make this happen.

Holistic, comprehensive approaches to urban development will help to manage the ripple effects of focused strategies that may address a particular set of local needs, but neglect, or even exacerbate other priorities. Ultimately, being deliberate and forward-thinking would be essential in advancing the next chapter in urban (and human) development, in Harlem, and elsewhere.

ENDNOTES

INTRODUCTION

1. This issue became particularly visible around the experiences of well-known African Americans who were passed over by yellow cabs. In November 1999, the actor Danny Glover, in particular, brought light to the situation. He filed a complaint against New York's Taxi and Limousine Commission, which regulates taxi service. Glover, his daughter, and a friend had been in Harlem, and he was refused by numerous available yellow cabs before one finally picked him up.
2. Details on the Abraham Lincoln Houses, named after Abraham Lincoln, were obtained from the New York City Housing Authority (http://www.nyc.gov/html/nycha).
3. John Bess, interview, 9/25/01.
4. Mary Baker, interview, 3/4/02.
5. Ibid.
6. "Jim Crowism Laid to Hospital Staff," *New York Times,* May 11, 1935.
7. "Lehman Calls Harlem a Rebuke to the North," *Washington Post and Times Herald,* Washington, DC, June 4, 1956.
8. Mary Baker interview, 3/4/02.
9. Ibid.
10. Malcolm X made this statement in his "The Ballot or the Bullet" speech on April 3, 1964, in Cleveland, Ohio.

CHAPTER 1

1. Ric Burns and James Sanders, *New York: An Illustrated History* (New York: Knopf, 1999), 323.
2. Howard Dodson, Christopher Moore, and Roberta Yancy, *The Black New Yorkers: The Schomburg Illustrated Chronology*, The Schomburg Center for Research in Black Culture (New York: John Wiley and Sons, 2000).
3. Ibid., 4.
4. Ibid., 20.
5. Ibid., 15.
6. Ibid., 15.
7. Ibid., 28.
8. Ibid., 52.
9. Ibid., 46. By 1860, 80 percent of the cotton shipped from the South went to New York.
10. Ibid., 60.
11. Ibid., 98.
12. Ibid., 75.
13. Ibid., 76.
14. Ibid., 92.
15. Ibid., 93.
16. Michael Henry Adams, *Harlem Lost and Found: An Architectural and Social History* (New York: The Monacelli Press, Inc., 2002), 255.
17. Dodson et al., 26.
18. Ibid., 55.
19. Gilbert Osofsky, "Harlem: The Making of a Ghetto," in *Harlem: A Community in Transition,* ed. John Henrik Clarke (New York: Citadel Press, 1964), 16.
20. Burns and Sanders, 325.
21. Osofsky in Clarke, 18.
22. Ibid., 19.
23. Ibid., 21.
24. Ibid., 23.
25. Dodson et al., 126.
26. Burns and Sanders, 324.
27. Ibid., 326.
28. Osofsky in Clarke, 25.
29. Cheryl Lynn Greenberg, *Or Does it Explode: Black Harlem in the Great Depression* (New York: Oxford University Press, 1991), 29.
30. Dodson et al., 167.
31. For a more in-depth discussion of the Caribbean presence in Harlem during the first half of the twentieth century, see: Richard B. Moore, *Caribbean Militant in Harlem: Collected Writings 1920—1975,* ed. W. Burghart Turner and Joyce Moore Turner (London: Pluto Press, 1988).
32. So much has been written about the Harlem Renaissance. This book cannot even attempt to capture the vast dimensions of the period. Two of the better known works on the Renaissance include: David Levering

Lewis, *When Harlem Was in Vogue* (New York: Random House, 1981) and Nathan Irving Huggins, *Harlem Renaissance* (New York: Oxford University Press, 1971).

33. This moniker is not to be confused with that attributed to musician, Robert Johnson, "King of the Delta Blues."

34. Burns and Sanders, 334.

35. Dodson et al., 188.

36. Langston Hughes, "My Early Days in Harlem" in *Harlem: A Community in Transition,* ed. John Henrik Clarke (New York: Citadel Press, 1964).

37. Laconia Smedley, interview, 9/10/01.

38. Ibid.

39. Vicky Gholson, interview, 2/7/02.

40. Rivka Gewirtz-Little, "The New Harlem," *The Village Voice,* 18-24 September 2002.

41. Kenneth Clark, *Dark Ghetto: Dilemmas of Social Power* (New York: Harper and Row, 1965) extensively discusses the state of Harlem's social conditions during the early 1960s.

42. Dodson et al., 209.

43. Ibid., 208.

44. Ibid., 212.

45. Adams, 257

46. Dodson et al., 229.

47. Henry Louis Gates and Cornel West, *The African American Century: How Black Americans Have Shaped Our Country* (New York: Touchstone, 2000), 183.

48. Greenberg, 121.

49. John H Mollenkopf, *The Contested City* (Princeton, NJ: Princeton University Press, 1983), 117—119.

50. Dodson et al., 228.

51. Quote taken from Eve Edstrom, "Cry of Despair is Answered," *The Washington Post Times Herald,* 8 March 1964.

52. Kenneth Clarke, "HARYOU: An Experiment," in *Harlem: A Community in Transition,* ed. John Henrik Clarke (New York: Citadel Press, 1964), 212.

53. Hope Stevens, "Economic Structure of the Harlem Community" in *Harlem: A Neighborhood in Transition,* ed. John Henrik Clarke (New York: Freedomways, 1964), 106.

54. Stevens, 110.

55. Jennifer Lee, "From Civil Relations to Racial Conflict: Merchant-Consumer Interactions in Urban America," *The American Sociological Review* 67, no.1 (2002), 77-98. Lee argues that most interactions between consumers and merchants in Black communities are rather cordial, and that too much has been made of those instances when they reach high levels of tension.

56. Eugene Knickle Jones of the Urban League uttered this phrase. It was quoted in: Cheryl Lynn Greenberg, *Or Does it Explode: Black Harlem in the Great Depression* (New York: Oxford University Press, 1991), 18.

57. A substantial discussion of the history and character of the wealth gap between Blacks and Whites can be found in: Melvin Oliver and Tom Shapiro, *Black Wealth/White Wealth* (New York: Routledge, 1996).

58. Vicky Gholson, interview, 2/7/02.

59. This story is told and analyzed in: Philip Kasinitz and Bruce Haynes, "The Fire at Freddy's," *Common Quest* 1, no. 2 (Fall 1996), 24–34.

60. All of this data is from the year 2000 report from the United States Census Bureau.

61. This does not necessarily mean that eighteen thousand Harlem residents suddenly had no more need for public assistance. The number of people on Medicaid, in fact, doubled. But with welfare reform in 1996, caseloads have been reduced for a number of reasons that often do not mean that former welfare recipients are self-sufficient. Many poor people may be intimidated from applying for public assistance, as policy has made it clear that the goal is to take people off of public assistance. Moreover, with caseload reduction being a motivating force for local governments, some people have simply been moved off. A discussion of this can be found in: Kenneth J. Neubeck & Noel A. Cazenave, *Welfare Racism: Playing the Race Card Against America's Poor* (New York: Routledge, 2001).

62. Data provided by New York City Community District 10.

63. All data from the Corcoran Group's, a New York City-based real estate brokerage firm, mid-2001 report. Housing included in the sample included shells and townhouses requiring reconstruction along with already renovated housing. Therefore, it is likely that the rise in prices could be more dramatic in the coming years, as much of this housing stock will be refurbished. So many units in Harlem have been abandoned over the years, that it was probably essential for Corcoran to include essentially undeveloped properties in their survey. Moreover, one of the trends in housing sales in Harlem has been the purchase of homes at modest prices that can be thoroughly redeveloped or even demolished, and ultimately rebuilt.

64. From the 1996 New York City Housing and Vacancy Survey, as cited in: Julia Brash, "Gentrification in Harlem," (Urban Planning Thesis, Columbia University, 2000). Vacancy surveys are sponsored by the New York City Department of Housing Preservation and Development.

65. HMDA Data.

66. Ibid.

67. All of this tourism data is from: *Upper Manhattan Tourism Market Study: A Study of Visitors to Upper Manhattan, including their Economic Impact and Local Spending* (New York: Upper Manhattan Empowerment Zone Development Corporation, December 2000).

68. Amy Waldman, "In Harlem, A Hero's Welcome for New Neighbor Clinton," *New York Times*, 31 July 2001.

69. Ibid.

70. David Levering Lewis, "Harlem's Visible Man," *New York Times*, 2 August 2001.

71. Former Upper Manhattan Empowerment Zone director, Deborah Wright as quoted in: Craig Horowitz, "The Battle for the Soul of Harlem," *New York*, 27 January 1997.

72. *Upper Manhattan Empowerment Zone Annual Report: 2001*, 13.

73. David Dinkins, interview, 11/27/01.

74. Ibid.

75. Ibid.

76. All figures from: *Upper Manhattan Empowerment Zone Annual Report: 2001*, 10–13.

77. Ibid., 14, 15.

78. Ibid., 16, 17.

79. Ibid., 18.

80. Ibid., 24.

81. Ibid., 18.

82. For further details on the various projects under development and the various developers behind them, see: David Dunlap, "The Changing Look of the New Harlem: As Brand Names Move Uptown Not Everyone is Happy," *New York Times,* 10 February 2002. The major developers are not indigenous to Harlem, although they partner with local developers through the Empowerment Zone and various Community Development Corporations.

83. For a deep discussion of the significance of Harlem to people of African descent, and the uniqueness of the neighborhood because of its international symbolism, see: John L Jackson, *Harlemworld: Doing Race and Class in Contemporary Black America* (Chicago: University of Chicago Press, 2001).

CHAPTER 2

1. Anthony Love Rhodes, "Town Meeting Demands Action," *HarlemLive*, <http://www.harlemlive.org/>. (HarlemLive is an online news source produced by Harlem youth.)

2. Rivka Gewirtz-Little, "The New Harlem," *The Village Voice,* 18–24 September 2002.

3. Rebecca Webber, "The New Gentrification," *The Gotham Gazette,* 11 December 2000.

4. Vajra Kilgour, "Tenants Protest Gentrification in Harlem," *Tenant Net,* November 2000, <www.tenant.net>.

5. Quotes taken from: Rob Gurwitt, "Up in Harlem," *Preservation,* July/August 2002, 82.

6. Cynthia Simmons, interview, 6/11/01.

7. Laconia Smedley, interview, 9/10/01.

8. Ibid.

9. Anne C. Kubisch, Patricia Auspos, Prudence Brown, Robert Chaskin, Karen Fullbright-Anderson, and Ralph Hamilton, *Voices From the Field II: Reflections on Comprehensive Community Change* (New York: Aspen

Institute Roundtable on Comprehensive Community Initiatives for Children and Families, 2002).

10. One can find gentrification addressed primarily through the people and real estate dimensions in works such as: Neil Smith, *The New Urban Frontier* (New York: Routledge, 1996). Gregory Squires rightfully maintains that race drives disinvestment from urban communities in: Gregory Squires, *Capital and Communities in Black and White* (New York: State University of New York Press, 1994). This work does address the business dimension through lending, but less through the sort of retail industry thrust in Harlem's recent development.

11. Rebecca Solnit and Susan Schwartzenberg, *Hollow City* (New York: Verso Books, 2002). This book addresses the "vanishing places" in San Francisco that have transformed the richness of the city.

12. Vicky Muniz, *Resisting Gentrification and Displacement* (New York, Garland Publishing, 1998), 33.

13. Melvin Oliver and Tom Shapiro, *Black Wealth/White Wealth* (New York: Routledge, 1995). This book demonstrated that inequality between African Americans and Whites should be measured by wealth more than income. The true reality of inequities between these races is far more stark when looking at wealth rather than income.

14. Angela Blackwell, "Holding on to Harlem," *New York Times,* 12 April 2001, Op Ed. Blackwell's organization, PolicyLink, in conjunction with the National Community Building Network and others have been discussing issues of equitable development in every major city in the United States. They have been finding significant similarities in the characteristics of gentrification. Harlem, because of its size and other aforementioned characteristics, may take longer to gentrify than many other areas. This is partly because of its extensive public housing, as will be discussed later in this book.

15. Vicky Gholson, interview, 2/7/02.

CHAPTER 3

1. The following statistics were found at: U.S. Census Bureau Public Information Office, "Income Stable, Poverty Up, Numbers of Americans With and Without Health Insurance Rise, Census Bureau Reports Number of People Living in Poverty Increases in the U.S.," *U.S. Census Bureau News,* 24 August 2004.

2. "Poverty: 2002 Highlights," *U.S. Census Bureau,* 26 September 2003, <http://www.census.gov/hhes/poverty/poverty02/pov02hi.html>.

3. See: Manuel Pastor, Peter Dreier, J. Eugene Grigsby, and Marta Lopez-Garcia. *Regions That Work: How Cities and Suburbs can Grow Together* (Minneapolis, MN: University of Minnesota Press, 2000). This book analyzes sprawl and the growth of metropolitan regions. As a result of regional growth, they maintain, it is important to forge regional development strategies that can provide low-income communities access to the resources in entire regions. Of course, the cooperation and will of

those in possession of most of the resources is required to make any such attempts real. They provide some examples of regional development strategies in the book. Also see: Myron Orfield, *Metropolitics: A Regional Analysis for Community and Stability* (Washington, DC: Brookings Institution, 1997). This book also addresses the dynamics of metropolitan regions.

4. See: William Julius Wilson, *When Work Disappears: The World of the New Urban Poor* (New York: Random House Vintage Books, 1996). This book addresses issues of urban isolation—the separation of urban communities from jobs and other resources.

5. Melvin Oliver and Thomas Shapiro, *Black Wealth/White Wealth: A New Perspective on Racial Inequality* (New York: Routledge Press, 1995). This book highlighted the true picture of the gap between Blacks and Whites by focusing on wealth (net worth) rather than just income, which only scratches the surface.

6. "Dow Breaks 10,000 But Typical Household Wealth Down Since 1983," *United for a Fair Economy*, 29 March 1999.

7. Ibid.

8. Salim Muwakkil, "The Need to Bridge a Wealth Gap Before it Grows too Wide for America to Survive," *Chicago Tribune*, 14 February 2000.

9. For further details and more specific data, see: U.S. Department of Commerce, *Falling through the Net: A Report on Telecommunications and Information Technology Gap in America* (Washington, DC: US Department of Commerce, July 1999).

10. Ibid.

11. See: John H. Mollenkopf, *The Contested City*. (Princeton, NJ: Princeton University Press, 1983). This book thoroughly analyzes how the urban policies of much of the twentieth century negatively impacted low-income urban residents.

12. *Out of Reach 2002* (Washington, DC: National Low Income Housing Coalition, 2002). This document is an extensive report on the state of housing, particularly focusing on the prospects for low-income communities.

13. Ibid.

14. Ibid.

15. Ibid.

16. Katherine S. Newman, *No Shame in My Game: The Working Poor in the Inner City* (New York: Russell Sage Foundation, 1999), xiv.

17. National Low Income Housing Coalition, 2002.

18. Lance Freeman and Frank Braconi, "Gentrification and Displacement in New York City," *Journal of the American Planning Association*, 70, no. 1 (Winter 2004): 39-53.

19. Maureen Kennedy and Paul Leonard, *Gentrification: Practice and Politics* (New York: Local Initiatives Support Corporation Center for Home Ownership, 2001).

20. See: Amy Domini, *Socially Responsible Investing: Making a Difference and Making Money* (Chicago: Dearborn Trade, 2001).

21. See: Edmund Burke, *Corporate Community Relations: The Principle of the Neighbor of Choice* (Westport, CT: Praeger, 1999).

22. James E. Austin, *The Collaboration Challenge* (New York: The Drucker Foundation, 2000).

23. Ibid.

24. Matt Moore, "Poll: More Companies Duck Social Causes," *Associated Press*, 17 September 2002.

25. Michael Porter, "The Competitive Advantage of the Inner City," *The Harvard Business Review*, May/June 1995, 55–71.

26. For a thorough discussion of the literature addressing the relations between urban communities and local small businesses see: Jennifer Lee, "From Civil Relations to Racial Conflict: Merchant-Customer Interactions in Urban America," *American Sociological Review*, 67, no. 1 (2004): 77–98.

27. *Survey of Minority-Owned Business Enterprises* (Washington, DC: U.S. Census Bureau, 1997), 12.

28. Ibid., 9.

29. Ibid., 10.

30. Taken from: "Statistics about Business Size (including Small Business) from the U.S. Census Bureau," (Washington, DC: U.S. Census Bureau, 1997). also 1997 figures.

31. *Survey of Minority-Owned Business Enterprises* (Washington, DC: U.S. Census Bureau, 1997), 10.

32. Ibid., 11.

33. Ibid., 15. Figures suggest that when comparing African American businesses with all U.S. firms in a variety of business categories, such as agriculture, construction, manufacturing, transportation, wholesale, retail, finance, and services, Black-owned businesses are closest in construction (outdistanced by three times), and furthest apart in manufacturing (outdistanced by 16.6 times).

34. Mamadou Chinyelu, *Harlem Ain't Nothin' But a Third World Country: The Global Economy, Empowerment Zones, and Colonial Status of Africans in America* (New York: Mustard Seed Press, 1999).

35. Ibid., 124.

36. One example: Robert Allen, *Black Awakening in Capitalist America*. (Trenton, NJ: Africa World Press, 1990).

37. One example: Manning Marable, *How Capitalism Underdeveloped Black America* (Boston, MA: South End Press, 1983).

38. One notable discussion around this issue takes place in this landmark: Frantz Fanon, *The Wretched of the Earth* (New York: Grove Press, 1963).

39. *The Upper Manhattan Empowerment Zone Annual Report: 2001*, 22.

40. Upper Manhattan Empowerment Zone, *EZONE Newsletter*, no. 2 (Second Quarter 2002).

41. These points were taken from: "Investing in Business in Upper Manhattan," *Upper Manhattan Empowerment Zone*, 2005, <www.umez.org/brisktext.htm> (7 September 2005).

42. Information taken from: Amy Waldman, "Vendors Angry at Evictions from City Mall in Harlem," *The New York Times*, 16 August 2001, sec. B.

43. See: Peter Medoff and Holly Sklar, *Streets of Hope: The Fall and Rise of an Urban Neighborhood* (Boston, MA: South End Press, 1994).

CHAPTER 4

1. David Dinkins, interview, 11/27/01.
2. Lorraine Gilbert, interview, 9/19/01.
3. Minnette Coleman, interview, 5/01.
4. Robert Roach, interview, 6/13/01.
5. Ibid.
6. Ibid.
7. Minnette Coleman, interview, 5/01.
8. Ibid.
9. John Bess, interview, 9/25/01.
10. Nelson Antonio Denis, "Beware Primrose Pathmark," *New York Daily News*, 25 April 1995, 21.
11. Ibid.
12. Ibid.
13. Editorial, "Pathmark to Progress," *New York Daily News*, 30 May 1995.
14. Editorial, "At Last, the Right Path," *New York Daily News*, 2 August 1995.
15. Terry Pristin, "Big vs. Local in Harlem Supermarket Proposals," *New York Times*, 15 June 1999.
16. Terry Pristin, "Construction is to Start in the Fall on Central Harlem Supermarket," *New York Times*, 3 July 2002.
17. Gail Aska, interview, 5/11/01.
18. Robert Roach, interview, 6/13/01.
19. Lorraine Gilbert, interview, 9/19/01.
20. Editorial, "Good Business," *New York Daily News*, 5 October 1999, 32.
21. Laconia Smedley, interview, 9/10/01.
22. Gail Aska, interview, 5/11/01.
23. Vicky Gholson, interview, 2/7/02.
24. Tourist industry employment data from: *Upper Manhattan Tourism Market Study: A Study of Visitors to Upper Manhattan including their Economic Impact and Local Spending* (New York: Upper Manhattan Empowerment Zone, December 2000), 31.
25. *Upper Manhattan Empowerment Zone Annual Report: 2001*, 44.
26. Example: PA Jagorsky, *Poverty and Place* (New York: Russell Sage Foundation, 1997).
27. John Bess, interview, 9/25/01.
28. Robert Roach, interview, 6/13/01.
29. Laconia Smedley, interview, 9/10/01.
30. Ibid.

31. All of this crime data was taken from the New York Police Department's "Compstat" on its website: http://www.nyc.gov/html/nypd/.

32. All of this information on support for cultural institutions was taken from *The Upper Manhattan Empowerment Zone Annual Report: 2001*, 28-33.

33. Laconia Smedley, interview, 9/10/01.

34. Ibid.

35. Minnette Coleman, interview, 5/01.

36. Corcoran.com Neighborhood Report.

37. All figures taken from the 2000 Census Demographic Profile of New York City Community Districts.

38. David W. Chen, "City Rent Board Again Opts for Ambiguity," *New York Times*, 4 May 2005.

39. Laconia Smedley, interview, 9/10/01.

40. Minnette Coleman, interview, 5/01.

41. John Bess, interview, 9/25/01.

42. Minnette Coleman, interview, 5/01.

43. Cynthia Simmons, interview, 6/11/01.

44. John Bess, interview, 9/25/01.

45. Reggie James, interview, 6/19/01.

46. Tyletha Samuels, interview, 5/11/01.

47. Deborah Faison, interview, 2/21/02.

48. Lorraine Gilbert, interview, 9/19/01.

49. Ibid.

50. Ibid.

51. Vicky Gholson, interview, 2/7/02.

52. In rem units are located in structures owned by the City of New York. The units are in rem as a result of actions taken by the city against owners who failed to pay taxes on the properties for one or more years. Many of these units were once rent controlled or rent stabilized. However, they are now exempt from both of these regulatory systems during the period of city ownership.

53. Ibid.

54. Columbia University Professors Lance Freeman's and Frank Barconi's (of the Citizen Housing and Planning Council) 2002 study cited in: "The Gentry, Misjudged as Neighbors," *New York Times*, 26 March 2002. This article suggests that gentrification does not lead to the displacement of low-income people. Their study suggests that low-income families are, in fact, more likely to stay in gentrifying as opposed to nongentrifying neighborhoods. Vigdor's 2001 study similarly suggests that various improvements in local conditions encourages residents to stay.

55. A discussion of the influence of the unrest of 1992 Los Angeles on the Empowerment Zone legislation can be found in: Dennis E. Gale, *Understanding Urban Unrest: From Reverend King to Rodney King* (Thousand Oaks, CA:, Sage Publications, 1996).

56. Mary Baker, interview, 3/4/02.

57. Ibid.

58. Laconia Smedley, interview, 9/10/01.
59. Mamadou Chinyelu, *Harlem Ain't Nothing But a Third World Country* (New York: Mustard Seed Press, 1999), 76.
60. Interviews with Shabbazz Market Vendors, 4/8/02.
61. Ibid.
62. Dee Soloman, interview, 2/24/02.
63. Dee Soloman, interview, 1/24/02.
64. Ibid.
65. Deborah Faison, interview, 2/21/02.
66. Ibid.
67. Gail Aska, interview, 5/11/01.
68. Reggie James, interview, 6/19/01.
69. Ibid.
70. Ibid.
71. Ibid.
72. *The Upper Manhattan Empowerment Zone Annual Report: 2001*, 34.
73. Ibid., 35.
74. John Bess, interview, 9/25/01.
75. Cynthia Simmons, interview, 6/11/01.
76. Quote taken from: Herb Boyd, "Record Shack's Rents Soar Off Charts," *Amsterdam News,* 7 February 2003.
77. Cynthis Simmons, interview. 6/11/01.
78. Laconia Smedley, interview, 9/10/01.
79. Smedley was referring to Mart 125, a shopping mall for small, independent businesses, which was in the heart of activity on 125th Street. The mart has since been dissolved, making way for new businesses.
80. Cynthia Simmons, interview, 6/11/01.
81. Anonymous developer, interview, 5/23/01.
82. Tyletha Samuels, interview, 5/11/01.
83. Ibid.
84. Gail Aska, interview, 5/11/01.
85. We chose five women's clothing items and six men's items, identified the regular price and sale price of each of the items in each of the three stores. The prices were the same across the board.
86. John Bess, interview, 9/25/01.
87. Vicky Gholson, interview, 2/7/02.
88. Gail Aska, interview, 5/11/01.
89. Lorraine Gilbert, interview, 9/19/01.
90. Williams, Grant, "Library and Harlem Programs are Priorities for Clinton," *Chronicle of Philanthropy,* 17 October 2002, 9. Descriptions of Clinton's foundation's various programs were all indicated in this article.
91. The youth included: Tamika Smith, 15; Krystle Lewis, 15; Angel Martinez, 15; Ibn Mitchell (age not indicated); Taree Jones, 18; Tiffany Colbourne, 16; Melissa Samuels, 16; Brittany Bishop, 15; Franklin Bennet, 16. Barbara, an adult, and staff chaperone was also in the room.
92. Youth (Tamika) from Wadleigh focus group, 11/13/01.
93. Youth (Angel) from Wadleigh focus group, 11/13/01.

94. Youth from Wadleigh focus group, 11/13/01.
95. Ibid.
96. Youth from Wadleigh focus group, 11/13/01. This youth, although perceptive, underestimates the monthly rent of a studio apartment facing Central Park, which likely rents for significantly more than $1,300. And by the publishing of this book, it will probably be impossible to find a studio apartment in Harlem for $700.
97. Youth from Wadleigh focus group, 11/13/01.
98. Ibid.
99. Ibid.
100. Ibid.
101. Ibid.
102. Ibid.
103. Ibid.
104. Ibid.
105. Ibid.
106. Ibid.
107. Ibid.
108. For a more in depth discussion of the perils of sprawl, see: Manuel Pastor, et al., *Regions that Work* (Minneapolis, MN: University of Minnesota Press, 2001). But the book also provides specific examples of cities that have fostered equitable development by forging a greater shared interest between cities and suburbs.
109. John Bess, interview, 9/25/01.
110. Anonymous, interview, 11/1/01.
111. Ibid.
112. Ibid.
113. Ibid.

CHAPTER 5

1. Gail Aska, interview, 5/11/01.
2. Minnette Coleman, interview, 5/01.
3. Vicky Gholson, interview, 2/7/02.
4. Ibid.
5. Ibid.
6. Ibid.
7. Ibid.
8. All of this information about the decision-making structure of the UMEZ was provided for us by the UMEZ office itself.
9. Daniel Yankelovich, *The Magic of Dialogue: Transforming Conflict into Cooperation.* (New York: Simon & Schuster, 1999).
10. Ibid., 42.
11. Deborah Faison, interview, 2/21/02.
12. Ibid.
13. Ibid.
14. Abdul Salaam, interview, 11/29/01.

15. Ibid.
16. Ibid.
17. Rivka Gewirtz-Little, "The New Harlem: Who's Behind the Real Estate Gold Rush and Who's Fighting It?" *Village Voice,* 18–24 September 2002.
18. Gail Aska, interview, 5/11/01.
19. John Bess, interview, 9/25/01.
20. Ibid.
21. Tyletha Samuels, interview, 5/11/01. Bargain World was a discount convenience store, which was once a staple in the community. It recently closed.
22. Tyletha Samuels, interview, 5/11/01.
23. Laconia Smedley, interview, 9/10/01.
24. Ibid.
25. This information was taken from the New York City Department for the Aging's list of "Frequently Asked Questions" about the SCRIE program.
26. John Bess, interview, 9/25/01.
27. Gail Aska, interview, 5/11/01.
28. Ibid.
29. Laconia Smedley, interview, 9/10/01.
30. Ibid.
31. Cynthia Simmons, interview, 6/11/01.
32. Minnette Coleman, interview, 5/01.
33. Ibid.
34. Congressman Charles Rangel's website: http://rangel.house.gov.
35. *Upper Manhattan Empowerment Zone Annual Report: 2001,* 27.
36. UMEZ Spring 2002 Nonprofit Workshop Series Brochure.
37. Lorraine Gilbert, interview, 9/19/02.
38. Dee Soloman, interview, 1/24/02.
39. Cynthia Simmons, interview, 6/11/01.
40. Vicky Gholson, interview, 2/7/02.
41. Gail Aska, interview, 5/11/01.
42. Laconia Smedley, interview, 9/10/01.
43. Ibid.
44. Cynthia Simmons, interview, 6/11/01.
45. Minnette Coleman, interview, 5/01.
46. Ibid.
47. Robert Roach, interview, 6/13/01.
48. For further discussion about higher education/community partnerships, and their significance to community development, see: David Maurrasse, *Beyond the Campus: How Colleges and Universities Form Partnerships with Their Communities* (New York: Routledge, 2001).
49. Robert Roach, interview, 6/13/02.
50. Community Impact trains students and other members of the Columbia community to volunteer locally; the Urban Technical Assistance Project has been working with residents to develop plans; the Dental School

maintains an extensive clinic. The Community Affairs office of the University developed a website that will help those external to Columbia find out more about the various programs on campus. In addition to the various university-sponsored programs, several classes and student organizations have forged collaborative projects with Harlem residents. Tensions persist partly because of issues around real estate—Columbia being the largest local landlord.

51. Cynthia Simmons, interview, 6/11/01.
52. Reggie James, interview, 6/19/01.
53. Minnette Coleman, interview, 5/01.
54. Ibid.
55. ACE was created by former Columbia University professor Mark Gordon, through a nonprofit management course at Columbia's School of International and Public Affairs. As a way of teaching students how to manage nonprofits, an actual organization was created. I am now the professor of record on this course. Now that the tourist guide is completed, ACE is in the process of developing other projects that can leverage the university's resources on behalf of residents and community organizations in Harlem.
56. Tourist guide information from: *Upper Manhattan Tourism and Marketing Study* (New York: Upper Manhattan Empowerment Zone, December 2000), 19.
57. Robert Roach, interview, 6/13/01.
58. Ibid.
59. Cynthia Simmons, interview, 6/11/01.
60. Minnette Coleman, interview, 5/01.
61. This information was received from the Department of Environmental Protection of the City of New York.
62. Abdul Salaam, interview, 11/29/01.
63. Reggie James, interview, 6/19/01.
64. Anonymous, interview, 11/1/01.
65. Deborah Faison, interview, 2/21/02.
66. Ibid.
67. Ibid.
68. Mary Baker, interview, 3/4/02.
69. Ibid.
70. Laconia Smedley, interview, 9/10/01.

CHAPTER 6

1. Karen Phillips, interview, 9/19/01.
2. Ibid.
3. Ibid.
4. Ibid.
5. Anonymous, interview, 11/1/01.
6. Ibid.
7. Ibid.

8. The Abyssinian Development Corporation, Development and Communications Department, "The Revitalization of Ennis Francis Houses," *Beyond Borders*, 31 March 2005, 4.
9. Harlem Congregations for Community Improvement.
10. Anonymous, interview, 11/1/01.
11. *The Upper Manhattan Empowerment Zone Annual Report: 2001*, 36–37.
12. Deborah Faison, interview, 2/21/02.
13. Ibid.
14. Vicky Gholson, interview, 2/7/02.
15. Abdul Salaam, interview, 11/29/01.
16. Ibid.
17. Harlem Children's Zone website: http://www.hcz.org.
18. Lee Farrow, interview, 8/2/01.
19. Ibid., 8/2/01.
20. Jennifer Steinhauer, "Once Vilified, Squatters Will Inherit 11 Buildings," *New York Times*, 20 August 2002, sec. A.
21. Lee Farrow, interview, 8/2/01.
22. Ibid.
23. Ibid.
24. Community Pride Focus Group Participant, 8/9/01.
25. Ibid.
26. Ibid
27. Ibid.
28. Ibid.
29. Ibid.
30. Ibid.
31. Ibid.

CHAPTER 7

1. *PolicyLink*. website. May 24, 2005. Market Creek Plaza: Overview. http://www.policylink.org/Projects/MarketCreek/.
2. Ibid.
3. Ibid.
4. Webber, Rebecca, "The New Gentrification" in *The Gotham Gazette*, 11 December 2000.
5. Williamson, Thad, David Imbroscio, Gar Alperovitz. 2002. *Making a Place for Community: Local Democracy in a Global Era*. Routledge, New York.
6. Ibid.
7. PolicyLink and Pratt Institute Center for Community and Environmental Development. *Increasing Housing Opportunity in New York City: The Case for Inclusionary Zoning*. Fall 2004.
8. Williamson, Thad. *Making a Place for Community: Local Democracy in a Global Era*.
9. Ibid.

10. Hibbard, Michael, and Susan Lurie. "Saving Land but Losing Ground: Challenges to Community Planning in the Era of Participation." *Journal of Planning Education and Research.* 20 (2000): 187–195.

11. Margerum, Richard. "Collaborative Planning: Building Consensus and Building a Distinct Model for Practice." *Journal of Planning Education and Research.* 21 (2000): 237–253.

12. Wyatt, Edward. "Even Critics Say Some Designs for Downtown Aren't So Bad," *New York Times,* July 23, 2002.

13. Ibid.

14. Wyatt, Edward. "Officials Rethink Building Proposal for Ground Zero," *New York Times,* July 21, 2002.

15. These statistics were taken from a "Preliminary Report" of the July 20, 2002, event at the Jacob Javits Convention Center in Manhattan, organized by the Civic Alliance to Rebuild Downtown New York. The process itself was designed and facilitated by a nonprofit organization, called America Speaks.

APPENDIX

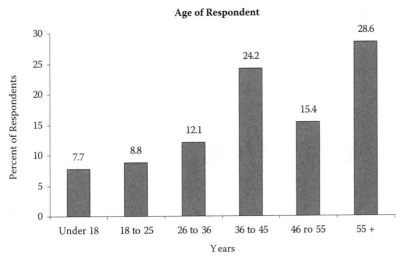

Age of Respondent

Figure A. Age

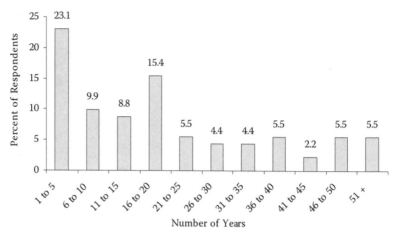

How many years have you lived in Harlem?

Figure B. Years of Residence in Harlem

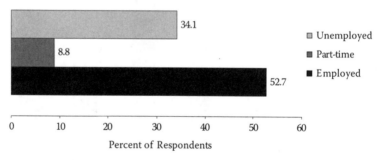

Figure C. Employment Status

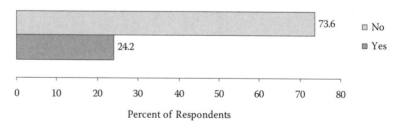

Figure D. Property Ownership

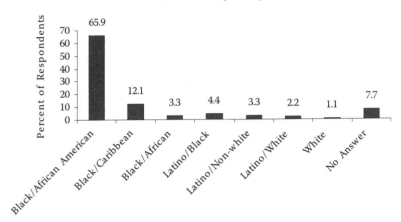

Figure E. Race/Ethnicity

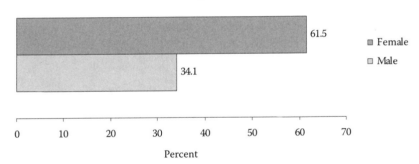

Figure F. Gender

INDEX